Tracing Your Naval Ancestors

Tracing Your Naval Ancestors

Bruno Pappalardo

PUBLIC RECORD OFFICE

Readers' Guide No. 24

First published in 2003 by

Public Record Office
Kew
Richmond
Surrey
TW9 4DU

www.pro.gov.uk/

ISBN 1 903365 37 6

A catalogue record for this book is available from the British Library

Front cover illustrations: Ratings training, August 1904 (COPY 1/476); ratings cleaning the deck of a ship, *Illustrated London News*, (ZPER 34/148)

Back cover illustration: Photograph of HMS *Agincourt*, launched in 1865 (ADM 176/10)

Printed in Great Britain by The Cromwell Press Ltd., Trowbridge, Wiltshire.

Contents

Illustrations

Acknowledgements

This guide has been in preparation for some time, so I would like to take the opportunity to acknowledge the many people who have helped me to complete it.

To begin with, I would like to thank my uncle, Giacomo Villaricca, for interesting me in naval matters.

Particular thanks are also due to William Foot, for first encouraging my interest in naval records, and also for explaining the intricate workings of the Admiralty digests and indexes; guidance which still proves useful to the present day. Moreover I would like to thank the late Garth Thomas for his advice and help in the preparatory work for this guide. I am also indebted to the work of N.A.M Rodger, author of *Naval Records for Genealogists*.

Special thanks are also due to many of my colleagues, the staff of other offices, and fellow researchers for their advice, feedback and encouragement. In particular: Keith Bartlett; Amanda Bevan; Alan Bowgen; John Carr; John Cassidy; Stella Colwell; Jane Crompton; John Fisher; Sheila Gopaulen; Guy Grannum; Chris Heather; Abi Husiany; Hilary Jones; Peter Keat; Jan Keohane, Anne Kilminster; Sheila Knight; Aidan Lawes; Sarah Leach; Peter Le Fevre; Malcolm Mercer; Ann Morton; Paul Moxon; Roger Nixon; Bob O'Hara; Rob Perez; William Spencer; Lesley Thomas; Chris Watts; and Colin Williams.

I would also like to thank both Peter Leek and Kathryn Sleight for their efforts and patience in fine tuning this guide and seeing it through to publication.

Finally, but not least, I would not have been able to complete this work without the support of my mother, father, brother, mother- and father-in-law, and my wife Laura and children Sara and Marco who have provided me with the inspiration and impetus to see this book through to completion.

Introduction

From the seventeenth to the nineteenth century the Royal Navy was one of Britain's largest employers, though the number of men serving in the navy contrasted significantly between times of war and peace. For example, the highest total employed during the seventeenth century was 48,514 in 1695; the number dropped as low as 6,298 in 1725; and peaked at 142,098 in 1810. In 1811 the estimated population of Great Britain was 12,609,864, of which 6,340,214 were male. Out of this total, 130,866 (roughly one male in 48) served in the navy; and this ratio underestimates the popularity of the navy as a career, bearing in mind that many men would have been unable to join, being either medically unfit or too young or too old. As a result, there is a good chance that one of your ancestors served in the Royal Navy – and your ancestors do not necessarily have to have been British, as it was not uncommon for the navy, particularly with regard to its ratings, to employ men of all nationalities.

The purpose of this guide is to provide a comprehensive overview arranged by subject of the numerous records held by the Public Record Office (PRO) relating to men and women who served in the Royal Navy, or in the naval reserves or auxiliary forces formed to assist it, from 1660 to modern times. By providing details of the content, date range and series or document references of the various records, it aims to help researchers evaluate which ones are relevant in tracing the career history or family background of an individual officer or rating. This should make it possible to plan research and conduct searches in a more focused way, so that it is easier to locate the most appropriate sources.

Topics covered range from service records, ships' pay books and musters, pensions, medals and medical records to discipline and courts martial. Also included are two case studies: the one (in section 3.4) showing how to locate details of a rating who served before 1853, the other (in 2.13) tracing the career of a commissioned officer who saw active service between 1799 and 1853. These case studies provide practical guidance on how to use the vast array of records at the PRO to find genealogical and career information about officers and ratings who served in the navy. Chapter 6 – which is devoted to the various naval reserves and auxiliary forces, including the Royal Naval Reserve, Royal Naval Volunteer Reserve, Royal Naval Division, Royal Navy Air Service, Women's Royal Naval Service and Queen Alexandra's Royal Naval Nursing Service – provides extensive details about recently released service records of men and women who served during the First World War.

This guide does not cover naval records prior to 1660, nor those relating to civilian employees of the Admiralty, naval dockyards – described in PRO information leaflet MO 41 – or the Royal Marines, which are the subject of Garth Thomas's *Records of the Royal Marines* (PRO, 1994). Although some merchant navy and coastguard records are touched on, they are not covered in great detail, as these are described more comprehensively in *Records of Merchant Shipping and Seamen* by K. Smith, C.T. Watts and M.J. Watts (PRO, 1998) and, for the coastguard service, in PRO information leaflet MO 44.

The Public Record Office is the repository of one of the most complete archives in the world, dating back to the Domesday Book in 1086 and (at the time of writing) extending up to the 1970s. It holds the records for the central government of the United Kingdom (primarily of England and Wales, as Scotland and Northern Ireland have their own central record offices), as well as the records of the law courts of England. In addition, it is a major international archive, because of its vast holdings on former British colonies and on foreign relations over eight centuries. The PRO also holds the largest collection of records of interest to family and naval historians relating to the administration and government of the Royal Navy, naval reserves and auxiliary forces and to those who served in them. Other key sources, such as the record collections of the National Maritime Museum, Royal Naval Museum and Fleet Air Arm Museum, are mentioned where relevant throughout this guide. Addresses, phone numbers and websites for these and other organizations of interest to naval genealogists are given in Appendix 2.

Public records are not normally made available for reading until 30 years after the date of their final creation; thus a file opened in 1961 and closed in 1971 becomes available in 2002. Some documents have much longer closure periods to safeguard personal confidentiality – an obvious example being service records, which are closed for 75 years.

Service records – the main source of information readily associated with those who served in the armed forces – were not maintained by the Royal Navy with the family historian in mind. No centralized records of service were kept for seamen (ratings) until 1853. Service records for officers began to be systematically kept only from the 1840s, and as a result are patchy and incomplete. Researchers seeking information about officers should begin their search by consulting the printed sources described in sections 2.1 and 2.2.

Those looking for genealogical information about ratings who served before the mid nineteenth century will generally have to use records for which comprehensive alphabetical indexes of names do not exist. Before 1853 the Royal Navy did not offer ratings a full-time career: they were employed and discharged according to the manning requirements of the navy at the time, with no guarantee that they would be re-employed. Consequently, for the majority of these men the only service records are the ships' musters and pay books described in 4.1, of which some 250,000 have survived and are held by the PRO.

Finally, it should be mentioned that some sections of this guide – particularly the overview of naval history in Chapter 1 – include material that appeared in a more condensed form in the PRO Pocket Guide *Using Navy Records* by the same author.

Using the PRO

The Public Record Office (PRO) is the national repository for government records in the UK. Its main site at Kew holds the surviving records of government extending back to the Domesday Book (1086) and beyond. Currently it holds approximately 9 million records, which occupy more than 175 kilometres of shelving; another 2–3 kilometres of documents are added at the beginning of each calendar year. The PRO at Kew is generally the best place to go to in order to search for information about an ancestor who served in the armed forces.

Contact details

Public Record Office
Kew
Richmond
Surrey
TW9 4DU

Website: www.pro.gov.uk/

General telephone number: 020 8876 3444

Enquiries and advance ordering of documents (with exact references only):
Telephone: 020 8392 5200

Fax: 020 8392 5286
Email: enquiry@pro.gov.uk
PRO catalogue (PROCAT) website: http://catalogue.pro.gov.uk/

Opening times

(closed Sundays, public holidays, and for annual stocktaking – usually the first week of December)

Monday	9 a.m. to 5 p.m.
Tuesday	10 a.m. to 7 p.m.
Wednesday	9 a.m. to 5 p.m.
Thursday	9 a.m. to 7 p.m.
Friday	9 a.m. to 5 p.m.
Saturday	9.30 a.m. to 5 p.m.

Note that the last time for ordering documents for same-day production is 4 p.m. on Monday, Wednesday and Friday; 4.30 p.m. on Tuesday and Thursday; and 2.30 p.m. on Saturday.

The Public Record Office is about 10 minutes' walk from Kew Gardens Underground Station, which is on London Transport's District Line and the North London Line Silverlink Metro service. It is situated just off the South Circular Road (A205), and there is free parking. Facilities include self-service lockers, for which a (refundable) £1 coin is needed, a restaurant, a bookshop, an extensive reference library, and an Education and Visitor Centre.

The PRO may seem a confusing place on your first visit, but staff are knowledgeable, friendly and happy to help. You do not need to make an appointment to visit, but a reader's ticket is required to gain access to the research areas and to order documents. To obtain a reader's ticket, you will need to bring some means of personal identification, such as a banker's card, passport or full UK driving licence, if you are a British citizen; and a passport or national identity card, if you are not.

To protect the documents, many of which are unique, eating, drinking and smoking are not permitted in the reading rooms, and security is tight. You can take a laptop computer into the reading rooms as well as pencils, a notebook and up to 10 loose sheets of paper; the use of pens, rubbers and mobile phones is not allowed.

Identifying and ordering documents

To view a document at the PRO, either in its original form or on microfilm, you need to identify it by its document reference. PRO document references usually consist of three parts: department code, series number and piece number. When they are transferred to the PRO, the government records selected for permanent preservation are normally kept together and assigned a department code reflecting their provenance. For example, records created by the Admiralty commence with the department code **ADM**. Each collection of records is identified by a series number (to pick a random example, the series containing the majority of lieutenants' passing certificates is **ADM 107**), and each document or 'piece' within a series has its own individual piece number (for example, **ADM 107/3** contains lieutenants' passing certificates for the years 1712–45).

To place an order for an original document held by the PRO you need a reader's ticket, a seat number (available from the Document Counter in the Document Reading Room) and a full document reference (for the document mentioned above, it would be **ADM 107/3**). Original documents are ordered via a computerized ordering system and are usually delivered after 30 minutes. Documents on microfilm can be accessed on a self-service basis in the Microfilm Reading Room.

Document references can be found through the PRO website (www.pro.gov.uk) or by using the printed *PRO Guide* and series lists, copies of which are available in the PRO reading rooms. The website allows readers to access PROCAT (the PRO's online catalogue), which can be searched using keywords such as a person's name or the name of a ship. More specific searches can be carried out by adding dates and series references. If a PROCAT search is successful, document references relevant to your research will be listed on screen.

From the website – which includes information about where the PRO is, opening times and how to gain access – you can download record information leaflets (there are over 100 to choose from) and lists of independent researchers. PROCAT can also be accessed on computer terminals in the PRO reading rooms at Kew and in the Census and Wills Reading Room at the Family Record Centre (FRC) in London.

For more information about ordering and using PRO documents, see *Tracing Your Ancestors in the Public Record Office* by Amanda Bevan (PRO, 6th edn 2002), which is available in the reading rooms and can be purchased from the bookshops at the PRO and FRC or via the PRO's internet bookshop (www.pro.gov.uk/bookshop).

History and organization of the Royal Navy

It is difficult to use naval records for genealogical research without having an understanding of the origins and history of the Royal Navy, the way it was organized, and how this developed over time. A general overview of the period up to 1914 follows. Those with a deeper interest in the navy's history and organization will find recommendations for further reading in the Bibliography at the end of this book.

1.1 History of the Royal Navy

1.1.1 Origins of the Royal Navy

The origins of the Royal Navy lie in the merchant shipping of medieval England. The king had ships of his own but called on the merchant fleet as the need arose. Successive kings granted trading privileges to a number of ports on the south coast, known as the Cinque Ports (originally Dover, Hastings, Hythe, Romney and Harwich, to which Rye and Winchelsea were added later). In return for these privileges, the king was able to call upon the Cinque Ports for help in defence of English maritime interests. At this time, it was possible to convert a ship easily from trading to defensive use. This was done whenever required, more or less on the personal authority of the king.

The beginnings of a structured navy can be traced from the time of the Tudors. Henry VII personally owned a fleet of seven ships, which were used for trading as well as defence, and this fleet was greatly expanded by Henry VIII. The Tudors were quick to grasp the implications of the discoveries of the New World and the importance of having a strong navy to protect the nation's interests and territories from attack by rival European countries. In 1546 Henry VIII set up an organization, subsequently known as the Navy Board, to be responsible for the civil administration of the navy, including its ships and the royal dockyards that he had authorized to be built at Portsmouth, Chatham and Plymouth. Advances were made in the design of the ships, and their armaments were augmented. As a result, when the Spanish Armada set sail in 1588, the Royal Navy was strong enough to meet it.

Although there now existed a royal fleet and an organization to oversee it, there was as yet no permanent body of officers and men (ratings) to serve in it. Officers and ratings were employed only as and when necessary. In times of peace there was no need to have as many ships as in wartime, so thousands of men would be laid off, until the next emergency arose. The problem of how to man ships was one that the navy had to grapple with until as late as the nineteenth century, when it was partially solved by the introduction of continuous service for ratings in 1853.

The early Stuarts were not as interested in the navy as the Tudors had been, and during the earlier part of the seventeenth century the navy was dogged by poor administration and by scandal and corruption, all of which hampered its efficiency and growth.

With the outbreak of the English Civil War in 1642, a navy of 35 ships committed itself to Parliament. By the time of James II's dethronement in 1688, it had increased to 151 ships. The growth of the navy during this time and the recognition of its importance was mainly due to the naval-minded kings Charles II and James II (who, as lord high admiral, personally took command of the fleet in the Second Dutch War) and to the influence and work of Samuel Pepys. The navy was built up partly to protect the increasing number of merchant ships involved in shipborne trade, but also in response to the threat of Spain and France and because of the wars with the United Provinces of the Netherlands in 1652–4, 1664–7 and 1672–4, caused by economic rivalry over fishing and trade. Whereas previously it had been possible to adapt merchant ships for wartime use, new tactics – in which squadrons of ships formed lines of battle and fought each other at closer distances with heavier and more potent guns – highlighted the need to have ships specifically built for such purposes. Consequently the navy and merchant navy began to separate, as their roles became increasingly distinct. It is to this time that many of the features associated with the modern navy can be traced; and many of them can be attributed to Pepys, who was Clerk of the Acts to the Navy Board in 1660–73 and First Secretary of the Admiralty in 1673–9 and 1684–9.

Under Pepys, the Naval Discipline Act, incorporating the Articles of War and brought into force in 1661, gave the navy a uniform disciplinary code of conduct, enforced by courts martial. In 1677 professional examinations were introduced for would-be lieutenants. Those who qualified, along with the existing service officers, now had the possibility of a permanent naval career. Pensions, albeit in a limited form, were introduced for some officers in 1672. In addition, a system of half pay (a fee paid to retain the services of officers who were not employed) was introduced in 1688, although similar arrangements for ratings were not brought in. Around this time the navy, now with its own specially made ships, a recognizable body of professional officers, its own separate identity and the backing of Charles II, began to be known as the Royal Navy.

1.1.2 The impact of the Glorious Revolution, 1688

From 1689 to 1815, peace and stability in Europe depended on a delicately shared balance of power between the Netherlands, France, Spain and England, which was maintained by diplomacy, treaties, military strength, monarchical family ties, and alliances made with one another or with smaller, weaker countries.

England's position in Europe was largely dictated by its monarchy, internal political situation, economy and military strength and by relations with its European neighbours. All these factors impacted on the size of the Royal Navy, the number of men required to man it, and how it was deployed.

In the 1670s Louis XIV's France was trying to tip the balance of power in its own favour by invading the Netherlands. But England seemed less willing to pit itself against the Netherlands, a Protestant country – ruled by William of Orange, nephew of Charles II and James II – that was determined to defend itself against France, a Catholic country that appeared to pose a greater threat. In 1678 anti-Catholic and anti-French feelings in England were fanned by the 'Popish Plot', a conspiracy allegedly supported by the Pope and Louis XIV, which aimed to kill Charles II, so that his devout Catholic brother, James, Duke of York, could become King of England.

Charles II insisted that Mary, James's eldest daughter and heir, was brought up as a Protestant, and in 1677 she married William of Orange, which strengthened ties between England and the Netherlands. For the time being, James's second marriage, to the Catholic princess Mary Beatrice of Modena, whose family was backed by Louis XIV, had produced no children. But three years after James's accession to the throne (as James II, on the death of Charles II in 1685) a son, James Francis Edward Stuart, was born, who would be brought up a Catholic and was in line to become the next monarch, instead of Mary. This caused great concern to those fearful of a Catholic French takeover, as James II sought to restore the power of the Catholic church.

In 1688 Parliament urged William of Orange and his wife to use military force to depose James II, and promised support. William, although eager to have England on his side against France, was concerned that such an act might render his own country liable to a French invasion. However, Louis XIV believed that William would become embroiled in a long war in England. He therefore decided to attack the Palatinate and south Germany in September 1688, and invade the Netherlands later.

When, in November 1688, William landed in England, he met no resistance from James's II army, and James and his family fled to France. Although Mary's claim to the English throne was stronger than William's, in February 1689 Parliament decided that they should rule England jointly. At the same time, royal powers were reduced by a Bill of Rights, which stipulated that monarchs could not ignore parliamentary laws and that future monarchs were not to be Catholic or marry Catholics.

William III's accession set in place British foreign policy for the period from 1689 to 1815, which was designed to prevent France gaining political and military supremacy in Europe. Aware that his accession would provoke a French reaction, in May 1689 William III, at the head of a 'grand alliance' consisting of the United Provinces (the Netherlands), the Holy Roman Empire, Spain and Savoy, promptly declared war on France.

This change in British foreign policy, to which the Royal Navy was integral, had major implications for the way it was deployed. Previously the navy had mainly been concerned with guarding home waters, serving as the first line of defence against threatened invasion, which was most likely to come from France. But now it also had to protect Britain's growing empire – with distant colonies in the West Indies, North America and India – and her mercantile interests and shipping routes, while taking part in a European power struggle and race for lucrative new trade routes and undiscovered or underdeveloped countries to colonize or trade with. So that the navy could perform this role effectively, it needed overseas dockyard facilities – eventually acquired by diplomacy (for example, Lisbon in 1703) or military action (for example, Antigua in 1729) – that could service, supply and maintain naval ships in the Mediterranean and West Indies without them having to return to the nearest British port, which was Portsmouth. Moreover, it meant that a large navy had to be kept in readiness for quick mobilization whenever or wherever it was required. The necessity of protecting trading interests would eventually bring Britain into conflict with Spain (in 1739–48) and most significantly, periodically throughout 1689–1815, with France – which, under Louis XIV and later Napoleon, aimed for complete domination of Europe.

1.1.3 Developments in the Royal Navy 1689–1815

In its efforts to maintain supremacy at sea between 1689 and 1815, the Royal Navy adopted the latest scientific and technological advances in its ships, or sought to sponsor them, and carried out work that would contribute to its effectiveness. This was a prerequisite for keeping ahead of its maritime rivals, and a policy it would adhere to in the future. The navy was quick to use new scientific instruments, such as the quadrant and sextant, which enabled better geographical accuracy to improve navigation. Great advances were made in cartography when, in 1681, Greenvile Collins was appointed by the Admiralty to survey the coasts of Britain and produce new charts to replace the Dutch ones then in use. He was later appointed hydrographer to the King, and many of his plans featured in the *Coasting Pilot* of 1693. This led to the creation, in 1795, of a hydrography department at the Admiralty, which produced the Admiralty Charts that the whole world later was to rely on for navigation purposes.

The problem of how to determine longitude, to enable the reckoning of a ship's position at sea, was solved by the clockmaker John Harrison – who was finally rewarded for his efforts with £20,000 in 1773, the Admiralty having sponsored research in this field by offering the reward as early as 1714. Studies of health at sea, in particular by the naval surgeon James Lind, sought to prevent diseases such as scurvy, typhus and yellow fever. Lind had discovered in 1747 that a regular intake of lemon juice prevented scurvy, but it was only regularly issued in the navy from 1795.

The Royal Navy also undertook some celebrated feats of navigation and exploration that added significantly to what was known about the geography of the world. Among these were Captain George Anson's circumnavigation of the world in 1740–4, from which he brought to England riches worth £500,000 (though at a terrible price, 1,051 of his crew of 1,995 having died from scurvy); Captain Bligh's journey of 3,618 miles in an open boat as a result of the mutiny on the *Bounty* in 1789; and Captain James Cook's epic voyages of exploration between 1768 and 1779, which led to the charting of the coasts of New Zealand and East Australia, the discovery of

Hawaii, and the disproving of theories about the existence of a vast undiscovered southern continent (*Terra Australis incognita*). Cook's discoveries were instrumental in Britain deciding to colonize Australia and New Zealand, to replace the North American colonies lost during the American War of Independence (1775–83).

At home, buildings for Admiralty use were erected in Whitehall in 1699. Work continued on the Royal Naval dockyards in Portsmouth, Deptford, Woolwich, Chatham and Plymouth. In 1673 *Sailing and Fighting Instructions* – the Royal Navy's first publication of this kind – was issued by James, Duke of York (later James II). James's book stressed the importance of maintaining the line in battle. Revised in 1691, it formed the basis of British naval tactics up to 1783. Another important publication, *Regulations and Instructions relating to His Majesty's Service*, was first issued in 1731. An officers' training academy was opened in Portsmouth in 1733, and in 1748 uniforms for officers were introduced.

The Royal Greenwich Hospital, built specifically for naval seamen who were injured or too old to serve in the navy, admitted its first pensioners in 1705. A dedicated seamen's hospital, Haslar Hospital in Gosport, the largest brick building in the world, started to admit patients in 1754; and another naval hospital, in Plymouth, opened in 1761. The Royal Navy's fleet increased substantially, from 270 ships in the early part of the century to 500 ships in 1793; and the number of men required to man the enlarged fleet rose from 48,000 in 1713 to 142,000 in 1813. Various naval dockyards overseas (for example, in Halifax, Nova Scotia, founded in 1749) ensured the maintenance of ships in foreign waters. Regular servicing of ships at these bases, using techniques such as careening, to scrape weeds and barnacles from hulls, ensured optimum sailing speeds and prevented the build-up of shipworm, which ate away at wooden hull timbers. Copper sheathing encasing ships' hulls also helped to eradicate this problem; introduced in 1761, it was fitted with more regularity during the 1780s. In 1796 a semaphore system for relaying messages, developed by Sir Home Popham and Reverend George Murray, was accepted by the Admiralty and installed in 15 stations from London to Deal.

1.1.4 Officers and ratings in the age of sail, 1689–1815

Britain's defeat of France at the end of the Napoleonic Wars – in which the navy played a crucial part, epitomized by victories in battles such as the Glorious First of June (1794), Cape St Vincent (1797), the Nile (1798), Copenhagen (1801) and Trafalgar (1805) – gained her undisputed supremacy of the seas.

This was achieved through the efforts of officers and ratings whose conditions of service had remained much the same for over a century. Ratings worked and slept in cramped conditions, often without seeing families or friends for several years at a time, and rarely being granted shore leave because of fear of desertion. Hundreds of men – sometimes as many as 600 or 700 – would sleep below deck in shifts not longer than four hours, in hammocks which naval regulations stated could only be 14 inches wide. Although ships tended to be larger and carried more guns, they still relied on sail for movement. In wartime, there were usually not enough volunteers to man the ships. Poor pay (seamen's wages did not increase between 1653 and 1797) and bad food – which James Lind described as 'extremely gross, viscid, and hard to digest' – were hardly incentives to join the navy. If a ship's complement was below strength, the shortfall was redressed by 'impressment' (forcible recruitment), which did not bode well for morale. Enforced by courts martial, discipline was strict and frequently harsh. Most offences on board naval ships would result in a man being flogged; five or six dozen lashes were often inflicted as the punishment.

The nature of work on board ships in the age of sail was very hazardous and exhausting. Seamen had physically to haul in the anchor, gun carriages and canvas sails, which increased in weight when wet. Men were often injured or killed as a result of falling from the rigging, and by cannon shot or flying wooden splinters in battle. Accidents were frequently caused by men hitting their heads on low beams or being hit by loose cannons. No doubt some accidents occurred because the men were issued with half a pint of rum a day. Ratings discharged from ship because of injury received no state help, nor did their next of kin. Generally ratings did not receive systematic training and were offered no job security; at the end of a ship's commission there would be no guarantee of further employment, and there were no automatic long-service pensions. They had to purchase their own slops (clothes) from the purser, and any medical treatment they received on board was deducted from their wages. James Lind blamed ratings' 'tainted apparel' for the spread of diseases such as typhus. Wages were usually paid at the end of a ship's commission, which could last many years, and sometimes were not paid at all. Dr Johnson quipped that 'no man will be a sailor who has contrived enough to get himself into a jail; for being in a ship is being in jail, with the chance of being drowned. A man in a jail has more room, better food and commonly better company.'

Officers did not face the same harsh working conditions as ratings. During wars, with more ships in commission, there was a better chance of employment. Promotion to the rank of lieutenant was dependent on passing a qualifying examination, introduced in 1677, and also on having served a mandatory number of years at sea (see 2.6). Those that qualified for a lieutenancy by passing the examination were appointed by selection, as were existing lieutenants seeking further employment. In peace time, when there tended to be a relatively limited number of lieutenant's vacancies, those with 'interest' – an influential social or political background or family links with the Admiralty – generally had a head start over others in securing employment. Promotion to captain was also on the basis of selection. Consequently, officers without 'interest' could spend many years without promotion. Once an officer reached the rank of captain, further promotions were based on seniority to that rank. Because the navy had no official method of retiring its officers, the only opportunity for promotion from the rank of captain was if officers occupying higher ranks died or left the service because of a disciplinary offence. This archaic system of promotion produced huge bottlenecks in the promotion chain and created numerous problems for the Admiralty. When not on active employment, officers received half pay, a fee paid to secure their services.

Most officers came from well-to-do families and entered the service as 'captain's servants'. This was the rating given to 'young gentlemen' serving a form of naval apprenticeship under the patronage of a captain – who more often than not took them on to oblige 'influential' friends or relatives. Sometimes they were as young as eight years old. Because they would inevitably miss much of their schooling, in 1702 schoolmasters were appointed to ships and in 1733 the Royal Navy Academy was opened in Portsmouth to provide the 'young gentlemen' with schooling and training in preparation for going to sea.

1.1.5 *From* Victory *to* Dreadnought, *the transition from sail to steam*

After the Napoleonic Wars Britain's military strength, wealth and trade were without equal. The nation could now look forward to a long period of peace and stability, comfortable in the knowledge that it possessed the strongest navy in the world. Former enemies realized that it was more advantageous to trade with Britain than to enter into renewed conflict with her and, apart from one instance (the Battle of Navarino, in 1827), the Royal Navy would not be involved in any large-scale naval battle until after the outbreak of the First World War.

Consequently, during this period Britain adopted foreign policies that reflected her new status as the leading world power – including a policy of free trade. To ensure that legitimate trading ships of all nationalities could ply the seas without interference, the Royal Navy was now primarily deployed in a 'policing' role rather than for offensive purposes. Emblematic of this new role was the part played by the navy in enforcing the ban on the slave trade, which had been declared illegal in Britain in 1807 and by the Congress of Vienna in 1815. This involved stopping ships suspected of slave running, and freeing any slaves found aboard. To protect trading interests and foster stability, the navy was also responsible for combating piracy, particularly along the North African coast (which in 1817 resulted in the bombardment of Algiers), and for preventing localized conflicts escalating into large-scale wars.

Given the navy's new role, it was no longer necessary to keep it on a wartime footing. From 1815 the government and the Admiralty, as they had done after every war previously, scaled the navy down – but this time to its lowest and weakest level in over a century. By 1817, it numbered just 131 ships and 20,000 men.

The Industrial Revolution brought the introduction of steam engines in agriculture, factories and transport. Such engines were already in use in ships in the early nineteenth century; and in 1817 the *Savannah* became the first steam-assisted vessel to cross the Atlantic, a voyage which took 26 days. It was only a matter of time before ships that were reliant on human muscle power and the natural elements for movement would be superseded. The Royal Navy, as always at the cutting edge of technology, kept a watching brief on this intriguing innovation. Initially it showed a certain resistance to steam-powered ships, still favouring its 'wooden walls of England'. However, in 1822 the navy brought into service its first paddle steamer,

Comet, to tow ships out of harbour in unfavourable weather conditions. With paddle wheels, it was difficult to position guns along the sides of a ship, which meant a reduction in firepower capability. In contrast, the invention of the screw propeller, placed below the water line at the stern, made for a more manoeuvrable ship and no loss of gunpower. The first steam battleship to be built incorporating this new technology was the *Agamemnon*, in 1853. However, ships of its type soon became obsolete. French battleships used in the Crimean War (1853–5) showed the value of wrought-iron armour protection. Britain, aware that a rival European maritime power had taken the lead in ship design, responded with HMS *Warrior*, the Royal Navy's first ship built entirely of iron and at that time the largest ship in the world. This sparked an arms race, as ironclad warships increased in size and thickness of armour and were equipped with larger and more powerful guns. The early ironclads had been fitted with sails, but in the early 1880s sails were finally dispensed with and steel was used both for armour and for ship construction. The technological advances of the late nineteenth century in rapid-fire gunnery and the manufacture of rifled guns and torpedoes dictated the need for purpose-built battle cruisers. In the shape of dreadnoughts powered by turbines, these revolutionized naval warfare and took it into the twentieth century.

With these technological advances, the Royal Navy required officers and ratings such as engineers, wireless operators, electricians and specialists in gunnery who could work effectively in the new ships. Because of this requirement the navy had to begin to provide systematic training of a kind not previously given to men serving in the navy. A gunnery school, HMS *Excellent* at Portsmouth, was set up in 1830 to provide training to selected seaman gunners on contracts of 'five or seven years renewable on expiration'. These first steps taken by the Admiralty towards offering some ratings a permanent career marked the beginning of the creation of a full-time navy, which was fully realized in 1853 with the introduction of continuous service for ratings. From 1853 boys joining the service could sign on for 10 years, and boys or ratings already serving were encouraged to commit themselves to continuous service. Benefits that resulted from the introduction of continuous service included increased pay, paid leave and improved sick pay; free uniforms were issued to ratings from 1859; and ratings who served 22 years in the navy under the continuous service scheme became eligible for a long-service pension.

Boy entrants to the service were now given systematic training both at HMS *Excellent* and on two dedicated training ships, HMS *Illustrious* at Portsmouth (from 1854 until 1857) and HMS *Implacable* at Devonport (from 1855). From the 1860s, these training ships were augmented by another five.

Employment opportunities for officers after 1815 were very scarce, owing to the smaller numbers of ships required for service in peacetime. In 1814 there had been 713 ships in active service; by 1820 this had been reduced to 134. In January 1818, out of 5,887 commissioned officers, only 597 were in active service. This situation was exacerbated by the lack of an official method for retiring officers. At various dates from 1836 officers became eligible for pensions on reaching a specific age or seniority (either automatically or on application) – thus easing the promotion blockage and in time addressing the problem of having very elderly officers in positions of command at sea.

Before 1854 the selection of officer cadets was mainly a privilege exercised by captains and admirals, which could be traced back to the days of captain's servants (see 1.1.4). However, from 1857 all naval cadets were to receive training on HMS *Illustrious* before going to sea (the Royal Naval Academy for would-be officers having closed in 1837). Torpedo training was provided from 1872 in HMS *Vernon*, in Portsmouth; and engineer officers received their training in Keyham from 1888.

More enlightened attitudes in the navy meant a pay increase from 1859 for men who did not draw their rum ration (which had been halved in 1825); libraries on board ships from 1838; the abolition of flogging in 1871; and for ratings and warrant officers, the possibility of promotion to commissioned officer ranks in 1903.

From 1903, with the introduction of a new system of training known as the Selborne Scheme, all future executive officers entered the service and trained together until they reached a point where they had to decide which branch of the service they wanted to serve in.

1.2 Organization of the Royal Navy

In the Middle Ages the navy was managed by the King in Council, and at various times after 1360 through an official known either as the lord admiral, high admiral or admiral of England, or from 1627 as the lord high admiral. Day-to-day administration was effected by subordinate keepers or clerks of the kings' ships. The lord high admiral generally commanded the navy in person or by deputy and was responsible for policy, strategy and fighting personnel. Occasionally in the seventeenth century the office of lord high admiral was not filled. In such instances his duties of governing the navy were taken on by a Board of Admiralty – an arrangement which, except for one instance, became permanent from 1708.

In 1546 a group of 'officers of marine causes' was appointed by letters patent to be responsible under the lord admiral for the civil administration of the navy. Later these officers became known as the Principal Commissioners of the Navy, or the Navy Board. The Board's duties, which comprised shipbuilding and maintenance of ships, supplies and stores, contracts and auditing accounts, were shared by a number of principal officers.

To help the Navy Board cope with the problems of providing for and provisioning the expanding navy (which was becoming one of the biggest, most expensive and technically advanced organizations of its time), an intricate, sometimes overlapping, system of administrative boards emerged. There was the Board of Admiralty, which in 1708 was officially recognized as being responsible for governing the navy; the Sick and Hurt Board, formed in 1653, which was responsible for medical care and the exchange of prisoners of war; the Victualling Board, set up in 1683, which supplied food and oversaw the pursers who distributed it on board ships; and the Transport Board, first appointed in 1686, whose main function was the ferrying of troops overseas.

By 1832 the Navy Board had asserted its authority over matters of naval administration, but it was then abolished and its duties transferred to the Board of Admiralty. Control of the Board of Admiralty's various subordinate departments was given to naval lords (from 1904 known as sea lords) and a civil lord, with a parliamentary and permanent secretary. It remained in this form until 1 April 1964, when it became the Admiralty Board of the Defence Council of the Ministry of Defence.

1.3 Officers and ratings

Basically the personnel employed by the navy can be divided into two groups: officers and ratings (seamen). Before starting a search for information about anyone who served in the navy, it is useful to establish whether the individual concerned was an officer or a rating, as the records held by the PRO relating to these two categories of naval personnel are in most cases kept separately. A general overview of the various officer ranks and ratings used by the navy from the mid seventeenth to the nineteenth century (of which some still exist) is given below. More detailed information about this topic can be found in *Naval Records for Genealogists* by Dr N.A.M. Rodger (PRO, 1998).

The Royal Navy's officers were not part of a permanent corps. They were appointed either by a sovereign's commission, and regulated by the Admiralty, or by a warrant from a naval administrative body such as the Navy Board. Continuous employment was not guaranteed, so once the appointment had lapsed, officers went onto half pay, if they were entitled to it, until they were re-employed.

1.3.1 Commissioned officers

There are many different types of officer, but generally they fall into two categories: commissioned officers and warrant officers. Commissioned officers are known as such because they are the only officers who can hold commissions. In the past they have collectively been called sea officers, fighting officers, or the military or executive branch of the service. They are responsible for the command of individual ships, fleets and stations, and their rank structure is more clearly defined than that of other officers. At the top of the rank structure are the flag officers (the various types of admiral and the rank of commodore), followed by captain and, finally, lieutenant. These were added to, at various dates, by the introduction of the ranks of commander, lieutenant commander and sub-lieutenant, and by the change of status of some warrant officers to commissioned rank.

1.3.1.1 Admiral of the fleet

The origin of the rank of admiral of the fleet can be traced to 1360, when Sir John Beauchamp was appointed 'Admiral of the King's Southern, Northern and Western

Fleet'. This appointment gave the command of the English navy to one person for the first time. However, it was not until after 1707 that the navy had successive admirals of the fleet. Meanwhile, sole command of the navy was at various times given to the lord admiral, high admiral or lord high admiral (a title that originated with the appointment of George Villiers, first Duke of Buckingham, in 1627).

Up to 1864 the overall command of Royal Navy ships was the responsibility of either the lord high admiral or an admiral of the fleet. When the lord high admiral or the admiral of the fleet was serving at sea, he took the place of the admiral of the red (see below) and would fly either the royal standard (lord high admiral) or the Union flag (admiral of the fleet) from his ship.

Until 1863 the admiral of the fleet held office until his death. From 1863 the Royal Navy was allowed to have three admirals of the fleet, who from 1870 were expected to retire at the age of 70. During the First and Second World Wars, the numbers of admirals of the fleet increased due to promotion. In 1940 all admirals of the fleet were placed on the active list for life.

1.3.1.2 Admiral

The title of admiral probably reached Britain as a result of the crusades – when the rank of admiral was used to indicate the commander of the fleet, or sometimes the person in charge of a ship. The first official use of the title in England was in relation to William De Leybourne, previously the 'Captain of the King's sailers and mariners', who in 1297 was appointed 'Admiral of the sea of the King of England'.

In the seventeenth century the ever growing Royal Navy was divided into three squadrons: the Van, identified by white ensigns; the Centre, with red ensigns; and the Rear, with blue ensigns. Each squadron was commanded by an admiral, who was responsible for formulating battle plans and sending commands to other ships in their squadron by means of flag signals.

As the three squadrons grew in size, it became increasingly difficult for one admiral alone to be in complete control of a squadron. The ranks of vice admiral and rear admiral were therefore introduced for each of the squadrons. But even nine admirals proved insufficient, and by the 1740s provision was made to have more admirals.

The three flag officers (admiral, vice admiral, and rear admiral) each flew an ensign denoting the colour of their squadron. The precedence of seniority of these squadrons was red, white and blue. Up to 1804, there were nine flag officer ranks, the admiral of the fleet (if appointed) being the most senior and the rear admiral of the blue the most junior.

With the introduction of the rank of admiral of the red in 1805, the number of flag ranks increased to 10. Admirals held their rank for life, and promotions based on the seniority of the squadrons occurred only when an admiral died. This rank structure remained unchanged until 1864, when the three squadrons were abolished and the flag ranks reduced to four (admiral of the red, admiral, vice admiral, rear admiral). At the same time, use of the white ensign was extended to all HM ships.

1.3.1.3 Commodore

Promotion from captain to rear admiral was based on seniority and proved to be inflexible. However, the introduction in the seventeenth century of the rank of commodore allowed the Admiralty to promote capable captains on a temporary basis to a specific duty – such as commander-in-chief of a naval station or to take charge of a detached squadron – even though they lacked the seniority necessary to become an admiral. Last in the hierarchy of flag officers, at sea commodores fly a broad pennant to show their rank. At the end of their commission, they revert to the rank of captain.

1.3.1.4 Captain

Traditionally the rank given to the commanding officer of a ship and the most senior rank below flag rank, the courtesy title of captain is also applied to any officer in charge of a naval vessel – for example, a lieutenant in charge of a sloop.

Captains appointed to command HM ships rated 1–6 ('post ships', see 2.11.4) were given the rank of post captain – which was used to distinguish them from those addressed as captain as a courtesy title.

The promotion of captains to rear admiral was based on when a captain had attained post rank. In a bid to ensure that only able captains would be promoted, in 1747 the Admiralty introduced a system whereby unsuitable and elderly captains were promoted to an 'unspecified squadron' popularly known as the 'yellow squadron'. These officers – commonly known as 'yellow admirals' – were entitled to the half pay of a rear admiral but did not have any prospects of future employment or promotion. This provided the remaining captains with opportunities for promotion, based on grounds of seniority and ability.

1.3.1.5 Commander

First used around 1667, the rank of master and commander was adopted for captains of sixth-rate ships. These ships were considered too small to have both a master and captain, so their duties were combined in the one rank. In later years, sixth-rates were also commanded by post captains, though the rank of master and commander was still used. The rank was established by 1747, and by the 1750s it was recognized as the natural progression from lieutenant to captain. In 1794 the 'master and' fell out of use, and the rank of commander was formally introduced.

Officers promoted to the rank of commander were given the command of a ship that was smaller than a post ship but larger than the vessels commanded by lieutenants. This meant that the rank carried the status but not the full rank of captain. It was only from 1827 that the rank of commander was used to indicate the second in command of a ship, as it still is today. Throughout the nineteenth century commanders were addressed as captain, even though they did not hold post rank. From 1794, commanders could be promoted to the rank of post captain. Lieutenants could not receive a commander's commission unless they had served two years as a lieutenant.

1.3.1.6 Master of the fleet

Occasionally the Admiralty appointed an officer to be in charge of navigating a fleet. The post of master of the fleet, which ranked below commander, was created by an order of 1805.

1.3.1.7 Lieutenant commander

Before the official introduction of the rank of lieutenant commander in 1914, it would be used to indicate a lieutenant who was in command of a ship. From 1914, any lieutenant who had eight years' seniority was promoted to the rank of lieutenant commander.

1.3.1.8 Lieutenant

The rank of lieutenant is considered to be the first step in the career of a commissioned officer. Its existence can be traced back to the time of the Armada, though by the end of the sixteenth century it had fallen out of use. In the 1620s the rank was reintroduced, with the aim of appointing 'young gentlemen for sea service'. Lieutenants were considered to be 'gentlemen', regardless of their social background. Like other commissioned officers, a lieutenant received a new commission for each new appointment. The commission often indicated his position on board – for example, a first lieutenant would be second in command of a ship, after the captain. Some ships carried more than one lieutenant. These would be distinguished as first, second and third lieutenant. Numbered lieutenancies are no longer used.

Promotion to the rank of lieutenant depended on selection by the Admiralty or by commanders-in-chief of foreign stations. As already mentioned (see 1.1.5), in times of peace lieutenant's vacancies tended to be scarce. At the turn of the nineteenth century there were three principal ways in which lieutenants could be promoted: through 'interest', using familial or political links with the Admiralty; through commanders-in-chief of foreign stations, when there were vacancies on board ships abroad (subject to the Admiralty's final approval); or as a reward for brave conduct in action. The Admiralty was responsible for appointing lieutenants within the North Sea, Channel surroundings and UK coastal areas.

1.3.1.9 Master's mates, mates and sub-lieutenants

Strictly speaking, mates and master's mates were ratings; but they were distinguished from common ratings because they both tended to be and were recognized as men in training to become officers. The rating master's mate – a senior petty officer (see 1.3.3), commonly referred to simply as 'mate' – was used for men aspiring to become a master, from whom they learned navigation. As navigation was a skill that commissioned officers had to be familiar with, many of them in the early stages of their career served as a master's mate.

From 1824 the rating of mate was adopted to identify would-be lieutenants, and those who aspired to be a master became known as master's assistants. In 1840 the rating of mate was established as an officer's rank, below that of lieutenant. Then in 1860 the rank of mate was renamed sub-lieutenant (a rank that had been used previously, between 1805 and 1815, to describe an officer who was second in command of a small ship commanded by a lieutenant).

1.3.1.10 Midshipmen and cadets

Although the terms midshipman and cadet are ratings, they were generally recognized as 'young gentlemen' (see 1.1.4) aspiring to be lieutenants. The status they were accorded was therefore very different to that of other ratings. The ways in which commissioned officers were recruited and trained and attained their ranks is described in more detail in 2.6 and 2.7.

1.3.2 Warrant officers

In terms of rank structure, warrant officers come after commissioned officers. Appointed by warrants from various naval administrative regulating bodies such as the Navy Board, most warrant officers kept accounts and carried out more specialized duties, for which they often had to serve an apprenticeship and pass a professional examination. These officers can be divided into groups according to their rank and status. The highest warrant officer rank was that of master. Next came surgeon, purser and chaplain (often referred to as civilian officers, because the work they performed at sea was similar to that undertaken ashore); and then gunner, boatswain and carpenter (known as standing officers, because they were responsible for ship maintenance and so stayed appointed to a ship even when it was in dock). The lowest level of warrant officers (the 'inferior officers') comprised surgeon's mate, armourer, sailmaker, schoolmaster, cook and master-at-arms; in the nineteenth century these were classed as ratings, but later they had the opportunity to advance to warrant and commissioned officer ranks. The inferior officers included caulkers and ropemakers from 1790 and later coopers, all of whom had the status of petty officers (see 1.3.3). It is important to note that some warrant officer ranks were transferred to commissioned officers' ranks in the mid nineteenth century, and that from 1903 it was possible for individual warrant officer ranks to achieve commissioned status.

1.3.2.1 Masters

A master was responsible for the navigation of the ship and was qualified to command HM ships on non-combatant duties. Appointed by warrant from the Navy Board, masters were professionally examined by Trinity House (established in 1517). In 1808 the rank of master attained commissioned officer status, being equal initially to that of lieutenant and then from 1814 to that of commander. In 1867 masters were renamed navigating officers. These ranks became redundant after 1883, as henceforth all commissioned officers were trained in navigation.

1.3.2.2 Physicians and surgeons

Surgeons had to pass an examination set by the Barber-Surgeons' Company (from 1745, the Surgeons' Company) before they could be warranted to ships by the Navy Board. They were responsible to the Sick and Hurt Board and were the only medical officers on board ships, whereas physicians were appointed to naval hospitals and fleets. The rank of physician was abolished in 1840 and replaced by deputy inspector of hospitals; this was changed to deputy inspector of hospitals and fleets in 1844, then to deputy inspector general of hospitals and fleets in 1859.

At various dates in the nineteenth century, diverse ranks senior to that of physician were introduced by the navy. At the top end, the rank of physician of the navy was introduced in 1832, only to be replaced by physician general of the navy in 1835. This was in turn altered to inspector general of naval hospitals and fleets in 1843, and to medical director general in 1844. Below this rank in terms of seniority, but above that of physician, was the short-lived rank of inspector of hospitals. This existed from 1805 to 1815 and was then reintroduced in 1840 – only to be replaced by inspector of hospitals and fleets in 1844, which in turn was replaced by inspector general of hospitals and fleets in 1859.

In 1843 surgeons became commissioned officers, and the rank of staff surgeon was introduced for surgeons with over six years' seniority. Then in 1875 the rank of staff surgeon was replaced by that of fleet surgeon.

Surgeons were sometimes assisted by surgeon's mates, serving a form of apprenticeship. These were renamed assistant surgeons from 1805 until 1873, when they became known as surgeons.

1.3.2.3 Pursers

Pursers were warranted to ships by the Admiralty but answerable to the Victualling Board. They were not professionally examined until the mid nineteenth century. Pursers were responsible for the supply and issue of victuals, such as food, tobacco and slops (clothes), and had to keep exact records (musters) of every person on board ship and the victuals they consumed. Some of the supplies issued by a purser were provided by the Victualling Board and some by the purser himself, for which he claimed reimbursement. From 1683, pursers were allowed to keep any 'savings' that could be made on ratings' rations.

In 1843 the rank of purser achieved commissioned officer status, the name being changed to paymaster and purser. In 1852 this was shortened to paymaster, although purser continued to be used.

Pursers often chose a purser's steward or purser's yeoman (both ratings) to assist in their work. Another rating who helped with book keeping and administration was the clerk (often helped by clerk's assistants), who was employed by the captain. Clerks were often in training for a purser's warrant.

At a more exalted level, flag officers employed secretaries to help with their paperwork. These secretaries, who were nominated by the admiral, were usually pursers that held the purser's warrant for the flagship (those duties being carried out by a deputy). From the nineteenth century, secretaries were assigned an officer's rank, which in terms of seniority was higher than that of purser.

1.3.2.4 Engineers

The earliest naval engineers were mechanics supplied by the firms that built ships' engines. The appointment of the first chief engineer and inspector of machinery took place in 1835. When engineer ranks were introduced in 1837, they did not initially include any commissioned or warrant officer ranks. Then in 1847 the most senior engineers became commissioned officers and were ranked as inspectors of machinery afloat (from 1877, inspectors of machinery) and chief engineers. The latter were further subdivided into first, second and third class, and from 1886 were known as fleet engineer, staff engineer, and chief engineer respectively. After these ranks followed assistant engineers (first, second and third class), who were appointed by warrant. In 1861 assistant engineers first class became known simply as engineers, while assistant engineers second and third class were redesignated first and second class. Under the Selborne Scheme, from 1903 lieutenants opting to become engineers were called lieutenants (E).

1.3.2.5 Boatswains

The rank of boatswain is one of the oldest used in the navy; it has its origins in medieval times. Warranted by the Admiralty but answerable to the Navy Board, the boatswain was responsible for the sails, rigging and rope. Up to 1731 he was also responsible for maintaining discipline on board ship – a duty that then passed to the master-at-arms, 'the ship's policeman'. Boatswains were often promoted from the rating of boatswain's mate.

1.3.2.6 Gunners

The rank of gunner can be traced to the fifteenth century. Gunners were examined by and answerable to the Ordnance Board. They were primarily responsible for the ship's guns and ammunition, which was supplied by the Ordnance Board. As warrant officers, gunners were assisted by armourers and yeomen of the powder room and by one quarter gunner or seaman gunner per four guns. Torpedo gunners, or gunners (T), who had specialist knowledge of torpedoes, mines and parts of ships' electrical systems, were added to the list of gunners in the 1880s.

1.3.2.7 Carpenters

Carpenters were warranted by the Admiralty and answerable to the Navy Board. Their duties consisted of the care and preservation of the ship's hull and mast. By the end of the eighteenth century, no person could be appointed as a carpenter to an HM ship without having served an apprenticeship to a shipwright and spent six months or more as a carpenter's mate on board an HM ship; in addition, good conduct certificates had to be produced. In battle, carpenters were to be particularly vigilant to spot any damage from shot, and have ready shot boards and wood to stop any leaks. Many carpenters worked for the Navy Board as civilian employees (shipwrights) in the dockyards before going to sea. In 1918 carpenters were renamed warrant shipwrights, as their work had ceased to be entirely concerned with timber.

1.3.2.8 Chaplains

In 1626 Charles I decreed that each ship of his fleet should have a chaplain. An inspector of naval chaplains was first appointed in 1702. Up to 1843 chaplains were considered to be warrant officers and were appointed by the Admiralty; from then on, they were classed as commissioned officers. No person could be appointed a chaplain by the Admiralty unless he was an ordained deacon and priest of the Church of England, over 35 years of age, and possessed a certificate from the bishop of the diocese in which he was last licensed.

An order in council of 1859 introduced four classes of chaplains, enjoying the same status as commissioned officers. For example, a chaplain with 10 years' service was on a par with a lieutenant. From 1859, the senior chaplain of Greenwich Hospital was to be recognized as the head of naval chaplains, having the title 'chaplain of the fleet' and ranking with a rear admiral. In 1902, the chaplain of the fleet was granted the ecclesiastical dignity of an archdeacon.

1.3.2.9 Schoolmasters and naval instructors

The rank of schoolmaster can be traced back to 1702, when as a rating with the status of midshipman he would receive £20 a year for instructing 'young gentlemen' (see 1.3.1.8), a duty often shared with the chaplain. Schoolmasters could not serve on HM ships unless they had passed an examination at Trinity House. In 1819 this qualifying examination was transferred to the Royal Naval College, and in 1822 the standard of the examination was raised. In 1836 schoolmasters attained warrant officer rank. From 1837 they became known as naval instructor and schoolmaster, and from 1842 simply naval instructor. In 1861 naval instructors attained commissioned officer rank, and from 1864 to 1903 their ranks were subdivided by seniority. With the introduction of the Selborne Scheme in 1903, the naval instructor branch was closed. It was revived in 1918, with naval instructors adopting the executive ranks of instructor lieutenant to instructor captain.

1.3.2.10 Cooks

Up to 1704, cooks were warrant officers. But after 1704, when their warranting body changed from the Admiralty to the Navy Board, their status declined and from 1838 they ranked as petty officers (see 1.3.3). Cooks were usually disabled seamen and often were untrained. In the 1740s their main responsibilities consisted of ensuring that meat supplies were stored properly and watered regularly and that food was carefully cleaned and boiled before being served. From 1838, like some other ratings, they had the opportunity to advance, over a period of time, to commissioned and warrant officer ranks.

1.3.2.11 Masters-at-arms

A master-at-arms was appointed by warrant from the Admiralty. His duties consisted of training petty officers and the ship's company in the use of small arms, overseeing the changing of the ship's guards and watches, ensuring that firearms were clean and in working order, searching vessels bringing provisions, and preventing seamen leaving the ship without leave. He was also responsible for reporting any misdemeanours committed on board to the officer of the watch. It was common for masters-at-arms to have previously served in the army, and they were often assisted in their duties by a corporal.

With the establishment of the Royal Marines in 1755, the need for seamen to be trained in musketry diminished. As a result, the duties of the master-at-arms changed and he became primarily responsible for policing the ship. In the nineteenth century his rank became that of a petty officer, but with the possibility of advancing to warrant and commissioned officer ranks.

1.3.3 Ratings

Below commissioned and warrant officers, in the naval hierarchy, come 'the people' (ratings). The term 'rating' is used to describe a seaman's status. Seamen were 'rated' according to their skills and ability and the kind of work they were expected to perform. Many types of rating have been used by the Royal Navy. It is not possible to describe each one in detail, but a general overview follows of the ratings most commonly used from the seventeenth to the nineteenth century. Further information about ratings can be found in Chapter 3.

At the top end of the ratings' structure are Chief Petty Officers (CPOs) and petty officers (senior ratings that have the same status in the navy as sergeants in the army). Midshipmen and master's mates were recognized as would-be commissioned officers and so their status was both different from and above that of other petty officers, such as quartermasters and quarter gunners. After the various petty officers came a huge variety of other ratings.

1.3.3.1 Master's mates

A master's mate, who was usually an experienced seaman, assisted the master of a ship (see 1.3.2.1). By the 1750s a master's mate was likely to be a superior midshipman waiting to pass his examination or to receive his commission.

1.3.3.2 Quartermasters

The duties of a quartermaster comprised steering the ship, stowing ballast, placing provisions in the hold, keeping time using the ship's watch-glasses, and overseeing the delivery of provisions to the purser's steward. Quartermasters were usually older seamen.

1.3.3.3 Gunner's mates and quarter gunners

Ranked after the gunner's mate, there was one quarter gunner for every four guns on board a ship. The main duties of a quarter gunner consisted of assisting the gunner, keeping the guns and carriages in working order, and ensuring that there were sufficient supplies for their use.

1.3.3.4 Captains of the top, waist, afterguard and forecastle

Although these are grand titles, the men assigned to these posts were in fact ratings. It was common practice in the navy to put some seamen in charge of specific areas of a ship during each watch. For example, in a fifth-rate ship with 36 guns and a complement of 250 men, four 'captains' would be appointed to the top (two to the main top and two to the mizzen mast), two 'captains' to the waist, two to the afterguard, and two to the forecastle. Seamen who held these 'rates' had extra responsibility but did not receive extra pay.

1.3.3.5 Able seamen

The system of rating seamen as 'ordinary' or 'able' was introduced in 1652. An able seaman was considered to be a 'thorough bred sailor' and 'one who is not only able to work, but is also acquainted with his duty as a seaman'. The rating of seamen was usually the responsibility of the captain, in consultation with the master and the boatswain. An able seaman had to be at least 20 years old, with five years' experience at sea. He was expected to have all the skills of an ordinary seaman and, in addition, be able to take over as the main helmsman, keeping the ship on course, and to 'heave the lead' (a process that enabled the master to gauge the depth of water for navigational purposes).

1.3.3.6 Ordinary seamen

The rating of ordinary seaman – introduced in 1652, along with that of able seaman – was generally recognized as the lowest rating on a ship. Boys were rated ordinary seaman at the age of 18 and were usually rated 'able' at the age of 21. An ordinary seaman was described 'as one who can make himself useful on board, but is not an expert or skilful sailor'. Seamen were not trained formally and developed their skills mainly through experience. Ships had miles of rope rigging, and good seamen were expected to be familiar with all the ropes and able to find them readily at any time of day or night and in every kind of weather. Ordinary seaman could tie many knots, prepare ropes, and run rigging up to the yardarm in all weather conditions – a small amount of supporting footrope being the only safeguard against injury or death through falling. In addition, seamen needed to be able to work the sails, row boats, hoist weights, raise and lower the anchor, help load guns and push them to the gun ports when required, and cope with life at sea with all its potential problems.

1.3.3.7 Landsmen

The rating of landsman was a 'rate' given by the Royal Navy to men serving on a warship who lacked sea experience. Ideally, men recruited to the navy should have had some experience of working at sea. However, especially during the seventeenth and eighteenth centuries, in times of war the demand for men was so great that nearly every man brought in by the press gangs was rated on board ship as a landsman. Because it could take up to two years to train landsmen in the skills of seamanship, their presence was often resented by both officers and seamen. However, no special provision was made for training landsmen, which was the responsibility of the captain. Some landsmen – for example, barbers and tailors – were able to perform duties on board ship in line with their previous trade. But many landsmen did not possess a skill or trade appropriate to sea service, and so had to perform tasks such as cleaning the decks and heaving ropes. The rate of landsman was discontinued in 1862, when it was replaced by ordinary seaman second class.

1.3.3.8 Boys and volunteers

The ratings of boy first, second and third class were introduced in 1794 to replace that of captain's servant (see 2.7). Those under the age of 15 were rated boys third class, and those aged 15 to 17 as second class. The rating of boy first class (subsequently called volunteer first class) was given to 'young gentlemen' (see 1.3.1.8) training to become officers.

2 Officers

2.1 The *Navy List* and *New Navy List*

Many details about an officer's career and personal background can be found in published sources. So as a first step, instead of searching original documents for information, it may be a more effective use of time to look through the *Navy List* (and the *New Navy List*, if relevant) and through biographical reference books and manuscript sources (see 2.2). They may also help you decide where to start when you are ready to search the records themselves.

By far the most important printed source for tracing details of commissioned and warrant officer careers is the *Navy List*. This began as *Steel's Navy List*, first issued in 1782, and is still published today. Produced four times a year, it includes seniority lists of officers by rank and from 1810 it lists the ships of the Royal Navy with the names of officers serving on them. Surname indexes appear in the *Navy List* from April 1847. Commissioned officers and masters are listed from 1782, surgeons from 1794, pursers from 1796, chaplains from 1815, mates from 1841, clerks from 1846, engineers from 1853, sub-lieutenants from 1861, naval instructors from 1862, boatswains, carpenters, gunners, midshipmen and cadets from 1870, and artificer engineers from 1898.

Confidential editions of the *Navy List* issued during the First and Second World Wars are available, in series **ADM 177**, in the Microfilm Reading Room (MRR).

Published between February 1841 and February 1856, the *New Navy List* contains similar information to the *Navy List* but also provides backdated information about officers' war service. Surname indexes appear in the *New Navy List* from February 1846.

Both the *Navy List* and *New Navy List* include content lists and keys to abbreviations used. In early editions of the *Navy List*, abbreviations are explained under the heading 'Contractions'.

Near complete sets of the *Navy List* and *New Navy List* are held in the Microfilm Reading Room.

2.2 Printed and manuscript sources

2.2.1 General biographical sources

Given that from the mid seventeenth to the nineteenth century many commissioned officers of note came from wealthy or aristocratic backgrounds, it is possible to find

Where serving	Name	Rank	Seniority	Where serving	Name	Rank	Seniority
	2 ALPHABETICAL LIST OF THE ACTIVE OFFICERS						
546	ABBAY Ambrose T. N....	L	1 Apr 09	34a	Aitken Robert	A E	1 Apr 03
113	Abbey Douglas W. ...	A C	15 July 12	202	Aitkenhead Thomas E.	E L	1 Apr 08
148a	Abbie Andrew A.	A E	1 Apr 11	114	Albert *His Royal Highness Prince*	Mid	15 Sept 13
118	Abbie William C.... ...	A E	1 Jan 12	110	Alcock Henry C.	L	1 Oct 99
531	Abbott Edmund G. ...	Mid	15 Jan 13	39	Alder George F. ...	S B	22 Feb 12
476	Abbott Ernest	Gr	25 Oct 06	218	Alderson Percy F. ...	S S	11 Feb 09
232	Abbott Frank M. (act)	S L	15 May 13	148a	Alderson William J. S.	C	30 June 08
349a	Abbott Frederick J.	Gr	11 Oct 12	Page } 534	Aldwell Gerald W. S. ...	E L	15 Sept 04
420	Abbott Robert J. (act)	Gr	20 Nov 12		Alexander Alfred G.	Mate	14 Feb 13
120	Abbott William St. G. (act)	S L	15 Sept 13	80	Alexander Caledon C. ...	Mid	15 Sept 12
191	Abell William G.	W.W	1 Jan 10	238	Alexander Charles O. ...	L	15 June 08
145	Abercrombie Cecil H....	L	31 Dec 08	505c	Alexander Frederick ...	E L	1 June 04
48	Abraham Felix	F P	1 Mar 11	385	Alexander George H....	B	18 Oct 99
	Abraham Gerald H.F. RM	L	1 Jan 04	438a	Alexander James W. ...	E L	1 June 04
473	Abrams William C. ...	A E	1 Feb 12	225	Alexander Philip G. BA	Ch	2 Jan 12
263	Acheson *The Hon.* Patrick G. E. C. MVO	L	31 Aug 04	234	Alexander Ralph C. BA	Ch	4 Mar 13
	Ackerman Francis A. RM	W O	10 June 12	520	Alexander Robert... ...	S B	1 Apr 02
	Ackerman John C. (act)	Gr	22 May 13	484a	Alexander-Sinclair Edwyn S. ... ...MVO	C	30 June 05
	Acland Edward L. D., MVO	E L	1 Aug 05	252	Alexander-Sinclair Mervyn B.	Mid	15 Jan 12
180	Acland Hubert G. D. ...	L	15 Nov 10	262	Alington Argentine H.	Cr	30 June 10
263	Acland Kenneth F. D.	L	15 June 11	20	Alison Archibald	L	15 Nov 10
	Acock Walter... ... RM	W O	2 Sept 03	484a	Alison Frederick B. (act)	S L	15 May 13
	A'Court *The Hon.* Herbert E H.	C	31 Dec 07	204	Alison Roger V.	L	1 Oct 06
C G	Acton Fitzmaurice ...	Cr	30 June 08		Allan Charles ...(act)	A E	1 Oct 13
260	Acworth Bernard... ...	L	30 June 07	265	Allan George ... ... RM	RMG	1 Sept 11
	Adair Charles W. RM { Proby 2ndLt } 1 Jan 12	Proby 2ndLt	1 Jan 12	185a	Allchorn Arthur J.(act)	A E	1 Sept 13
	Adair *Sir* William T., KCB, RM	Gen.	22 Feb 12	277	Allen Arthur C.	S L	30 Mar 13
6	Adair-Hall Harold D....	L	31 Dec 06	326c	Allen Bertram C. ...MVO	F P	21 Oct 08
452	Adam Charles K.... ...	S L	30 Oct 11	261	Allen Cecil C. A.	Mid	15 Sept 12
510	Adam Herbert A.... ...	C	30 June 10	492	Allen Charles H.	L	15 July 13
275b	Adam Lionel S. M. ...	L	1 Oct 10	11	Allen Ebenezer J.... ...	E L	1 June 04
259	Adams Arthur ...	Ch B	25 Oct 12	288	Allen Francis J. C. ...	L	15 Mar 08
131	Adams Bryan F.	L	31 Dec 09	303	Allen Frank H.	A E	1 Oct 10
106	Adams Ernest... (act)	B	11 Nov 12	261	Allen George B.	E L	1 May 10
217b	Adams Francis E.	S P	5 June 12	512	Allen George R. G. ...	L	15 Oct 12
364	Adams George E. ...	Car	29 Mar 11	552	Allen Hamilton C. ...	L	30 Sept 04
448	Adams Henry G. H. ...	L	30 June 01		*(Lent for duty under Australian Govt.)*		
389	Adams Henry J.	Car	29 Oct 03	159	Allen Jack R	A P	12 July 08
259	Adams John H.	E A	14 Aug 10	48	Allen James	A E	1 Nov 06
40	Adams Joseph A.... ...	Ch Cr	24 Mar 13	512	Allen John D.	Cr	31 Dec 06
121	Adams Percy...	Gr	8 Nov 11	524 } DY } Dev	Allen John R....	Cr L	16 June 13
583	Adams Samuel	Gr	4 July 00	476	Allen Matthew	S B	1 Nov 98
	(Lent for duty under Australian Govt.)			366	Allen Percival W.... ...	E L	1 Nov 08
258	Adams William R.	Gr	2 Apr 12	339b	Allen Ralph H.	S L	15 May 13
225	Addington Leonard G.	S L	30 June 13		Allen Thomas ... (act)	A E	1 Oct 13
151	Addison Albert P. ...	C	30 June 13		Allen Walter L.	Cr	30 June 10
385	Addison-Scott Duncan G. ... ... MB	S S	21 Nov 12	307	Allenby John N.	E L	2 Jan 03
180	Addy Ernest	W A	8 Aug 11	W.Coll.	Allenby Reginald A.MVO	R A	20 Mar 13
476	Adshead Geoffrey P.MB	S	19 Nov 07	127b	Allerton Thomas R.(act)	A E	1 Jan 13
237	Agar Augustine W. S.	L	30 June 12	482	Alleyne *Sir* John M.Bt.	L	15 July 10
252 } DY Cape	Aggar Edward J.... ...	Ch B	1 Apr 12	117	Alleyne Reynold M. ...	S L	15 Oct 12
326	Agnew Hugh L.	Mid	15 Jan 12	202	Alleyne Victor P.... ...	L	1 Oct 09
6	Ahearn William J. (act.)	A E	1 May 13	338	Allsup Claud F.	L	30 June 03
303	Ahearn William T. ...	Gr	4 Apr 00	12a	Allum Alfred J.	Gr	1 July 01
384	Ahern William	Ch B	1 Apr 12	385 } NOD	Altham Edward	Cr	30 June 13
385 } Coll	Ainslie Maurice A. BA	N I	26 June 94	170	Alton Ernest St. G. ...	F P	27 Sept 06
	Ainsworth Frank S. ...	E L	7 Jan 03	Sec } 175 } NH } Portl	Alton Francis C. ... CB	P in C	5 June 08
C G	Airey Frederick W. I...	F P	1 Aug 01	520	Alton Francis C.	S	6 May 10
391c	Aitchison John G. (act)	S L	15 May 13	145	Alton Wingfield W. ...	F P	4 Feb 05

Figure 1 Extract from the *Navy List* containing an entry for HRH Prince Albert (right hand column), the future King George VI. (*Navy List*, November 1913, p2)

personal and career information about them in standard biographical reference works such as the *Dictionary of National Biography, Burke's Peerage, Burke's Landed Gentry, Who's Who* (1917 to present day), *Who Was Who* (1897–1995) and the *British Biographical Archive* (1601–1929).

Another extremely useful source in this context is *The Times*, which the PRO holds on microfilm from 1790 to 2001. To find items such as obituaries, it can be searched quickly by name using *Palmer's Index to The Times 1790–1905* and the *Official Index to The Times 1906–1980* (both published by Chadwyck-Healey), which are available on CD-ROM in the PRO Library.

The *Medical Directory*, which is published annually, includes lists of naval medical officers, giving rank and dates of passing qualifying examinations, plus details of qualifications and, in some instances, where practising. The PRO Library holds an incomplete series of the *Medical Directory* from 1895 to 1987.

2.2.2 Published naval reference works

Naval biographical works tend to relate to commissioned officers, and so are vital sources when trying to track down information about them. The most important ones are:

- *Biographia Navalis*, by J. Charnock (London, 1796). Six volumes and one nominal index. Short biographies of Royal Naval officers, 1660–1794.

- *Marshall's Naval Biography*, by J. Marshall (London, 1823). Twelve books and a name index. Short biographies of flag officers, superannuated rear admirals, retired captains, post captains (see 1.3.1.4) and commanders, 1760–1823.

- *Campbell's Lives of Admirals*, by Dr J. Campbell (London, 1817). Eight volumes. A historical account of the Royal Navy from its beginning until 1816, including biographies of admirals.

- *British Admirals of the Fleet 1734–1995*, by T. A. Heathcote (Pen and Sword Books, 2002). Outlines the lives of 115 officers who have held the rank of Admiral of the Fleet since 1734.

- *The Commissioned Sea Officers of the Royal Navy 1660–1815*, edited by D. Syrett and R.L. DiNardo (Naval Records Society, 1994). Arranged alphabetically by name. Gives dates of seniority, promotion, retirement and death.

- *O'Byrne's Naval Biography*, by W.R. O'Byrne (London, 1849). Arranged alphabetically by name, this provides genealogical and career details of all commissioned officers alive in 1845. O'Byrne's original manuscript – which is often more comprehensive than the published volume – is held by the Manuscripts Department of the British Library.

- *The Trafalgar Roll*, by Colonel R.H. Mackenzie (George Allen & Company, 1913). Lists by ship all the officers that served at the Battle of Trafalgar, often with personal and career details about them.

- *The Sea Chaplains, A History of the Chaplains of the Royal Navy*, by G. Taylor (Oxford Illustrated Press, 1978). Lists names and dates of appointments of sea chaplains, 1651–1977.

All the books mentioned above are held by the PRO Library, and should be orderable from local libraries.

2.2.3 Manuscript sources

The miscellaneous manuscript sources listed below can be viewed in the PRO Library:

- *List of Flag Officers and Commissioned Officers of the Royal Navy 1660–88.* Manuscript index arranged in nominal order. Gives name, rank, ship's name, dates of appointment and, in some cases, date of death.

- *The Papers of Ships and Officers 1660–88*, compiled by Commander W.B. Rowbotham. Alphabetical list of ships with the names of commissioned officers who served on them, plus rank and date of commission.

- *Commissioned Officers 1660–88.* An updated copy of Charles Sergison's manuscript held at the National Maritime Museum (for address and contact details, see Appendix 2). Arranged in nominal order, it gives the ships the officer served on, rank and date of commission.

- *List of the Officers of the Royal Navy 1660–1750.* Manuscript with own surname index. Gives dates of seniority and death, and notes about career.

- *Indexes of Officers and Ships 1665–88.* Arranged by rank, provides details of ships served on, dates of promotion and, in some instances, date of death.

- *List of Chaplains 1626–1903.* Arranged chronologically. Gives chaplain's name, ship's name and year of appointment.

2.3 Commissioned and warrant officers' service records

The main source for tracing information about an officer's background and career is a service record. These records vary in their ease of use and the amount of detail they contain. Sometimes it may not be possible to trace an officer's service record because it has not survived, or due to the way these records were kept and compiled by the Admiralty. From the seventeenth to the mid nineteenth century the Admiralty did not maintain a central registry of officers' service records, although many of its departments did keep their own officers' records. As a result, the various series of records are often patchy, sometimes contain different details, and occasionally

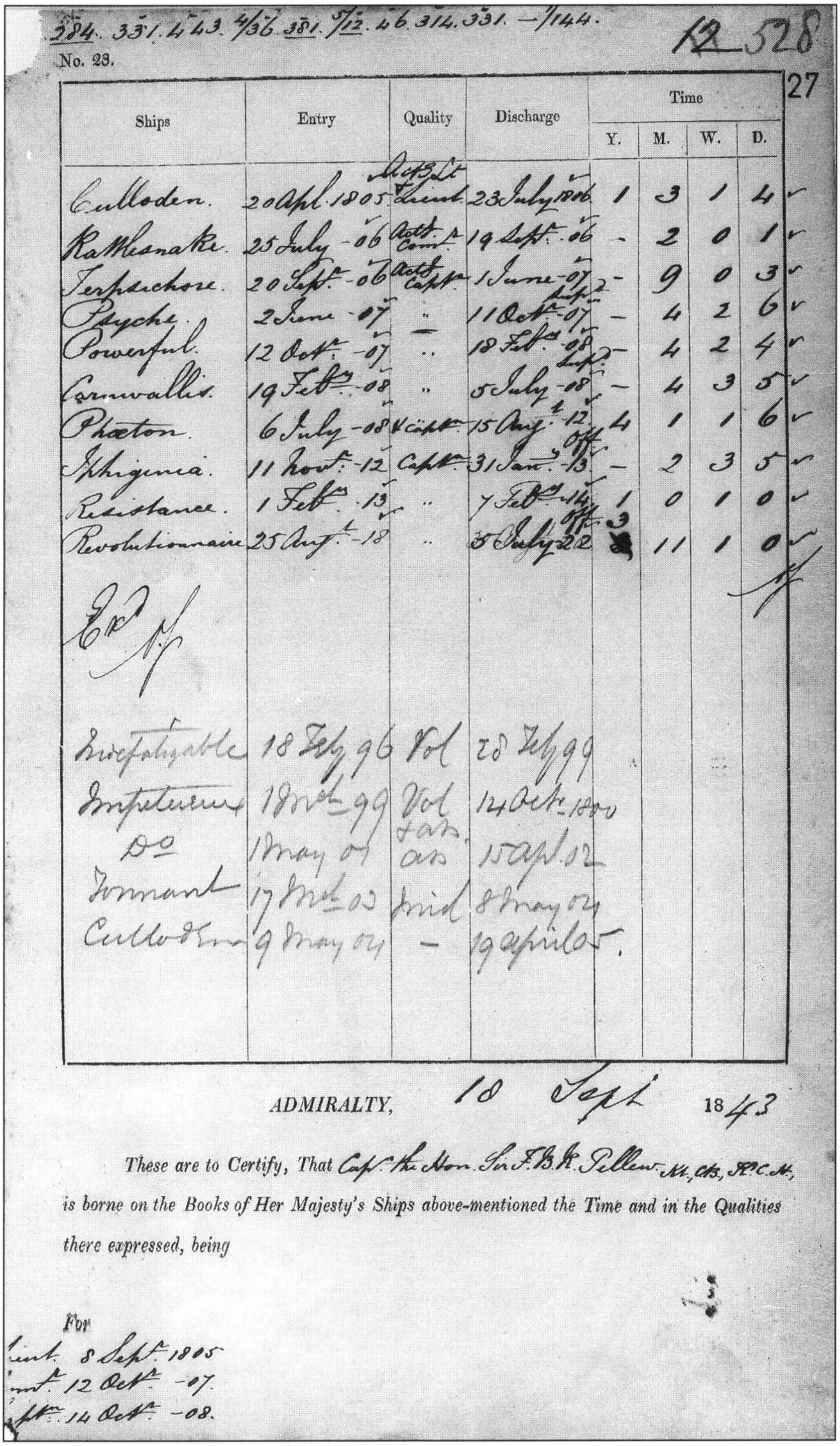

384. 331. 443. 4/36. 381. 5/12. 46. 314. 331. —/144.

No. 23.

12 528

27

Ships	Entry	Quality	Discharge	Time Y.	M.	W.	D.
Culloden.	20 Apl 1805	Actg Lt / Lieut.	23 July 1806	1	3	1	4
Rattlesnake.	25 July -06	Actg Comr	19 Septr -06	-	2	0	1
Terpsichore.	20 Septr -06	Actg Captn	1 June -07	-	9	0	3
Psyche.	2 June -07	–	11 Octr -07	–	4	2	6
Powerful.	12 Octr -07	..	18 Feby -08	–	4	2	4
Cornwallis.	19 Feby -08	..	5 July -08	–	4	3	5
Phaeton.	6 July -08	Captn	15 Augt -12	4	1	1	6
Iphigenia.	11 Novr -12	Captn	31 Jan -13	–	2	3	5
Resistance.	1 Feb -13	..	7 Feby -14	1	0	1	0
Revolutionnaire	25 Augt -18	..	5 July 22	3	11	1	0
Indefatigable	18 Feby 96	Vol	28 Feby 99				
Impetueux	18 Mch 99	Vol	14 Oct 1800				
Do	1 May 01	as	15 Apl 02				
Tonnant	17 Mch 03	Mid	8 May 04				
Culloden	9 May 04	–	19 April 05				

ADMIRALTY, 18 Sept 1843

These are to Certify, That Capt. the Hon. Sir F. B. R. Pellew. Kt, CB, KCH,
is borne on the Books of Her Majesty's Ships above-mentioned the Time and in the Qualities there expressed, being

For

Lieut. 8 Septr 1805

Comt. 12 Octr -07.

Captn 14 Octr -08.

Figure 2 Service record of Sir Fleetwood Broughton Reynolds Pellew. (ADM 196/5 p528); (see p70) overlap; also, you may sometimes find that there is more than one service record for an individual officer.

In most service records you can discover an officer's rank, names of ships served on, with dates of entry and discharge from each, total time served, and dates of promotion and death. Early service records tend to be less detailed – for example, it is only from the latter half of the nineteenth century that details such as an officer's date and place of birth, father's name and address, wife's name, date of marriage, and children's names and dates of birth may be found.

2.3.1 Officers' service records 1660–1913

There are some early service records, arranged in name order, for admirals (1660–88), captains (1660–88, but also including those with dates of seniority up to 1746), and commanders and lieutenants (1660–88) in **ADM 10/10**. Service records for the same officers, covering 1660–85, exist in **ADM 10/15**.

As mentioned above, from the end of the seventeenth century to the mid nineteenth century service records for officers were not kept systematically. Nevertheless, it is possible to piece together the career of officers who served during this period by searching the printed and manuscript sources described in sections 2.1 and 2.2, passing certificates (see 2.6), commission and warrant books (see 2.9), and ships' musters and pay books (see 4.1.1). Moreover, the *Calendars of State Papers* held in the Map and Large Document Room and the correspondence received and sent by the Admiralty (held in **ADM 1** and **ADM 2**) and the Navy Board (in **ADM 106**) contain much potentially useful information about officers, though due to the way they are arranged these records are not easy to search.

The main series of officers' service records are in **ADM 196**. Although extending from 1756 to 1931, they mainly relate to officers who served between 1840 and 1910. These records are available on microfilm in the Microfilm Reading Room, and there is a partial personal-name card index to them in the same room. When using this index, if you find a card or cards relating to an officer you are researching, note down the whole of the reference that appears in the top right-hand corner. This will enable you to locate the officer's service record more quickly. A typical reference from this index is **ADM 196/5** p528, which refers to a service record for Admiral F.B.R. Pellew (the subject of the case study in 2.13). In this example, **ADM 196/5** is the document reference for the microfilm that needs to be viewed, and p528 (which is not the same as the folio number stamped on the film) is the number of the page where Pellew's service record appears. If you cannot find the name of an officer in the personal-name card index, then it is worth checking the **ADM 196** series list to see if there are any relevant documents, as the card index to **ADM 196** is incomplete.

Various other service records for officers are scattered throughout Admiralty records. There are no comprehensive name indexes to them, but many contain integral surname indexes. A list of these records follows arranged by rank.

Rank	Date range	Documents	Remarks
Admirals	1843	**ADM 11/12**	Covers surnames with initial letters Mc–Z only, but contains backdated service details.
Captains	1843 1844	**ADM 11/12** **ADM 11/13**	Ditto. Ditto.
Commanders	1843 1846	**ADM 11/12** **ADM 11/11**	Ditto. Arranged in name order. Contains backdated service details.
Lieutenants	1846 31 Oct 1895 to 1 Oct 1898	**ADM 11/11** **ADM 196/137**	Ditto. Arranged by date of seniority. Contains a surname index.
Master's mates and midshipmen	1814	**ADM 6/182**	Arranged in two parts (A–K and L–Y), in folders, by initial letter of surname. Past service details, age and place of birth are given.
Inspectors of hospitals	1861–94	**ADM 105/75–76**	Both documents contain surname indexes.
Surgeons	1774–1886 1742–1893 1891–1904 1891–1913	**ADM 104/12–19*** **ADM 104/30–32, 38–42** **ADM 104/166–167** **ADM 6/443–444**	Name-indexed by **ADM 104/11**. Each document contains a surname index, except **ADM 104/44**, which is arranged in name order. Arranged by date of seniority as surgeon. No surname indexes. Each document contains a surname index.
Assistant surgeons	1795–1873 1803–1909	**ADM 104/20–28*** **ADM 104/33–42**	Name-indexed by **ADM 104/11**. Each document contains a surname index.
Gunners	1838–98	**ADM 196/167–170**	Each document contains a surname index.
Carpenters	1848–1912	**ADM 29/114–115**	Each document contains a surname index.
Boatswains	1848–1912	**ADM 29/116–119**	Each document contains a surname index.
Signal boatswains	1890–1912	**ADM 29/120**	
Paymasters	1891–1905	**ADM 6/443**	Contains a surname index. Is also name-indexed by **ADM 6/442**.
Chaplains	1812–1913	**ADM 6/440–444**	Each document contains a surname index except **ADM 6/444**.
Naval instructors	1891–1905	**ADM 6/443**	Contains a surname index.
Engineers	1839–62 1893–1905	**ADM 29/105–111** **ADM 196/130**	Name-indexed by **ADM 29/131**. Contains a surname index.
Assistant clerks and paymasters	1889–1910 1886–1902	**ADM 196/171** **ADM 196/172**	Contains a surname index. Contains a surname index.

* Contains many internal references that do not appear to relate to other existing documents – for example, 'brought from O.B folio 73'. Other references can be cross-referenced between surgeons' records in **ADM 104/12–19** and assistant surgeons' records in **ADM 104/20–28**.

If a service record for an officer cannot be found in **ADM 196** or in the records described in the table on p27, there are other records that may supply the details you seek. For example, the surveys and analyses of officers' service described in 2.4; warrant officers' certificates of service compiled by the Admiralty for Greenwich Hospital pensions, 1802–94, in **ADM 29** (see 2.5); and applications from officers for admission to the Greenwich Hospital as in-pensioners, 1790–1865, in **ADM 73** (see 2.5). It is also worth combing through the *Navy List* (see 2.1) and the various printed and manuscript sources described in 2.2. If these yield nothing, it may still be possible to piece together information about an officer's personal background and career, using other sources. Guidance on how to do this is given in the officer's case study in 2.13.

2.3.2 Officers' service records: First World War

The service records of executive officers (admirals, captains, commanders, lieutenant commanders, lieutenants, sub-lieutenants, mates, midshipmen, cadets) and warrant officers (carpenters, gunners, boatswains, warrant writers, signal boatswains, warrant telegraphists, warrant armourers, warrant electricians, instructors in cookery, torpedo gunners, warrant stewards, warrant shipwrights) who served in the First World War are in **ADM 196**.

Service records relating to executive officers who passed as midshipmen between 15 May 1912 and 1 May 1917 can be found in **ADM 196/117–124** (see table below). A surname index to the service records in **ADM 196/117–124** is available in the Microfilm Reading Room. This index provides a document reference and page number indicating where the service record of the officer will be found.

Another way of finding an executive officer's service record in **ADM 196/117–124** is to establish when he passed as a midshipman, since most executive officers passed through this rank at the beginning of their career. This passing date can be found in the *Navy List* (see 2.1). For example, the *Navy List* of November 1913 contains an entry for His Royal Highness Prince Albert (the future King George VI) (see p22). At the end

Date attaining rank of midshipman	Document reference
15 May 1912 to 15 January 1913	**ADM 196/117**
15 May 1913 to 15 January 1914	**ADM 196/118**
15 May 1914 to 2 August 1914	**ADM 196/119**
2 August 1914	**ADM 196/120**
2 August 1914	**ADM 196/121**
2 August 1914 to 8 September 1915	**ADM 196/122**
1 January 1916 to 17 July 1916	**ADM 196/123**
1 January 1917 to 1 May 1917	**ADM 196/124**

of his entry, under the rank column is the abbreviation 'mid' (for midshipman) and a date of seniority to that rank of 15 September 1913. You can use this date to locate his service record, since the table above gives the document reference (**ADM 196/118**) for midshipmen whose date of seniority is 15 September 1913. Most of these service records are arranged in passing-date order. Copies of the *Navy List* for 1782 to 1987 are held in the Microfilm Reading Room; from October 1847 they contain surname indexes that make them relatively easy to use.

The type of information given in First World War service records includes: date of birth (place of birth is not usually given); wife's name; date and place of marriage; name and profession of father (address sometimes given); dates of commission and promotion; details of rewards and distinctions and of examinations taken; dates of appointment and discharge from each named ship; comments by commanding officers regarding the officer's conduct, ability, professional knowledge and suitability for promotion; and dates of retirement and death. It is worth noting that the type of information given can vary between service records (particularly with regard to next of kin, which may be omitted altogether); that the records cover an officer's career in its entirety from the rank of midshipman upwards (so for some officers this would include service in and beyond the Second World War); and that references to overlapping service records can be found (for example, the records in **ADM 196/117–124** may make reference to **ADM 196/36–56** and **68**, which they follow directly in date order).

The main series of records of service relating to warrant officers who served in the First World War are in **ADM 196/156–161**, which cover warrant officers joining the navy between 1903 and 1931 (see table below). They are arranged by date of seniority to a particular warrant officer rank, and are partially name-indexed by **ADM 196/163**. A typical entry in this index would be '**J. Bellis, gunner, Volume 2 p13**' – which, as shown in the table above, refers to **ADM 196/156**, page 13. However, an alternative to using this index is to search these records by date of seniority to a particular rank, which you can find in the *Navy List* as explained above. It is also worth noting that **ADM 196/156–161** may contain cross-references to service records in **ADM 196/34–35**. Service records of warrant officers promoted to lieutenant between 1 January 1918

Date of seniority to rank	Document reference
1903–15	**ADM 196/156** (Volume 2). Indexed by **ADM 196/163**.
1915–16	**ADM 196/157** (Volume 3). Indexed by **ADM 196/163**.
1916–17	**ADM 196/158** (Volume 4). Indexed by **ADM 196/163**.
1895–1922	**ADM 196/159** (Volume 5). Indexed by **ADM 196/163**.
1922–6	**ADM 196/160** (no surname index).
1926–31	**ADM 196/161** (no surname index).

and 30 June 1931 are in **ADM 196/153**, which includes a surname index.

Details of further service records relating to executive and warrant officers who served in the First World War are given below. There is no overall name index to these records, but some are indexed by integral indexes or by separate index volumes. If there are no relevant name indexes, you will have to search the service records either by the date when the officer joined the navy or by his date of seniority or promotion to a particular rank. This type of information can be found by checking the surname indexes and seniority lists that feature in the *Navy List* (see 2.1 and above).

Lieutenants

Date of promotion to lieutenant (including supplementary lieutenants and sub-lieutenants)	Document reference
1 January 1913 to 1 June 1914	**ADM 196/152** (contains own surname index)

Engineers

Date of entry as probationary assistant engineer	Document reference
4 July 1905 to 7 August 1917	**ADM 196/131** (contains own surname index)
14 August 1917 to 18 November 1918	**ADM 196/132** (contains own surname index)
Date of entry as assistant engineer or engineer (temporary engineer officers)	
22 May 1878 to 22 January 1915	**ADM 196/133**
Date on becoming acting artificer engineer	
31 March 1911 to 10 September 1914	**ADM 196/134** (contains own surname index)
10 September 1914 to 1 March 1918	**ADM 196/135** (contains own surname index)
4 April 1918 to 26 March 1928	**ADM 196/136** (contains own surname index)

Gunners

Date of seniority as gunner	Document reference
30 March 1901 to 15 June 1914	**ADM 196/164** (contains own surname index)
1 August 1918 to 28 September 1918	**ADM 196/165** (contains own surname index)

Assistant clerks and paymasters

Date of entry as assistant clerk	Document reference
1911–20	**ADM 196/174** (contains own surname index)

Schoolmasters

Date of entry as schoolmaster	Document reference
1919–26	**ADM 196/177**

Surgeons

Date of seniority as surgeon	Document reference
21 November 1904 to 3 April 1914	**ADM 104/168**
1 January 1914 to 31 December 1926	**ADM 104/169** (includes short-service surgeons)
1914–16 (temporary surgeons)	**ADM 104/44**
1914–19 (temporary surgeons only)	**ADM 104/170** (contains own surname index)

If you are unable to find a service record for an executive or warrant officer who served in the First World War, you can use the *Navy List* to obtain a basic outline of his career (see 2.1). In addition, the summaries of confidential reports described in 2.12.2 provide a valuable complementary source.

2.3.3 Officers' service records since the First World War

Although some records mentioned above include details of officers serving beyond the Second World War, service records for executive officers whose service began after May 1917 and for warrant officers whose service began after 1931 are not available to the general public. However, information from records that have not yet been released can be provided to officers or, for a fee, to their next of kin. Applications for retired officers' service records should be addressed to the Ministry of Defence at the Navy Records Centre in Hayes, Middlesex (for address, see Appendix 2). Requests for service records of officers aged under 60 should be sent to the Naval Secretary (OMOBS) at the address given in Appendix 2.

A basic outline of the career of an officer who served in the navy after the First World War can be found by searching through the *Navy List* (see 2.1).

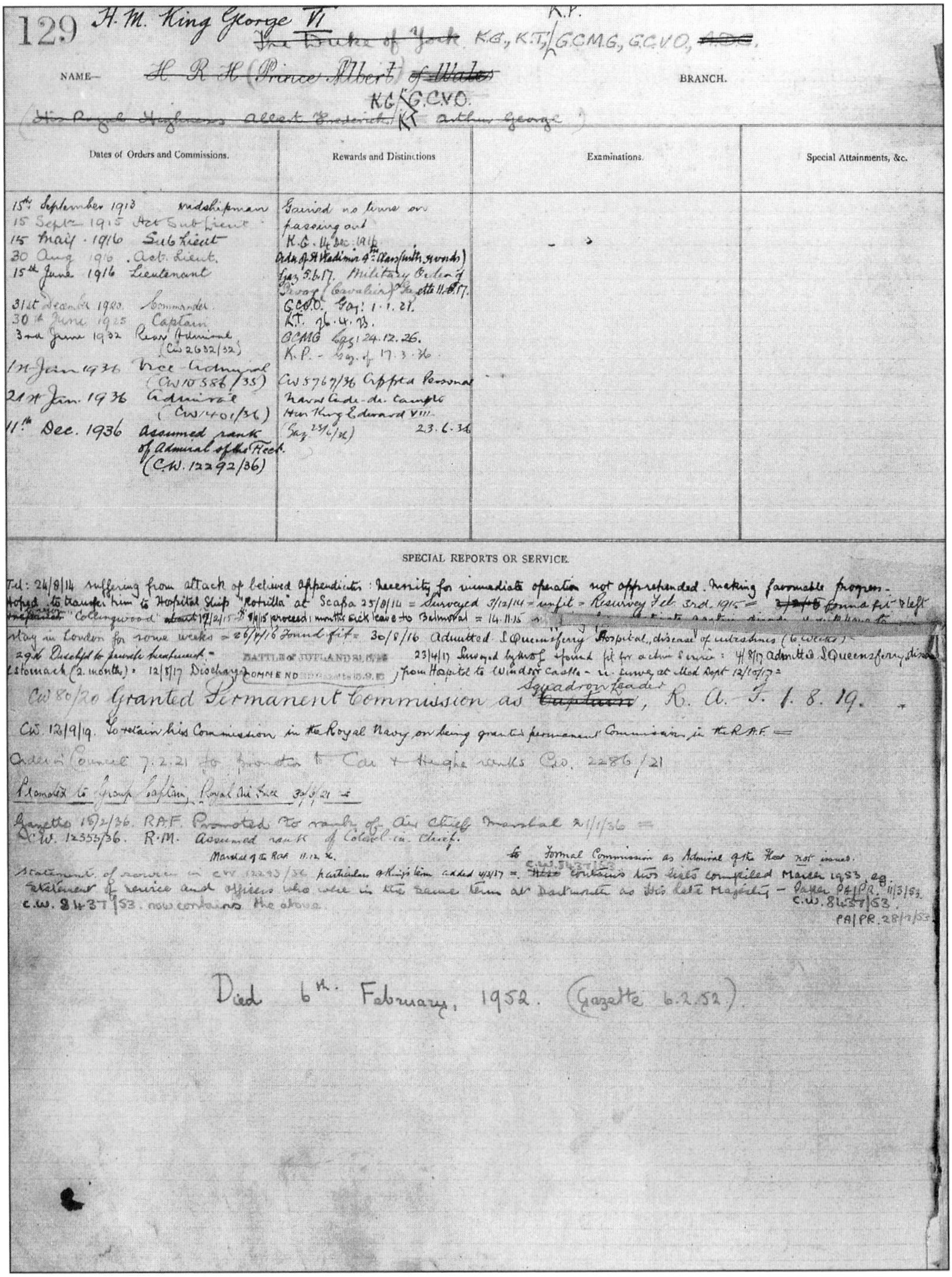

129 H.M. King George VI
~~The Duke of York~~ K.G., K.T., K.P., G.C.M.G., G.C.V.O., ~~A.D.C.~~

NAME— ~~H. R. H. (Prince Albert) of Wales~~ K.G. G.C.V.O. BRANCH.

~~(His Royal Highness Albert Frederick Arthur George)~~ K.T.

Dates of Orders and Commissions.	Rewards and Distinctions	Examinations.	Special Attainments, &c.
15th September 1913 Midshipman 15 Septr 1915 Act Sub Lieut 15 May 1916 Sub Lieut 30 Aug 1916 Act. Lieut. 15th June 1916 Lieutenant 31st December 1920 Commander 30th June 1925 Captain 3rd June 1932 Rear Admiral (CW 2632/32) 1st Jan 1936 Vice Admiral (CW 10586/35) 21st Jan. 1936 Admiral (CW 401/36) 11th Dec. 1936 Assumed rank of Admiral of the Fleet. (C.W. 12292/36)	Gained no time on passing out K.G. 14 Dec. 1916 Order of St Vladimir 4th Class (with swords) Gaz 5.6.17. Military Order of Savoy (Cavalier) Gazette 11.8.17. G.C.V.O. Gaz: 1.1.21. K.T. 26.4.23. GCMG Gaz: 24.12.26. K.P. – Gaz. of 17.3.36. CW 5767/36 Apptd Personal Naval Aide-de-Camp to His King Edward VIII. (Gaz 23/6/36) 23.6.36		

SPECIAL REPORTS OR SERVICE.

Tel: 24/8/14 suffering from attack of believed appendicitis: necessity for immediate operation not apprehended. Making favourable progress. Hoped to transfer him to Hospital Ship "Rohilla" at Scapa 25/8/14 = Surveyed 3/12/14 = unfit = Resurvey Feb. 3rd. 1915 = ... found fit & left "Collingwood" about 19/2/15 ... proceed 1 months sick leave to Balmoral = 14.11.15 ... stay in London for some weeks = 26/4/16 Found fit = 30/8/16 Admitted S Queensferry Hospital, disease of intestines (6 weeks) = 29th Discharged to private treatment = BATTLE of JUTLAND ... 23/4/17 Surveyed ... found fit for active service: 4/8/17 Admitted S Queensferry disease stomach (2 months) = 12/8/17 Discharged from Hospital to Windsor Castle – ... at Med Dept 12/10/17 = COMMENDED ...

CW 80/20 Granted Permanent Commission as ~~Captain~~ Squadron Leader, R.A.F. 1.8.19.

CW. 12/9/19. To retain his Commission in the Royal Navy on being granted permanent Commission in the R.A.F. =

Order in Council 7.2.21 for promotion to Cdr & higher ranks C.O. 2286/21

Promoted to Group Captain, Royal Air Force 30/6/21

Gazette 18/2/36. R.A.F. Promoted to rank of Air Chief Marshal 21/1/36 =
C.W. 12353/36. R.M. Assumed rank of Colonel in Chief.
Marshal of the R.A.F. 11.12.36.

Statement of service in CW 12293/36 ... Formal Commission as Admiral of the Fleet not issued. C.W. 8437/53 contains two lists compiled March 1953, e.g. statement of service and officers who were in the same term at Dartmouth as His late Majesty – Paper PA/PR. 11/3/53. C.W. 8437/53. C.W. 8437/53. now contains the above. PA/PR. 28/7/53

Died 6th. February, 1952. (Gazette 6.2.52)

Figure 3 Service record of King George VI. (ADM 196/118 f129)

2.4 Surveys and analyses

After the Napoleonic wars the manning levels of the Royal Navy shrank from 145,000 to 19,000 men, and from 713 ships in active service in 1814 to 134 in 1820. With limited job opportunities and an excess of officers, the Admiralty had to ensure that it employed the most competent. Lacking adequate information about the ages and previous service of its officers, the Admiralty sent out survey forms requesting them to provide such information. Some officers failed to receive their forms or neglected to return them, and not all of the forms that were returned have survived. Moreover, the surveys can be unreliable, as officers sometimes supplied their service details from personal recollection, not from official records. It is worth noting that the 1846 survey returns often give officers' addresses, which can be used as data for census searches (see 5.2).

If you are planning to search these records, it is useful to know the rank of the officer and whether he was alive at the time of the survey. A comprehensive list by rank, date and type of survey is given in the table below. Although there are original name indexes to some surveys (as noted in the remarks column of the table), if you are searching the 1817 and 1846 surveys it is easier to use the printed name indexes (additional finding aids to **ADM 9**, volumes 1 and 2 respectively) available on open access in the Research Enquires Room.

ADM 6/66 contains stray, rough and duplicate returns to the survey of officers' ages carried out in 1822.

Rank	Survey date	Document references	Remarks
Admirals	1822 1828 1846	**ADM 6/73–83** (age) **ADM 9/1** (service returns) **ADM 9/18–61** (service returns)	 Name-indexed by **ADM 10/1**. Name-indexed by **ADM 10/6–7**.
Captains and commanders	1817 1822 1846	**ADM 9/2–3** (service returns) **ADM 6/73–83** (age) **ADM 9/18–61** (service returns)	Name-indexed by **ADM 10/2–5**. Name-indexed by **ADM 10/6–7**.
Lieutenants	1817 1822 1831 1846	**ADM 9/6–17** (service returns) **ADM 6/73–83** (age) **ADM 6/84–85** (age) **ADM 9/18–61** (service returns)	Name-indexed by **ADM 10/2–5**. Name-indexed by **ADM 10/6–7**.

Masters	1822 1833–35	**ADM 106/3517** (age) **ADM 11/2–3** (age)	Each document contains a surname index. Name-indexed by **ADM 10/6–7**.
	1851	**ADM 11/7–8** (service returns)	
	1855, 1861	**ADM 11/9** (service returns)	
Mates	1846	**ADM 9/18–61** (service returns)	Name-indexed by **ADM 10/6–7**.
Gunners	1816–18	**ADM 11/35** (age/service)	
Boatswains	1816–18	**ADM 11/36** (age/service)	
Carpenters	1816–18	**ADM 11/37** (age/service)	
Pursers	1836	**ADM 6/193–196** (service)	Name index in **ADM 6** series list. Each document contains a name index.
	1852	**ADM 11/42–43** (service)	
Paymasters	1852, 1859	**ADM 11/42–44** (service)	Each document contains a surname index.
Chaplains	1833–34	**ADM 11/41** (service)	

Analyses of officers' service (see example on p36) were compiled by the Admiralty with the aim of comparing their ages and previous service so that the most suitable would be employed. Many of these analyses date from the mid nineteenth century, when choosing between officers for employment and promotion was a great problem for the Admiralty. Various analyses relating to flag officers, captains, commanders and lieutenants can be found in **ADM 11/10** (for 1780–1847) and in **ADM 11/64** (for 1844). Later analyses for these officers, covering 1893–1900, are in **ADM 11/80**, which contains a surname index. Analyses concerning lieutenants serving between 1813 and 1846, giving name, age, names of ships served on and time served, can be found in **ADM 6/174**, which includes a name index. Similar analyses of masters' services between 1777 and 1847 are to be found in **ADM 11/6**, which has an index of surnames and ships, and in **ADM 11/10** for the years 1793–1847. Analyses for 1742–1817 regarding surgeons, assistant surgeons and surgeon's mates are in **ADM 11/40**, which includes a surname index.

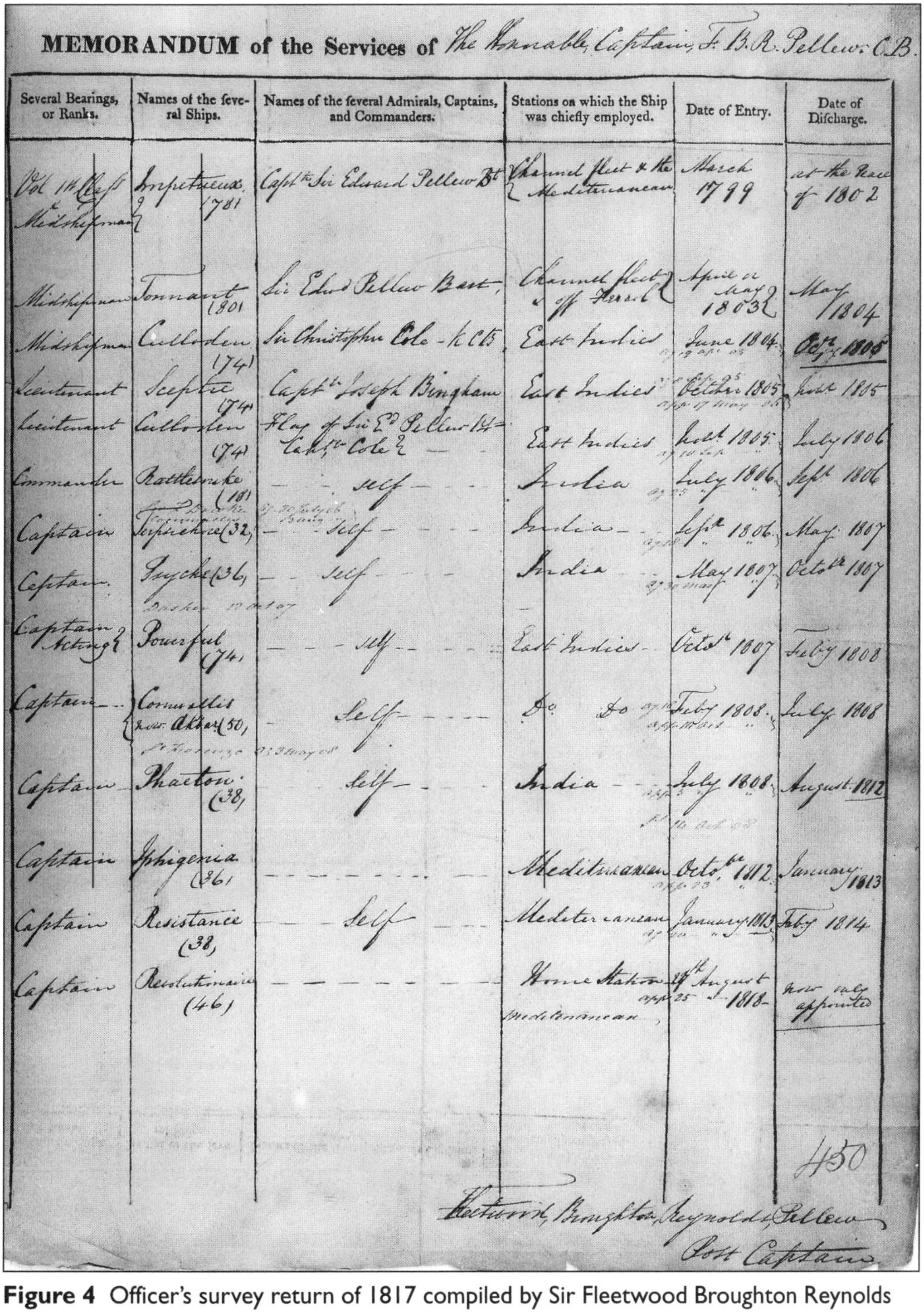

MEMORANDUM of the Services of *The Annable, Captain, F. B. R. Pellew. C.B.*

Several Bearings, or Ranks.	Names of the several Ships.	Names of the several Admirals, Captains, and Commanders.	Stations on which the Ship was chiefly employed.	Date of Entry.	Date of Discharge.
Vol 1st Class Midshipman	Impetueux (74) 1781	Captn Sir Edward Pellew Bt	Channel fleet & the Mediterranean	March 1799	at the Peace of 1802
Midshipman	Tonnant (80)	Sir Edwd Pellew Bart	Channel fleet & off Ferrol	April & May 1803	May 1804
Midshipman	Culloden (74)	Sir Christopher Cole K.C.B.	East Indies	June 1804	Octr 1805
Lieutenant	Sceptre (74)	Captn Joseph Bingham	East Indies	October 1805	June 1806
Lieutenant	Culloden (74)	Flag of Sir Ed Pellew Captn Cole	East Indies	July 1805	July 1806
Commander	Rattlesnake (18)	self	India	July 1806	Septr 1806
Captain	Terpsichore (32)	Self	India	Sept 1806	May 1807
Captain	Psyche (36)	Self	India	May 1807	Octr 1807
Captain Acting	Powerful (74)	self	East Indies	Octr 1807	Feby 1808
Captain	Cornwallis now Akbar (50)	Self	Do Do	Feby 1808	July 1808
Captain	Phaeton (38)	Self	India	July 1808	August 1812
Captain	Iphigenia (36)		Mediterranean	Octr 1812	January 1813
Captain	Resistance (38)	Self	Mediterranean	January 1813	Feby 1814
Captain	Revolutionaire (46)		Home Station Mediterranean	24th August 1818	now only appointed

Fleetwood Broughton Reynolds Pellew

Post Captain

450

Figure 4 Officer's survey return of 1817 compiled by Sir Fleetwood Broughton Reynolds Pellew. (ADM 9/3 p450); (see p71)

P.	Rank.	Seniority.	Date of 1st Entry.	Passed for Lieutenant.	Seniority as		Age, April 1, 1844.	
					Lieutenant.	Commander.	Y.	M.
+Pechell, Sir Samuel John Brooke, Bart., KCH.	C	16 June 1808					59	
Pechell George Richard	C	26 Dec. 1822					54	9
Pechell Charles	Mt	14 Aug. 1840					23	3
Pedder George Murray M'Kenly	L	30 Sept. 1809					57	
Pedder William	L	21 June 1824					43	10
Pedlar George	Cr	12 Oct. 1814					54	4
Pedler John	M	15 Feb. 1808						
Peel Edmund	Cr	21 Dec. 1841					43	10
~~Peel Jonathan Howarth~~	L	16 Aug. 1820						
Peirse Edward	Cr	10 Nov. 1842					30	2
*Pelham, Hon. Frederick Thomas	C	3 July 1840					35	8
Pelham, Hon. Dudley Worsley Anderson	C	26 Oct. 1840					34	
Pell, Sir Watkin Owen, Knt.	C	1 Nov. 1813					56	6
+Pellew, Hon. Sir Fleetwood Broughton Reynolds, Knt., KCH.	C	14 Oct. 1808					54	4
Pellew, Hon. Pownoll Fleetwood	L	30 Dec. 1843					21	
Pelly Richard Wilson	L	20 July 1836					30	9
Penfold George Stuart	L	15 Feb. 1823					45	8
Pengelley Charles	Cr	20 Sept. 1814					60	
Pengelley John	L	8 Feb. 1815					50	6
Pengelly Henry	L	21 Mar. 1812					51	6
Pengelly Robert Lamport	L	9 Dec. 1826					46	
Pennefather William Westby	L	22 Aug. 1821					48	
Penn John	M	12 Oct. 1831						
Penn James	M	23 Nov. 1841						
Pennell Follett Walrond	C	14 July 1828					40	
Pennington William	M	26 Sept. 1811						
Pennington Henry	S M	27 Feb. 1843						
Penrose Thomas	M	1 July 1796						
Penruddocke George	Cr	15 June 1814					59	6
Pentland James Murray	L	13 July 1824					43	9
Peppin Matthew	L	10 Jan. 1837					46	
Perceval Richard	L	6 April 1815					50	
Perceval Michael Henry	Mt	21 May 1840					24	3
+Percy, Hon Josceline	R B	23 Nov. 1841					59	2
Percy, Hon. William Henry	C	21 Mar. 1812					56	6
Perkins Henry Augustus	L	16 Mar. 1814					50	6
Perkins Charles James	Mt	30 Dec. 1837					28	10
Perriam John	M	3 Dec. 1812						
Perry James Clewlow	L	3 Mar. 1828					45	
Petch William Tatton	L	27 June 1814					55	
Petch Charles Adolphus	L	13 June 1828					47	6
Petley John	Cr	23 Dec. 1843					62	
Petley John Eaton	S M	1 Nov. 1839						

Figure 5 Part of an analysis of the services of commissioned officers which contains an entry for Sir Fleetwood Broughton Reynolds Pellew. (ADM 11/64); (see p73)

2.5 Certificates of service

There are several series of certificates of service, one of which is **ADM 29/1–96**. These certificates were compiled by the Navy Pay Office on behalf of warrant officers (and ratings) applying for pensions, gratuities or medals, and also when applications were made for the deletion of 'run' (desertion) from service records or the admission of children to Greenwich Hospital School. Many of these applications relate to orphaned children – so it can be assumed that the warrant officer or rating on whose behalf the application was submitted was no longer alive when the claim was made.

It is worth noting that although the service certificates in **ADM 29/1–96** are described as covering the period 1802–94, these dates actually relate to when the certificates were issued – which could be many years after a warrant officer or rating had left the service. Furthermore, some of the records are incomplete and it is possible to find more than one certificate of service for an individual.

The certificates in **ADM 29/1–96** for 1802–68 are name-indexed by **ADM 29/97–100**, and those for 1868–94 by **ADM 29/101–104**. All these documents can be viewed on microfilm in the Microfilm Reading Room. For advice on how to use these indexes and information about what the certificates contain, see 3.2.1.

Further certificates of service, covering 1790–1865, can be found in **ADM 73/1–35**. These accompany applications by warrant officers for admission as in-pensioners to the Royal Greenwich Hospital. Although dating from 1790, some applications include details of service 40 years or more earlier. Arranged by date of application and alphabetically by initial letter of surname, they provide details of character, name of last ship served on, age on joining and discharge from the navy, and the amount of time served. Sometimes they are annotated with the date of admission to the Greenwich Hospital.

Other certificates of service include those relating to boatswains in **ADM 6/121**, covering 1803–4; masters and pursers in **ADM 11/88**, for 1847–54; engineers in **ADM 29/112**, for 1870–3; boatswains, carpenters and gunners in **ADM 29/121**, for 1870–82; mates and sub-lieutenants in **ADM 107/71–75** for 1802–48, and in **ADM 11/88** for 1847–54; midshipmen and master's mates in **ADM 6/121** for 1803–4, and in **ADM 6/182** for 1814; and clerks and schoolmasters in **ADM 6/121**, for 1803–4. **ADM 11/88**, **ADM 29/121** and **ADM 107/71–75** contain surname indexes.

2.6 Passing certificates 1660–1902

In 1677, in an attempt to bring more professionalism and expertise to its commissioned officer ranks, the Admiralty introduced examinations for men serving in the navy who wanted to become lieutenants. The aim of these exams was to test whether prospective lieutenants had the necessary experience and skills to undertake the duties expected of them. An applicant at this time could not take the examination unless he was aged 20 or over and had served three years at sea. By 1728 this requirement had been increased to six years, and by the end of the eighteenth century three of the six years were to be

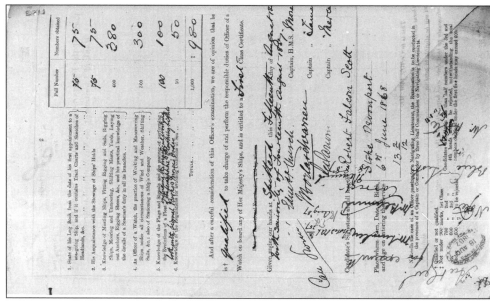

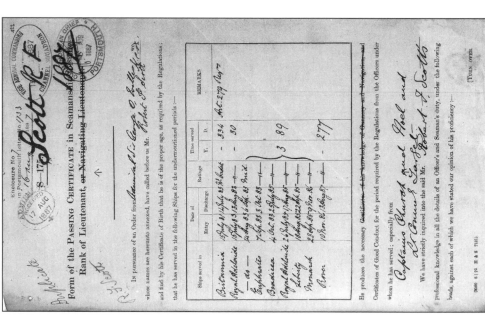

Figure 6 The Antarctic explorer Robert Falcon Scott lieutenant's passing certificate. Such certificates are key sources in tracing officers' personal backgrounds and the early stages of their careers. (ADM 13/222 pp422–4)

served as a midshipman or as a master's mate. Admiralty regulations specified that no one was to be rated midshipman unless he had served three years at sea and was in all respects qualified for such an appointment.

From the mid-seventeenth century onwards, similar qualifying examinations were brought in for warrant officer ranks, junior officers and certain specialist ratings.

Individuals taking these examinations had to provide senior examining officers with evidence about themselves – such as age, date and place of birth and the names of ships served on – which is usually recorded on passing certificates. It is worth noting that passing certificates may be accompanied by baptismal or birth certificates. This is certainly the case with lieutenants' passing certificates from 1779.

2.6.1 Searching the records

Bearing in mind that most commissioned and warrant officers would have taken a qualifying examination, passing certificates are a vital (though often overlooked) source for tracing the initial stages of an officer's career. Copies of commissioned and warrant officers' passing certificates are in a variety of series held by the PRO. Some can be found easily via personal-name indexes, but many are grouped together by rank and arranged by the date on which the examination was passed.

Having successfully passed their qualifying examinations, many officers had to wait some time for their first commission or warrant – in some cases, several years. The date of their first commission or warrant is considered a date of seniority, and so can be used as a starting date for your search if you are trying to establish when an officer passed his qualifying examination. Dates of seniority are given in many of the printed sources listed in 2.1 and 2.2.

Some men were promoted to the rank of lieutenant following an act of bravery, or thanks to patronage or family ties. In such cases there will not be a passing certificate, but the paperwork about the promotion may be found in **ADM 1**, **ADM 12** (see Chapter 7), **ADM 106** and the various State Papers Domestic series.

If an officer's age or place of birth is not given in a passing certificate dated after 1761, it may be possible to locate this information in the musters and pay books of ships the officer served on before taking the qualifying examination. PRO document references to ships' musters and pay books (see 4.1.1) can be easily found by entering the name of a ship and the dates the officer served on it into the PRO's online catalogue, which is accessible in the PRO reading rooms and via the website, www.pro.gov.uk.

The following table shows details of officers' passing certificates held by the PRO and identifies those that can be searched using personal-name indexes.

Rank	Date range	Document references	Remarks
Boatswains	1810–13 1851–9 1860–87	**ADM 6/122** **ADM 13/83, 85** **ADM 13/193–194**	
Carpenters	1856–60 1861–87	**ADM 13/84** **ADM 13/195**	
Clerks and assistant clerks	1852–5 1856–67 1856–99	**ADM 13/75** **ADM 13/76–78** **ADM 13/196–199**	Clerks only.
Engineers	1863–1902	**ADM 13/200–205**	Nominal indexes to these records can be found in the Research Enquiries Room and the **ADM 13** series list.
Engine room artificers	1877–86	**ADM 13/206**	
Gunners	1731–1812 1856–63 1864–87	**ADM 6/123–129** **ADM 13/86–87** **ADM 13/249–250**	There are gaps in the records for 1749–59, 1783–7 and 1798–1802.
Lieutenants	1691–1902	**ADM 1/5123/3** **ADM 6/86–118** **ADM 13/88–101, 207–236** **ADM 107/1–63**	There are known gaps in these records for 1677–90 and 1833–53. For a complete personal-name index to these records, see B. Pappalardo, *Royal Navy Lieutenants' Passing Certificates 1691–1902* (List and Index Society vols 289–290), which is available in the PRO Library or can be purchased from the List and Index Society c/o the PRO.
	1795–1812	**ADM 107/64–69**	Registers each with a surname index recording the results of candidates taking the exam for the rank of lieutenant.
	1801–10	**ADM 30/31**	Certificates of young gentlemen failing to pass for lieutenancy. A name index to **ADM 30/31** is held in the Research Enquiries Room.
	1810–32	**ADM 107/69–70**	Lists of gentlemen examined at home ports who have passed or been rejected.

Masters and other navigating officers	1660–1830	ADM 106/2908–2950	Masters only.
	c. 1800–50	ADM 6/135–168	Dossiers relating to individual masters.
	1825–31	ADM 106/3518	Masters only.
	1829–65	ADM 11/22	Mates and sub-lieutenants only. Contains surname index.
	1851–5	ADM 13/72	Masters and second masters only.
	1856–62	ADM 13/73	Second masters only.
	1859–63	ADM 13/74	Masters only.
	1869–85	ADM 13/238	Navigating lieutenants only.
	1857–66	ADM 13/102	Navigating midshipmen only.
	1865–81	ADM 11/89	Sub-lieutenants, mates and midshipmen. Contains surname index.
	1867–99	ADM 13/240–245	Midshipmen only.
	1895–7	ADM 13/251	Sub-lieutenants only.
Paymasters	1851–67	ADM 13/79–82	
	1868–89	ADM 13/247–248	
Pursers	1813–20	ADM 6/120	
Surgeons*	1700–1800	ADM 106/2952–2963	A name card index to these records is available in the Research Enquiries Room.

* Surgeons had to pass an examination set by the Barber-Surgeons' Company (from 1745, Surgeons' Company) before they could be warranted to ships by the Navy Board. The Surgeons' Company's examination books for 1745–1800 are now held by the Royal College of Surgeons; they record the surgeons' name and rank, the examiners' names and the date of the examination.

2.7 Training and examinations

From the mid seventeenth to the end of the eighteenth century, many commissioned officers began their career as captain's servants. These were usually the sons of a captain's relatives or friends, and went to sea under his patronage to serve a form of apprenticeship. It is in this capacity that most commissioned officers received their training – usually from the captain, aided by a schoolmaster.

Some commissioned officers entered the service under Admiralty patronage, as 'volunteers per order' (also known as 'King's Letter Boys') between 1676 and 1728 and as college volunteers between 1729 and 1816. Sometimes these would-be officers experienced problems in gaining the amount of time at sea needed in order to take the examination for lieutenancy (see 2.6), as captains were more likely to offer places on board their ships to their own protégés than to those sponsored by the Admiralty.

In a bid to ensure that its own protégés received training, the Admiralty opened the Royal Naval Academy at Portsmouth in 1733 (renamed the Royal Naval College in 1806) for 40 students to undertake a course of up to three years before they went to sea. The school did not prove successful – even though its intake was increased in 1806 and 1816 – and was closed in 1837. From 1839 to 1873, the college provided training courses for senior officers.

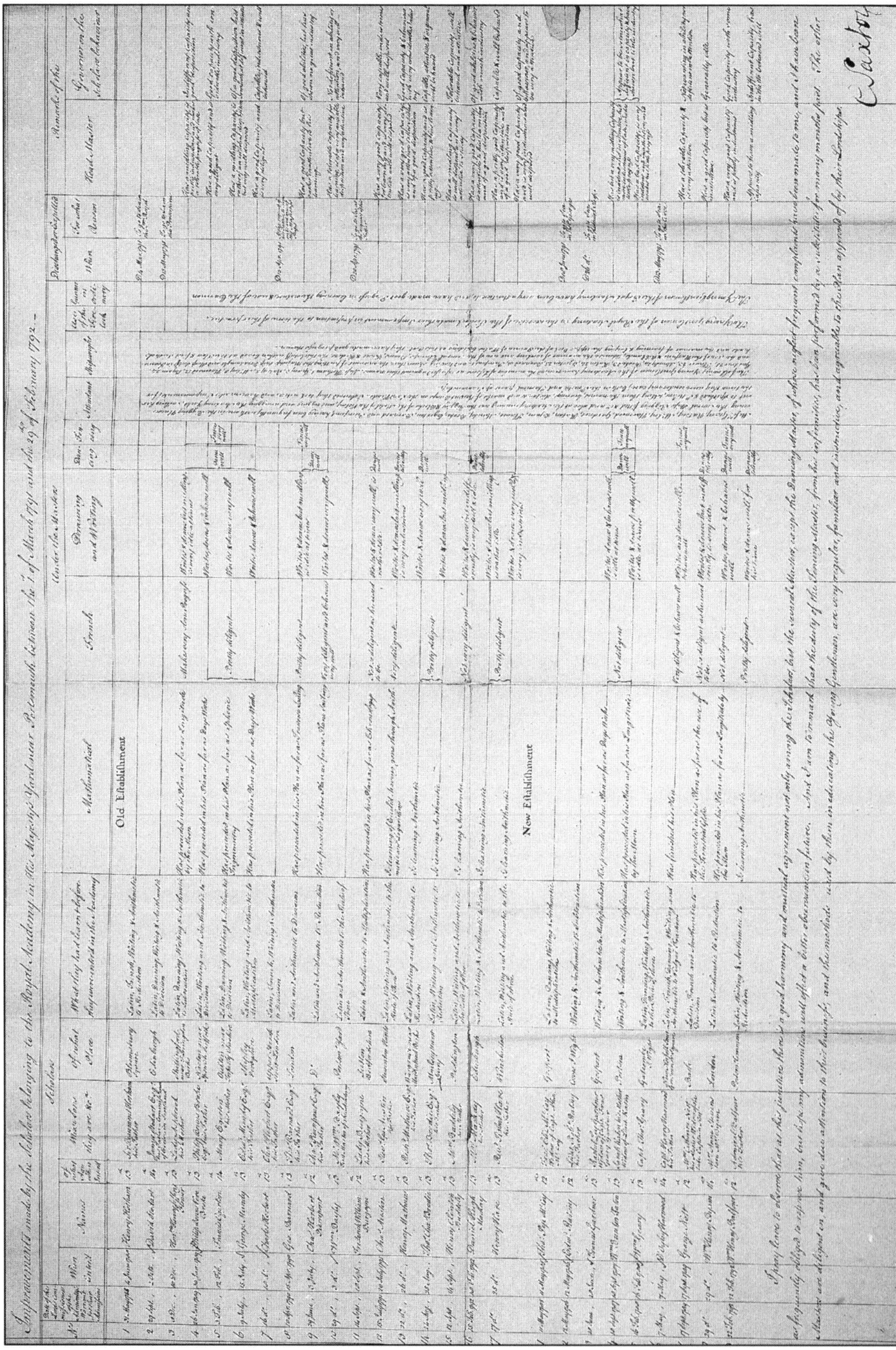

Figure 7 Copy of a list of scholars studying at the Royal Naval Academy during 1791–2. (ADM 1/3504)

Letters from the Commissioner of the Royal Naval Academy dating from 1773 to 1839 are located in **ADM 1/3504–3521**. These contain reports on candidates for admission to the Academy and on the progress of cadets being trained to become officers. A nominal list of the candidates and parents mentioned in **ADM 1/3504–3521** is available in the Research Enquiries Room.

You will find details of scholars warranted to the Academy in **ADM 6/427** for 1733–56 and in **ADM 6/185** (which has a surname index) for 1806–15. A register of candidates for the College between 1811 and 1836, with its own surname index, is in **ADM 11/53**; this gives the candidate's date of birth and his reason for leaving the college (for example, to serve on a ship).

Copies of birth and baptismal certificates of candidates for the College between 1813 and 1815 are in **ADM 7/1**, often accompanied by letters from parents or guardians.

Lists of candidates passing navigation and mathematics at the College between 1816 and 1818 are to be found in **ADM 6/119**. These give name, rank, age, birthplace, and ships served on and serving in.

Lists of officers studying at the College can be found in **ADM 11/73–78** for 1848–85, and in the *Navy List* (see 2.1) for the period between 1875 and October 1923. Records concerning students' college results for 1876–80 are located in **ADM 203/21–40**, while those for 1907–57 are in **ADM 203/41–44** (which include surname indexes).

As the Royal Navy began to implement the technological advances of the nineteenth century, such as steam engines and torpedoes, the training of officers became more comprehensive, structured and specialized. In 1857 the Admiralty decided that all naval cadets – a rank introduced in 1843 to describe those aspiring to become a lieutenant – would be trained in dedicated training ships.

Initially cadets were trained in HMS *Illustrious*. However, this ship proved to be too small and in 1859 HMS *Britannia* began to be used for training purposes. Between 1859 and 1862 *Britannia* was moored on Haslar Creek, Portsmouth. After that, it was stationed at Portland and, in 1863, on the River Dart in Dartmouth. In 1864 HMS *Hindustan* was moored with the *Britannia*. Then in 1869 the old *Britannia* was replaced by a larger *Britannia* (formerly *Prince of Wales*) to cope with the increasing numbers of naval cadets. As a result of the poor conditions on these ships, in 1900 the junior and senior colleges at Osborne and Dartmouth were built. The first cadets arrived there in 1903. Also in 1903, under the new system of training officers known as the Selborne Scheme, measures were introduced to enable cadets to obtain a full education, plus instruction for the specialist officer ranks that were now emerging in the navy. In 1921 Osborne College was closed down, and the staff and remaining cadets were transferred to the Royal Naval College, Dartmouth.

Various lists of cadets who trained on *Britannia* (with dates of birth, entry, and discharge and to what ship) can be found in **ADM 11/82–84** for 1857–76 and in **ADM 11/86** for 1875–88. Records relating to the exam results for 1877–1902 of cadets who studied on *Britannia* are located in **ADM 6/469–473**, which may also provide the cadet's date of birth and the address of parents or guardians. Lists of cadets studying at the Royal Naval College, Dartmouth, can be found in **ADM 203/104–137** for January 1931 to January 1942; in **ADM 203/151–178** for September 1946 to September

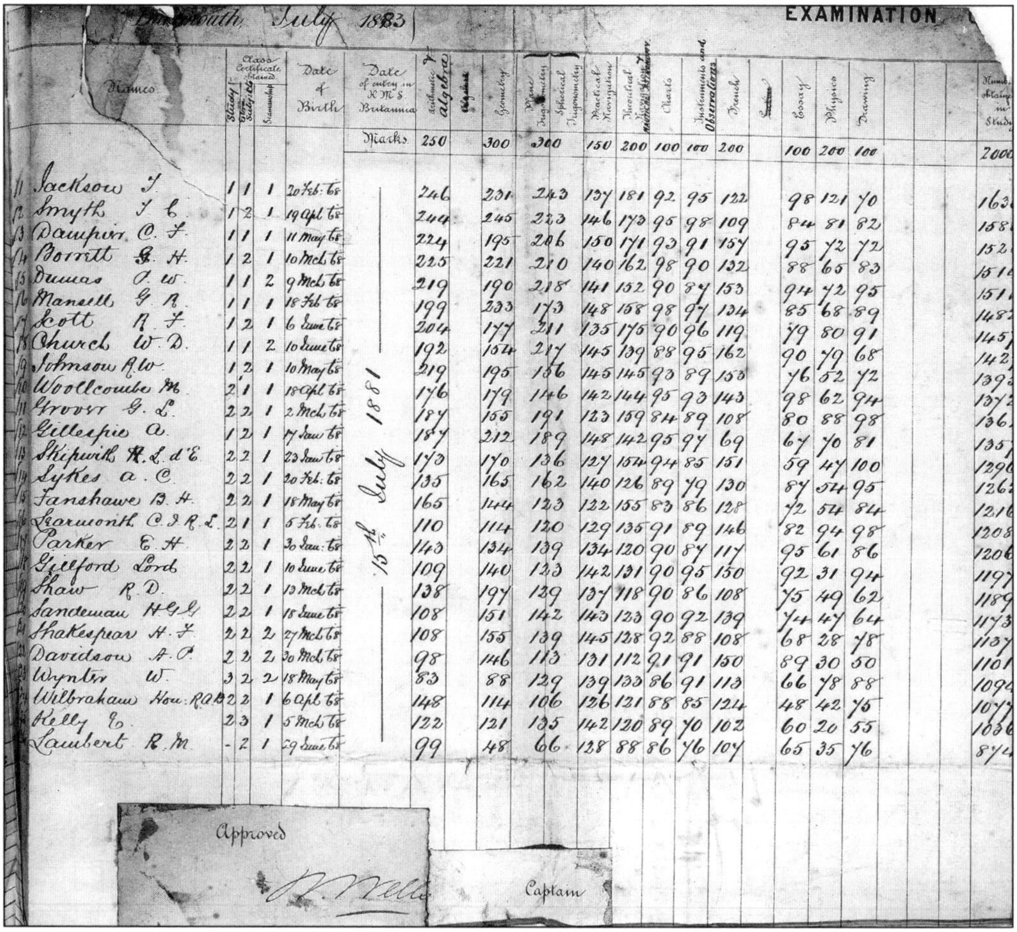

Figure 8 Extract of exam results of cadets who studied on HMS *Britannia*, July 1883. Entry number 7 relates to the famous Antarctic explorer, Robert Falcon Scott. (ADM 6/469)

1955; and in **ADM 203/179–191** for January 1956 to May 1964. Lists of cadets at the college at Eaton, Chester, are in **ADM 203/140–149**.

Lists of officers training on HMS *Ariadne* and *Trafalgar*, 1869–72, can be found in **ADM 11/84**. Lists of officers undertaking the torpedo training course on HMS *Vernon* are in **ADM 29/127** for 1882–90, in **ADM 11/79** for 1894–1902, and in **ADM 29/130** (warrant officers only) for 1896. Certificates of lieutenants passing gunnery exams are in **ADM 13/98–100** for 1864–6 and in **ADM 13/207–236** for 1868–1902.

Lists of officers qualifying in gunnery between 1833 and 1842 are to be found in **ADM 6/60**, which contains a surname index. The service records for 1838–98 kept by the HMS *Excellent* gunnery school, with surname indexes of gunners, are available on microfilm, in **ADM 196/167–170**, in the Microfilm Reading Room; these give the officer's date of birth and record career details up to 1902, including total time served, dates of entry and discharge from each named ship, and remarks about conduct, ability and knowledge.

A nominal list of engineers studying at Woolwich Steam Factory between 1848 and 1855, with dates of entry and discharge, is in **ADM 11/73**. Engineer cadets' examination results for 1899–1906 are in **ADM 7/931**.

Details such as date of birth and medical qualifications of surgeons and other medical staff taking examinations for entry into Haslar Hospital, 1844–1914, can be found in **ADM 305/71–72**.

ADM 29/127 and **130** relate mainly to warrant officers passed or rejected in navigation between 1889 and 1896.

An order in council of 4 June 1870 established recruitment by open competitive exam as the normal method of entry into the Civil Service. Records in **CSC 10** contain tables of marks and results issued by the Civil Service Commission listing the names of all assistant clerk, cadet, engineer student and paymaster cadet candidates that passed the exam, even if they did not enter the service. Tables of marks for 1870–6 are included in the Commission's annual reports in **CSC 4**. Up to 1895 the records give the marks attained by each candidate in various subjects, whereas later records simply state the total marks achieved. Naval exam results for 1923–64 are to be found in **CSC 10** records containing tables of marks designated 'B' (see **CSC 10** series list). **ADM 6/464** is a list of the first 65 candidates who passed or failed the competence exams held by the Civil Service in 1903.

2.8 Pay, expenses, and allotment and remittance registers

2.8.1 Full pay 1795–1905

Details of wages paid to officers when on active service are given in full pay records. Together with half pay records (see 2.8.2), these can be used – as they were originally – to piece together an officer's service record.

Full pay records for commissioned officers and for masters, chaplains and surgeons can be found in **ADM 24**, ranging from 1795 to 1905. For the period 1795–1829, the records in **ADM 24** are split into discrete groups of registers for each rank, with separate name indexes; from 1830 onwards, all officer ranks are combined and there are separate name indexes.

Records of full pay relating to engineers, boatswains, carpenters and gunners, 1847–94, can be found in **ADM 22**.

From 1795, full pay records usually list officer's names, amount of pay, and the name of the ship or station in which the officer was serving. Between 1830 and 1905, you may also find the reason why an officer left a ship (for example, because he had been placed on the half pay list) and either his agent's or his own address, which can be useful for census searches (see 5.2). Date of death is sometimes given, too.

2.8.2 Half pay 1667–1924

When an officer was not employed by the Admiralty he would be placed on the half pay list. Half pay was a sort of retainer paid to unemployed officers, so that their services would be guaranteed for future use. It was also used as a form of pension.

Half pay was initially paid to some flag officers and captains in the 1660s, then was gradually phased in for other officers – namely admirals in 1668, commodores in 1675, flag captains in 1668, captains of first-rate ships in 1674 and other captains in 1697, commanders in 1715, lieutenants in 1697, mates and sub-lieutenants in 1840, masters of first-rate ships in 1674 and other masters in 1697, surgeons in 1729, pursers in 1814, chaplains in 1817, and engineers in 1856. Half pay was abolished in 1938.

A search of half pay and full pay records can provide details of an officer's career. There are three main series of half pay records, most of them arranged in date order. The first series, **ADM 18/44–67**, covers the years 1667–89 and contains records for flag officers (1677–89), commodores (1675–89), captains (1674–89) and masters (1674–89). All of these except **ADM 18/51** include surname indexes. The second series, **ADM 25**, extends from 1693 to 1924, while the third series, **PMG 15**, ranges from October 1836 to March 1920. **ADM 25/3–256** (which cover 1700–1812) and **PMG 15/1–3** and **5–7** have surname indexes.

The details supplied in the earliest half pay records, **ADM 18/44–67**, are simply the officer's name, rank and rate of pay.

The records in **ADM 25**, which begin in 1693, list date of allowance of half pay, name and rank, names of ships served on with dates of entry and discharge, total time served, and to whom paid (often listing names of next of kin or agents). From 1735 they also indicate whether the officer has been re-employed; and from around 1851 death dates begin to be recorded, plus details of claims by next of kin for half pay arrears. This information is included until 1900, when the documents provide name, rank and dates of half pay payments. From 1900, the **ADM 25** half pay records are arranged by date and initial letter of officer's surname.

As well as recording the amount paid, the documents in **PMG 15** list name and rank, date of authority for half pay to begin, when paid, to whom (usually only place of residence given), and the date of the officer's death. From April 1840 these records also provide officers' addresses, which are useful for census searches (see 5.2). **PMG 15/9–148**, which cover 1840–1920, are arranged in year order and by initial letter of surname.

PMG 73/2 lists all officers on half pay in 1837, with their addresses.

2.8.3 Expenses (bill books)

The books in **ADM 18/1–155** range from 1642 to 1831 and contain details of bills drawn by the Navy Treasurer in payment for goods and services supplied at the order of the Admiralty or Navy Board. The payments for goods range from the purchasing by officers of items such as timber, canvas, hammocks, masts, medicines for the surgeon's chest, and rewards and gratuities; up to 1781 the books also contain details of salaries, pensions and half pay payable on the Navy Estimates. For example, an entry in **ADM 18/54** dated 1674 records the purchase of three tons of pork by Michael Boarsman, cook of HMS *Benbow*; and on page 208 of **ADM 18/46** there is an entry dated 1670 pertaining to 'wages paid to Thomas Frost' following his stay in St Bartholomew's Hospital as a result of wounds.

Documents **ADM 18/14–15, 17, 19–22, 24–28, 31–33, 36–37, 41–50, 52–118, 121–122, 128–137, 139–143** contain surname indexes; **ADM 18/16** and **29** include ship indexes; and **ADM 18/117–122** have subject-based indexes.

2.8.4 Allotment registers

The registers in **ADM 27/1–113**, which cover 1795–1851, list the names of boatswains, gunners and carpenters who allotted part of their pay for the maintenance of their wives or other relations under the provisions of the 1795 Naval Act. For more information concerning the content of these records, see 3.2.3. Names of men who allotted their pay can be traced in ships' musters and pay books (see 4.1.1).

2.8.5 Allotment declarations on promotion

The records in **ADM 27/114–120** consist of allotment declarations made on promotion by gunners, boatswains and carpenters between 1837 and 1852. For more information about the contents of these records, see 3.2.3.

2.8.6 Remittance registers

Arranged by ship's names, the registers in **ADM 26/39–54** cover 1838–51 and record payments to wives or relatives from wages and prize money due to boatswains, gunners and carpenters serving on ships in foreign waters. They usually provide the man's name and rank, his ship's pay book number (useful for searching ships' musters and pay books, see 4.1.1), the amount to be paid, name and address of next of kin, and the officer's signature.

2.9 Commission and warrant books 1695–1849

These books held in **ADM 6** can be used to trace the career of commissioned and warrant officers. Up to 1860 commissions and warrants were the only official method of appointing an officer to a ship; they were issued on each successive appointment. The records of commissions and warrants (1695–1849) are arranged mainly in date order and give the date, the officer's name, name of the ship he was appointed to, his

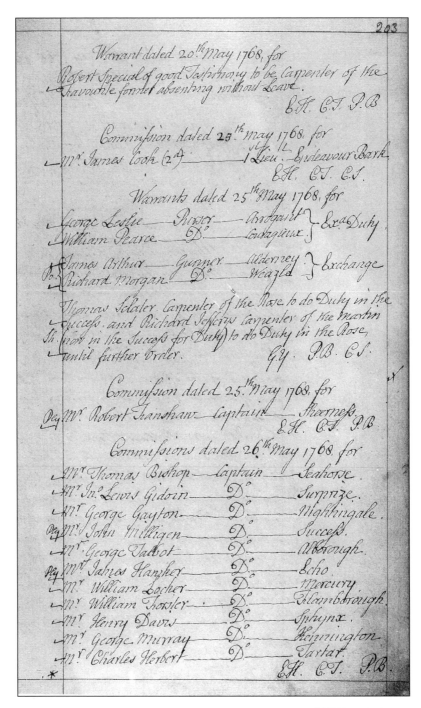

Figure 9 Part of the commission and warrant book of 1768, which shows the commission of James Cook (famous explorer) to the *Endeavour*. (ADM 6/20, p203)

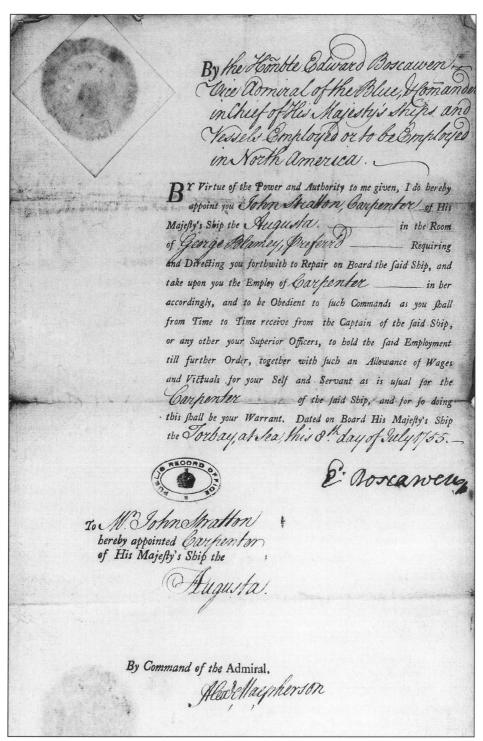

Figure 10 Copy of the original warrant of John Stratton, carpenter, dated 8 July 1755, signed by Vice Admiral Edward Boscawen. (ADM 6/63)

rank, and sometimes the reasons why the appointment was made. Original commissions and warrants, issued mainly during the Seven Years War (1755–63), can be found in **ADM 6/61–63**.

Manuscript name indexes to **ADM 6/3–22** and **ADM 6/61–72** are held in the Research Enquiries Room, along with a personal-name index to **ADM 6/15–16** and **22–23**.

2.10 Succession books and seniority lists

2.10.1 Succession books

Usually arranged by ship's name and by date, succession books provide another way to research the careers of commissioned and warrant officers. They often contain both surname and ship indexes, and under the ship's name generally list dates of appointment and discharge (with cause sometimes given) of named commissioned and warrant officers, thus forming the basis of a service record. In addition, they may list dates of seniority, retirement and death.

Flag officers

Succession books for flag officers from 1742 to 1808 are in **ADM 12/15**, which is arranged alphabetically by surname and station. Those for 1846–1903 and 1903–19, all of which contain surname and ship indexes, are held in **ADM 11/73–79** and **ADM 8/173–174** respectively. A later succession book relating to flag officers for 1913–19 is located in **ADM 6/461**.

Captains, commanders and lieutenants

Succession books for commanders and lieutenants, 1673–88, can be found in **ADM 6/425–426**, both of which contain surname indexes; **ADM 7/655** relates to captains and commanders from 1685 to 1725. The succession books for captains, commanders and lieutenants in **ADM 11/56–63** and **73–79** and in **ADM 8/173–174**, which extend from 1781 to 1909, all include surname indexes, while **ADM 11/58, 60–63** and **73–79** and **ADM 8/173–174** contain ship indexes too. An overlapping series of succession books for captains and lieutenants from 1780 to 1847 can be found in **ADM 11/65/1** to **ADM 11/70/3** and in **ADM 11/72/1–3**; these have integral surname and ship indexes (for example, **ADM 11/68/1** contains the index to **ADM 11/68/1–2**).

Sub-lieutenants

Succession books for sub-lieutenants can be found in **ADM 11/19** (1805–10), which is arranged by ship's name and includes a ship index. **ADM 11/83** (1865–70) contains its own index of surnames and ships. The ships and surnames in **ADM 11/84** (1870–7) are indexed by **ADM 11/85**. Those listed in **ADM 11/86** (1877–88) are indexed by **ADM 11/87**.

Masters and mates

ADM 106/2896–2897 and 2899–2901, all of which contain surname indexes, are succession books for masters and mates from 1733 to c. 1755 and from 1770 to c. 1807 (mates are not listed in ADM 106/2901). The surnames and ships listed in the succession books for masters (1812–49) in ADM 11/71/1–3 are indexed by ADM 11/71/3. Entries for mates can also be found in the succession books in ADM 6/175 (1802–3), which is arranged alphabetically by ship's name, and in ADM 11/23–30 (1815–53) and ADM 11/81–82 (1853–64), which all contain indexes of surnames and ships.

Boatswains, gunners, pursers, carpenters

The earliest succession books for boatswains, gunners, pursers and carpenters are in ADM 6/425–426, which cover the years 1673–88 and include surname indexes. Further succession books for these officers are located in ADM 106/2898 (for 1764 to c. 1784), ADM 106/2902–2906 (for 1785 to c. 1831) and ADM 11/65/1 to ADM 11/70/3 (for 1780 to 1849). The succession books in ADM 106/2898 and 2902–2906 all contain surname indexes, while those in ADM 11/65/1 to ADM 11/70/3 have integral surname indexes. A parallel series of succession books for these officers, covering 1812–39, can be found in ADM 11/31–33, all of which contain surname indexes.

A later series of succession books for boatswains, gunners and carpenters can be found in ADM 29/122 (for 1852–61) and ADM 29/125 (for 1869–81), both of which contain surname and ship indexes; in ADM 29/126–127 (for 1870–91), which are surname-indexed by ADM 29/128; and in ADM 29/129–130 (for 1890–6), which are surname-indexed by ADM 29/129. Further succession books for these officers, covering 1903–9, are located in ADM 8/173–174.

Medical officers

Succession books for 1733–55 for surgeons and surgeon's mates are located in ADM 106/2896–2897, both of which contain surname indexes. Surgeons (1782–3) are listed in ADM 7/762, which contains a index of ships; and both surgeons and assistant surgeons (1786–97) in ADM 106/2118, which is arranged alphabetically by surname. Further entries for surgeons and surgeon's mates (1790–1823) can be found in ADM 104/6–7, which include surname indexes. ADM 11/71/1–3 relate to surgeons and assistant surgeons for 1812–49 (ADM 11/71/1 serves as a surname index to ADM 11/71/1–3).

A series of succession books relating to surgeons, assistant surgeons and fleet and staff surgeons can be found in ADM 104/88–94, arranged alphabetically by ship or hospital. ADM 104/88 (which covers 1870–99) contains a ship and hospital index; ADM 104/89 contains a ship and hospital index to ADM 104/90 (both volumes cover 1900–11); ADM 104/91 contains a ship and hospital index to ADM 104/92 (both volumes cover 1912–16); and ADM 104/93 contains a ship and hospital index to ADM 104/94 (both of these cover 1917–24).

Engineers

Succession books for engineers can be found in **ADM 11/48–49** (for 1835–49) and **ADM 29/122** (for 1852–61), which all contain ship and surname indexes. There are further series of succession books relating to these officers in **ADM 29/126–127** (for 1870–91), which are surname-indexed by **ADM 29/128**; and in **ADM 29/129–130** (for 1890–6), which are surname-indexed by **ADM 29/129**.

Midshipmen, cadets and boys

The earliest succession book relating to midshipmen and cadets covers the period 1699 to 1756. Located in **ADM 6/427**, it includes a surname index. Later succession books in **ADM 11/23–30** (1815–52) have surname and ship indexes; **ADM 11/23–24** contain entries for boys for 1815–22. Other series of succession books relating to midshipmen and cadets can be found in **ADM 11/81–83** (for 1853–70), which contain surname and ship indexes. **ADM 11/84** (for 1870–7) is surname-indexed by **ADM 11/85**; and the surnames and ships in **ADM 11/86** (for 1877–88) are indexed by **ADM 11/87**. The succession book in **ADM 11/79**, which contains entries for midshipmen from 1894 to 1903, includes an index of surnames and ships.

Other officers

Succession books relating to cooks, 1673–83, can be found in **ADM 6/425–426**, both of which have surname indexes. **ADM 6/427**, which includes surname and ship indexes, contains entries for naval instructors, schoolmasters, chaplains, volunteers and masters-at-arms for the period 1699–1756.

2.10.2 Seniority lists

The main series of seniority lists is **ADM 118**, which covers the period 1717–1846. Arranged by rank, these documents give dates of seniority for the officers listed (i.e. the dates on which they received their first commission or warrant to a particular rank). This information was used by the Admiralty when assessing candidates for promotion. The lists are sometimes annotated to distinguish between officers on full and half pay, and in some instances they give date and place of death.

ADM 118 contains seniority lists for flag officers from 1748; captains, commanders and lieutenants from 1717; masters from 1748; surgeons from 1791; physicians and assistant surgeons from 1805; pursers, gunners, boatswains and carpenters from 1810; and chaplains, mates, midshipmen and cadets from 1834.

Some earlier seniority lists for captains have survived, in **ADM 6/424** for 1673–1754 and **ADM 7/549** for 1652–1737. The latter also includes commanders.

More seniority lists for surgeons can be found in **ADM 104/51–55** (1780–4), **ADM 104/56** (1787) and **ADM 104/58–65** (1797–1804). There are similar lists in **ADM 104/67–80** (1805–23) for physicians, surgeons and assistant surgeons; and in

ADM 104/81–84 (1868) for deputy inspectors of hospitals, staff surgeons, surgeons and assistant surgeons. Further seniority lists relating to deputy inspectors of hospitals, staff surgeons, surgeons and assistant surgeons are in **ADM 104/85** (1878) and **ADM 104/86** (1886). **ADM 104/87** (1886) ranges from the inspector general of naval hospitals and fleets through to assistant surgeons. All of the medical seniority lists in **ADM 104/51–87** contain surname indexes. **ADM 104/81** provides addresses for some of the officers listed. The lists in **ADM 104/86–87** give some dates of birth.

ADM 6/463 contains a seniority list for gunners from 1893 to 1924 that includes details about past service, qualifications, and dates of birth and pension. It has its own surname index.

A seniority list in **ADM 6/183** dated 1 October 1849 provides date of entry into the service for mates, midshipmen and cadets, plus their present rating and where serving (ship's name given).

2.11 Applications, appointments, and promotions

2.11.1 *Applications*

These documents mainly consist of officers' applications for employment, promotion or leave. They often provide information about why an application was made and in some instances give officers' addresses.

Flag officers, commanders, captains, lieutenants

Captains' and lieutenants' applications for employment, 1673–89 are in **ADM 6/428**. Applications from captains requesting to be superseded, between 1801 and 1803, are in **ADM 6/212**. Various applications from flag officers, commanders and captains between 1844 and 1850 can be found in **ADM 6/2**, which contains a surname index.

Applications from lieutenants for appointments and promotions, or to be superseded or for sick leave, for 1790 can be found in **ADM 1/5118/13–14** and **16**. Similar applications, including requests for leave to go abroad or to go onto half pay, are located in **ADM 1/5119/4–6** for 1791 and in **ADM 1/5120/4, 6** and **12** for 1792–3. A variety of lieutenants' applications can also be found in **ADM 6/170** (1799–1805); **ADM 6/212** (1801–3); **ADM 6/171–172** (1804–19); **ADM 6/2** (1844–50); and **ADM 6/181** (1846–54). Of these, **ADM 6/2, 171–173** and **181** contain surname indexes.

Masters

Applications from masters for appointments or promotion dated 1790 and 1792 are in **ADM 1/5118/14** and **ADM 1/5120/4**; requests made during 1792 for superannuation or to be placed on the half pay list on the grounds of ill health are in **ADM 1/5120/6**. Various applications from masters, ranging from 1844 to 1850, can be found in **ADM 6/2**, which contains a surname index.

Boatswains, gunners, pursers, carpenters

Applications from these officers for employment during 1673–89 are held in **ADM 6/428**; and there are further applications, covering 1770–90, in **ADM 6/187–189**. Promotion and employment applications for 1791–3 are in **ADM 1/5119/6** and **ADM 1/5120/4** (boatswains, pursers and carpenters only). Requests from boatswains, pursers and carpenters to be superseded, 1801–3, are located in **ADM 6/212**. Applications for promotion made by pursers and gunners in 1815 can be found in **ADM 1/5122/15**. Further miscellaneous applications from gunners, boatswains and carpenters for 1818–20 are in **ADM 6/190**, which contains a surname index. Applications from all these officers for employment or promotion during 1842–58, including addresses, are in **ADM 6/1**; similar applications from pursers only, 1844–50, are in **ADM 6/2**.

Surgeons

Applications made by these officers in 1792 for superannuation or to be placed on the half pay list on grounds of ill health are located in **ADM 1/5120/6**. Letters from surgeons seeking employment on convict ships, 1829–33, can be found in **ADM 6/186**. Various applications from surgeons submitted between 1844 and 1850 are in **ADM 6/2**, which contains a surname index.

Chaplains

Applications from chaplains for appointments, 1783–90, can be found in **ADM 6/187–189**. Requests to be superseded made by chaplains during 1801–3 are located in **ADM 6/212**, while applications for employment or promotion covering 1842–58 are in **ADM 6/1**.

Cooks

Requests from cooks for employment during 1673–89 can be found in **ADM 6/428**.

Paymasters, mates, clerks, second masters

ADM 6/2, which includes a surname index, consists of various applications from these officers for 1844–50.

Volunteers first class

ADM 6/198 consists of lists of questions answered by candidates applying for appointments as volunteers first class in 1830. This document gives each candidate's name, date and place of birth, plus type of education received, at what school and how long, father's name, residence and trade, and other personal details supplied by the applicant. It includes a surname index.

Midshipmen and masters-at-arms

Appointment and promotion applications from these would-be officers for 1790 can be found in **ADM 1/5118/14**.

2.11.2 Appointments

These records mainly relate to officers appointed to temporary or shore duties not covered by individual commissions or warrants (see 2.9). They usually provide details such as the officer's name and rank, date and type of appointment, and either a ship's name or a shore location, as appropriate. Details of officers' appointments can also be found in the *London Gazette* (see 4.7.6).

Flag officers

Lists of flag officers appointed to the America and West Indies station during 1795–1882 and 1795–1895 can be found in **ADM 128/8** and **114**. These give name, rank, period of command with dates, flagship, flag captain, secretary's name, and date of death. Further records of flag officers' appointments covering 1833–48 are in **ADM 11/72/3**; which in some cases gives date of death.

Commanders-in-chief

Appointment records regarding these officers are in **ADM 11/65/2** for 1780–4 (which is arranged by ship's name); **ADM 11/67/2** for 1795–1803; **ADM 11/68/3** for 1804–11; **ADM 11/69/3** for 1812–19; **ADM 11/70/3** for 1820–32; and **ADM 11/72/3** for 1830–48, which in some instances provides date of death.

Commodores

Records relating to commodores' appointments can be found in **ADM 11/70/3** for 1825–30 and in **ADM 11/72/3** for 1826–48.

Captains, commanders and lieutenants

Admiralty and Navy Board entry books concerning appointments of captains and lieutenants from 1696 to 1712 are held in **ADM 174/282**. Records relating to appointments of commanders and lieutenants for 1780–4 can be found in **ADM 11/65/2**. Records of appointments of these officers to the impress service, 1793–1800, and to cutters, tenders, signal stations and the impress service, 1803–15, are located in **ADM 30/34** and **ADM 11/14–18**, both of which contain surname indexes. Additional records of appointments relating to commanders and lieutenants, 1812–19, are held in **ADM 11/69/3**. Records of lieutenants' appointments for 1820–32 and of lieutenants with the temporary rank of commander are to be found in **ADM 11/70/3**. Further records of appointments of lieutenants and commanders for 1831–45 can be found in

ADM 11/72/3. Records of the appointment of 50 torpedo lieutenants, 1886–94, are in **ADM 11/78**.

Physicians, surgeons, assistant surgeons, surgeon's mates

The earliest records of appointments relating to surgeons are held in **ADM 106/2951**, covering 1671–4 and 1700–36. Appointments of physicians and surgeons for 1803–11 are in **ADM 11/68/3**. A variety of lists relating to medical officers can be found in **ADM 11/71/3**. These include records relating to the appointment of surgeons as superintendents of convict ships (1812–49); and assistant surgeons for service in Caledonia (1840–4), on emigrant transports (1843), in Sheerness and on the coast of Africa (February–April 1844), at Haslar Hospital (1844–9), Greenwich (1844–9) and Plymouth (1844–9), and in Malta (1845–7) and Jamaica (1845–9). Appointments of surgeons for service at Portsmouth for 1843–4 are in **ADM 11/70/3**, while **ADM 11/72/3** is a list of similar appointments for 1831–45. **ADM 105/38** contains lists of surgeons, supernumerary surgeons and assistant surgeons employed in January 1840 and 1842–7; and assistant surgeons in receipt of sea pay but not attached to ships on 1 January 1844. **ADM 105/39** contains various lists for 1847–51 relating to surgeons, assistant surgeons, supernumerary surgeons and assistant surgeons employed and not employed by the navy, surgeons employed in convict establishments and on cholera service, and surgeons who were candidates for shore establishments.

Pursers, gunners, boatswains, carpenters, chaplains, cooks, engineers

Records of appointments of boatswains, cooks, carpenters, pursers, gunners and chaplains for 1696–1712 are in **ADM 174/282**. Further records of appointments for pursers, boatswains, gunners and chaplains can be found in **ADM 11/65/2** and **ADM 11/69/3**, for 1780–4 and 1812–19 respectively. Details of chaplains' appointments for 1831–45 are located in **ADM 11/72/3**. Entries for the years 1885–90 for gunners, boatswains, carpenters, and engineers given torpedo appointments to ships, whose names have the initial letters M–Z, can be found in **ADM 29/127**.

Clerks and assistant clerks

Records of clerks' appointments for 1825–32 and 1833–42 can be found in **ADM 11/70/3** and **ADM 11/72/3**, while appointments of clerks to gun brigs and cutters during 1831–4 are in **ADM 11/27**. Assistant clerks' appointments for 1870–83 are in **ADM 7/927**.

Mates and secretaries

Appointments of mates during 1840–4 are recorded in **ADM 6/184**, while **ADM 11/27** gives appointments of mates to royal yachts for 1832. Records of the appointment of secretaries to commanders-in-chief for 1841–9 can be found in **ADM 11/72/3**; and of secretaries to flag officers, 1870–84, in **ADM 7/927**.

2.11.3 Candidates for promotion

These documents – which often include backdated information regarding a candidate's service history – were used by the Admiralty in the assessment of officers for promotion.

Captains, commanders and lieutenants

ADM 11/1 contains assessments of these officers for promotion dating from around 1841 to 1861, along with career details. The lists of commanders for promotion, 1879–95, in **ADM 7/929–930** include surname indexes and provide name, date of birth, entry into the service, ships served on, and dates of promotion, retirement and death. **ADM 178/172** lists captains serving in the Home Fleet in 1938 with dates of seniority going back to 1927; detailed assessments of their suitability for promotion to rear admiral are given, along with dates of birth and seniority and details of ships served on.

Masters

Trinity House letters concerning the suitability of candidates for the rank of master, 1702–1807, are in **ADM 6/134**. Similar letters for 1808–39 are located in **ADM 1/4314–4315**.

Surgeons

Victualling Board submissions concerning surgeons nominated for promotion during 1817–32 can be found in **ADM 105/1–19**. Various lists of assistant surgeons eligible for promotion, dating from 1824–42 and May 1847, are in **ADM 105/39**. These give name, seniority, time served, passing date for surgeon, dates of promotion, and in some instances date of death. **ADM 105/38** contains additional lists of assistant surgeons for promotion dated 1838, plus lists of deputy inspectors and surgeons dated 10 November 1846.

Engineers

ADM 196/71 lists candidates for appointment as engineers during 1837–9. As well as giving dates and names and addresses, it includes remarks about the candidates and records who examined them and reported on their suitability.

Paymasters and assistant paymasters

The analysis of paymasters' service for 1856 in **ADM 11/45** provides name, age in 1855, date of seniority, ships served on, time served on ships and sloops rated 1–6 (see footnote to 2.11.4), dates of appointment and discharge (with cause of), reports on character and handling of accounts, remarks such as whether unfit, and details of courts martial. An analysis for 1856 with similar details relating to assistant paymasters is in **ADM 11/46**.

2.11.4 Promotions

From the mid seventeenth century until the later part of the nineteenth century, promotions to the rank of lieutenant – and from that rank to captain – were made by the Admiralty on the basis of selection. In order to become a lieutenant, aspiring officers were normally required to have served in an active capacity for a specified number of years, known as 'sea time', and had to pass a lieutenancy examination (see 2.6). This meant that officers with friends or relations in positions of power at the Admiralty enjoyed a greater chance of promotion (see 1.3.1.8), since the Admiralty decided who would be employed on active duty.

As explained in 1.3.1.4, the term post captain was applied to captains appointed to command HM ships rated 1–6* (post ships), and was used to differentiate between officers who had actually reached the rank of captain and those called captain as a courtesy title. Promotion from captain to admiral was based on seniority, and was difficult to achieve since it largely depended on vacancies becoming available in the higher flag officer ranks as a result of death or courts martial. This situation arose because the number of individuals permitted to hold one of the flag ranks was set at 150 by an order in council of 1846, and because a retirement system for officers was only introduced at various dates from the 1830s.

The documents described below usually provide name, rank and date of promotion, and in some instances give the name of the ship to which an officer was being posted. Details of officers' promotions can also be found in the *London Gazette* (see 4.7.6).

Flag officers, captains, commanders, lieutenants

Lists of flag lieutenants (1820–32) and flag officers promoted can be found in **ADM 11/70/3**, plus promotions to captain (1820–32), commander (1820–30) and lieutenant (1820–31). Lists of flag lieutenants promoted to admiral and commodore during 1820–46 are located in **ADM 11/72/3**, along with promotions to lieutenant, commander, captain and flag officer between 1833 and 1841.

Assistant surgeons

ADM 105/39 contains a list of assistant surgeons promoted to the rank of surgeon during 1824–41, giving details of service and character, while **ADM 105/38** contains a further list of such promotions dated 28 May 1842. **ADM 105/39** also includes a list dated 18 November 1845 of assistant surgeons promoted for services in the River Panama action, and one dated 1 November 1848 of assistant surgeons promoted from

---

* Schemes for rating ships can be traced to the early 1570s, but were formally established in 1649. From 1751 to 1756, ships were rated according to the number of guns with which they were equipped. First-rate ships had 100–110 guns; second-rate, 84–100; third-rate, 70–84; fourth-rate, 50–70; fifth-rate, 32–50; sixth-rate, any number of guns, provided that a post captain commanded the ship.

the Royal Yacht since 1828. In **ADM 11/38** there is a list dated 22 August 1843 of assistant surgeons employed on duty in China who were subsequently promoted.

Assistant engineers

Records of engineers passing from third-class to first-class assistants during 1849–52 are in **ADM 29/108**. This document gives the officer's age, qualifications, a character reference, dates of passing, where passed, time served, and date of discharge.

Boatswains

Lists of officers promoted to boatswain for signal duties, under an order in council dated 28 November 1889, can be found in **ADM 29/127** and **130**.

Gunners (T)

Lists of men promoted to the rank of torpedo gunner during 1880–9 are in **ADM 29/127**.

Sub-lieutenants, mates, midshipmen

Lists of these officers promoted to the rank of lieutenant, 1826–81, with details such as date of birth, date of entry, when and where passed for seamanship, ship serving on, date when passed college and marks in gunnery and mathematics, can be found in **ADM 11/22** and **89**.

2.11.5 Promotion nominations

These records include both service history and personal details. They were used by the Admiralty to compare and assess the suitability of candidates for promotion.

Clerks, pursers, boatswains, carpenters, gunners

Arranged alphabetically, the lists in **ADM 11/38** cover 1803–28. They list name, date of certificate, where serving and place or address, with particular emphasis on candidates under 35 years of age.

Masters, mates, midshipmen

Lists of masters, mates and midshipmen nominated for the rank of lieutenant during 1814–16 can be found in **ADM 6/176–179**, while lists of midshipmen recommended for promotion during 1814–16 and 1846–54 are in **ADM 6/180–181**. There is a surname index in **ADM 6/181**.

Surgeons, assistant surgeons, chaplains, naval instructors

Various lists of surgeons and assistant surgeons nominated for promotion (dated 29

November 1842, 1 August 1843, 11 August 1843 and 22 February 1844) can be found in **ADM 105/38**. Similar records for 1854–1916 are in **ADM 104/45–50**, all of which contain surname indexes.

Reports of physical examinations of candidates for the ranks of surgeon, chaplain and naval instructor, 1870–1902, can be found in **ADM 6/468**, which contains a surname index. These provide details such as name, age, country, religion and qualifications, together with an assessment of fitness.

Assistant clerks

Lists of candidates nominated for assistant clerk ranks during 1882–1905 are in **ADM 6/448–449**. Both documents contain surname indexes and give date of application, boy's name, date of birth, father's rank and service dates and (where relevant) cause of father's death, together with any other claims, name and address of mother and guardian, total income of mother or guardian, and whether orphan has any means of his own.

Cadets

ADM 11/30 contains a list of candidates nominated for cadetships in accordance with an Admiralty Board minute dated 3 October 1848, covering the period from 1 October 1848 to 30 December 1852. **ADM 11/81** includes a list of candidates rejected for cadetships during 1851–8; names of candidates nominated for the Portsmouth flagship between 13 January 1853 and 9 July 1857, with date of birth and date and cause of discharge and to what ship; list of candidates nominated for cadetships as per the Board's minute of 1852, covering 1853–8; cadetships allowed to the colonies for 1855–60; and lists of flag officers' and captains' nominations for cadets, 1857–8. Also in **ADM 11/81** there is a list of cadets who passed under the new regulations introduced in February 1857 and who were bourne on (i.e. on the complement of) HMS *Illustrious* between 1857–9, with their date of birth, date of discharge to HMS *Victory*, and final date of discharge to a named ship.

A register of applications for cadet posts covering 1869–72 is in **ADM 6/447**, which contains a surname index. These include applicant's name, address and date of birth, plus applicant's references and patron's name.

Information relating to candidates nominated for cadetships during 1882–1905 can be found in **ADM 6/448** and **450–451**, which all contain surname indexes. In terms of content, these documents are similar to those described under assistant clerks above.

Further registers of applications for cadetships can be found in **ADM 6/464–467**, which cover 1898–1916. These documents all contain surname indexes. They usually provide the nominee's name and address, applicant's name and date of birth, claim (recommendations, details of next of kin, past service), school attended, and whether passed exam and marks attained.

NAME *Martin, Benjamin Charles Stanley* C.B.
D.S.O.

Services as Flag Officer

Seniority, &c.	Appointment	From
Admiral		
Vice-Admiral		
Rear-Admiral		
Captain	30 June 1935	
Commander	30 June 1931	
Lieutenant	13 Oct 1918	
Acting s/Sub-Lt 13 Oct 1916 Entered Service		
Date of Birth 18 July 1891		
Married 23 Mar 1918		

B.C.S. MARTIN. 14.4.42 – 30.9.43. (o)L.K., (d)(r)(g)7; (h)8, (e)6; (i)5; Commodore Martin's outstanding attributes are drive, determination and loyalty to his superiors. With these characteristics he can at times be somewhat ruthless in his treatment of subordinates. As Commodore at Durban he is the outstanding figure in that city's war effort, quite eclipsing the South African Brigadier who is the Fortress Commander, and as such he has drawn the admiration of the Prime Minister himself. Anyone less single-minded than Commodore Martin would long ago have fallen into one of the many pitfalls which await those British Officers who, possessed of initiative and energy find themselves playing an active part in South African affairs. I am convinced he would unflinchingly carry through to the end any task he might be given. His lack of recent sea experience would seem to weigh against his taking command of a squadron at sea, but for charge of landing operations on a defended coast, with his most robust physical strength, tireless energy and drive I consider he would be eminently suited. He knows what he wants done and is never muddle-headed. Promoted from the lower deck during the last war, he possesses a strong personality that should be made of further use and I strongly recommend him for promotion to Flag rank. (Sgd) Vice-Admiral Tait, 1.10.43.

B.C.S.MARTIN. (d)(r)(h)7; (e)6, (i)5; (g)8; (m)Yes: Commodore Martin has done a magnificent piece of work at Durban. Finding the city quite indifferent to the course of the war, he has by his energy galvanized the municipality and the local Fortress Commander, a South African Brigadier, into a realisation that South Africa is after all in the war and that Durban is a most important repair base for the Fleet. As time goes on, and the land war recedes further from the African continent, Commodore Martin's task has become more difficult. Yet his single-minded sincerity and forcefulness, though perhaps sometimes unimaginative, is still keeping the city concillors and the Fortress Commander from relaxing their efforts. General Smuts himself has told me that in his opinion South Africa owes much to Commodore Martin. He is not popular with his subordinates, being at times brusque and ruthless, but not one of them doubts he is actuated by motives of prosecuting the war. He has the defects of his qualities and upbringing in dealing with his own service contemporaries. He was promoted from the lower deck in the last war, and although he lacks recent sea experience, it would seem that he is a fitting subject to be the first promotion to Flag Officer since promotion was thrown open to the lower deck over thirty years ago. (Sgd.) Vice-Admiral C. Tait, 2.4.1944.

2.5.8.29.
by & 6'0".

Figure 11 Extract from the summaries of confidential reports relating to Sir Benjamin Charles Stanley Martin, Vice Admiral. (ADM 196/93, p1)

2.12 Other documentary sources

2.12.1 Addresses
(see also 5.2, regarding census returns)

As mentioned in 2.8.2, a register listing the names of flag officers, captains, commanders, lieutenants and mates on half pay in 1837, together with their addresses, can be found in **PMG 73/2**.

2.12.2 Summaries of confidential reports 1893–1943

Towards the end of the nineteenth century commanding officers were required to send confidential reports (form S206) to the Admiralty about junior officers' conduct, ability, professional knowledge, and suitability for promotion. These were sent at least once a year. The reports themselves do not appear to have survived, but summaries of them were kept by the Admiralty. These summaries contain genealogical and career information that can be used to supplement or fill in gaps in service records (see 2.3). Moreover, they often contain candid comments that create subjective pen portraits of individual officers, as well as illustrating the attitudes prevalent among the senior officers of the Admiralty of the period.

Thus for some officers not only is there a service record but also a document charting each significant promotion. Combining service records with summaries of confidential reports offers family historians the possibility of piecing together a very full record of an officer's life and career.

Summaries of confidential reports can be found in the documents referenced below, which are available on microfilm in the Microfilm Reading Room. They are arranged by date of promotion to a particular rank. To search them you therefore need to ascertain the date of seniority to that rank, either from service records or from the *Navy List* (see 2.3.2).

Admirals and captains

The summaries of confidential reports in **ADM 196/86–94** relate to the suitability of admirals and captains for promotion. They record service details from the rank of captain and admiral only. Photographs of officers can be found in **ADM 196/90–93**. A list of summaries of confidential reports pertaining to admirals and captains follows.

Date of seniority as captain	Document reference
1893–5	**ADM 196/86** (contains own surname index
1894–1902	**ADM 196/87** (contains own surname index)
1902–7	**ADM 196/88** (contains own surname index)
1907–14	**ADM 196/89** (contains own surname index)
1914–18	**ADM 196/90** (contains own surname index)
1918–26	**ADM 196/91** (contains own surname index)
1926–35	**ADM 196/92** (contains own surname index)
1935–41	**ADM 196/93** (contains own surname index)
1941–3	**ADM 196/94** (contains own surname index)

Commanders

The summaries of confidential reports in **ADM 196/125–128** relate to the suitability of commanders for promotion to the rank of captain. They record details of each officer's service as commander only.

ADM 196/129 is a name index to **ADM 196/125–128**. It provides, alongside each officer's name, a date of seniority and a page number that keys into **ADM 196/125–128**. A typical entry from this index would be '**John Cresswell 1929, page 21'**, indicating that his record will be found on page 21 of **ADM 196/128**.

Date of promotion to commander	Document reference
31 December 1908 to 26 December 1915	**ADM 196/125** (contains own surname index)
31 December 1915 to 30 June 1919	**ADM 196/126** (contains own surname index)
31 December 1919 to 31 December 1928	**ADM 196/127** (contains own surname index)
30 June 1929 to 30 June 1931	**ADM 196/128** (contains own surname index)

Lieutenants and sub-lieutenants

The summaries of confidential reports in **ADM 196/141–151** relate to lieutenants and sub-lieutenants, recording their service from cadets and midshipmen to commander. These records are indexed by name in **ADM 196/138–139**. A typical index entry would be '**Charles D. Rickett, volume 'B' 80'**, indicating that his record will be found on page 80 of **ADM 196/141**.

Date of entry	Document reference
15 July 1885 to 5 December 1892	**ADM 196/141** (Volume B, indexed by **ADM 196/138**)
15 July 1891 to 15 January 1897	**ADM 196/142** (Volume C, indexed by **ADM 196/138**)
15 January 1897 to 15 January 1902	**ADM 196/143** (Volume D, indexed by **ADM 196/139**)
15 January 1902 to 31 December 1918	**ADM 196/144** (Volume E, indexed by **ADM 196/139**)
15 September 1903 to 15 January 1908	**ADM 196/145** (Volume F, indexed by **ADM 196/139**)
15 May 1908 to September 1911	**ADM 196/146** (Volume G, indexed by **ADM 196/139**)
September 1911 to 15 January 1914	**ADM 196/147** (Volume H, indexed by **ADM 196/139**)
15 January 1914 to 11 April 1919	**ADM 196/148** (Volume I, indexed by **ADM 196/139**)
15 May 1916 to 15 May 1920	**ADM 196/149** (Volume J, indexed by **ADM 196/139**)
15 May 1920 to 15 January 1924	**ADM 196/150** (Volume K, indexed by **ADM 196/139**)
15 September 1924 to 25 August 1928	**ADM 196/151** (Volume L, indexed by **ADM 196/139**)

Mates and acting mates

Service details relating to mates and acting mates promoted to lieutenant and recording service to lieutenant commander can be found in the commanding officers' confidential reports listed below.

Date of becoming acting mate	Document reference
14 February 1913 to 1 December 1929	**ADM 196/154** (contains own surname index)
1 December 1930	**ADM 196/155** (contains own surname index)

Gunners

Date of seniority as gunner	Document reference
1881–1900	**ADM 6/462** (contains own surname index)
1900–12	**ADM 196/166** (contains own surname index)

Paymasters

Date of joining as assistant clerk or paymaster cadet	Document reference
1884–1933	**ADM 196/173** (arranged alphabetically by name)
1904–37	**ADM 196/175** (arranged alphabetically by name)
1903–39	**ADM 196/176** (arranged alphabetically by name)

2.12.3 Foreign officers

These records mainly relate to foreign officers admitted to the navy for the purpose of acquiring knowledge of navigation. Nominal lists of foreign officers serving in HM ships between 1871 and April 1904 can be found in the *Navy List* (see 2.1). They provide name, rank, name of ship serving on, and nationality.

An alphabetical register of pensions paid to French pilots during 1802–9 is in **ADM 30/40**. Miscellaneous correspondence relating to French pilots, 1803–9, can be found in **ADM 30/41**.

In **ADM 11/27–30** there are lists of foreign officers ranging from 1830 to 1852, which give name, date of entry, name of ship and in some cases nationality. Further information about foreign officers' service in HM ships is located in **ADM 11/81** for 1851–61; and in **ADM 7/912**, which contains a surname index, for 1852–1900.

2.12.4 Leave books

These documents usually record the date an officer applied for leave, for what period of time, in what service or to what place, and date of return.

A list of captains and lieutenants on leave, covering the years 1762–74, is in **ADM 106/2972**.

Records for 1783–1846 of officers granted leave while on half pay can be found in **ADM 6/207–211**. Lists of officers granted leave to go abroad while on active duty between 1804 and 1846 are in **ADM 6/200–206**. The records in **ADM 6/200–211** are usually arranged by date and initial letter of officers' surnames.

2.12.5 Letters
(see also Chapter 7)

Letters from unemployed admirals to the Admiralty ranging from 1693 to 1839 can be found in **ADM 1/577–607**. These are mainly about official business or the admiral's recent commands. Letters from admirals of various naval stations to naval secretaries are located in **SP 42/67–104** for 1700–72; and in **SP 42/18–19**, **22–29** and **105–110** for 1727–45.

ADM 1/1435–2738 contain captain's correspondence from 1698 to 1839, arranged by initial letter of surname and by year. They consist of letters from captains at sea and ashore, from captains reporting independently, and from those on half pay. Captains at sea usually reported to their commander-in-chief, who would summarize their reports or enclose them with his own. In this context 'captains' is to be understood in its eighteenth-century sense: that is, officers of the rank of post captain (see 1.3.1.4 and 2.11.4) or master or commander, but not lieutenants in command. Commodores on short-term duty are often treated as captains. Also included are letters from acting captains of HM ships up to 1705.

In **ADM 1/2739–3231** there are letters sent to the Admiralty between 1791 and 1839 by lieutenants in command of vessels not reporting to a senior officer and those on half pay or shore appointments (mates and, with some exceptions, sub-lieutenants are not included). Their correspondence is arranged by initial letter of surname and by year. Petitions, dated 1792 to 1800, from lieutenants, carpenters and midshipmen seeking promotion and rewards are in **ADM 1/5120/14**. Letters from lieutenants expressing willingness to serve in 1790 can be found in **ADM 1/5118/17**; otherwise, lieutenants' correspondence prior to 1791 appears to have been destroyed around 1808 during reorganization of Admiralty archives.

Admiralty and Secretariat out-letters, 1815–54, appointing, transferring or removing midshipmen, volunteers and other young gentlemen can be found in **ADM 2/1252–1281**. Appointment Branch out-letters, 1816–48, about the issue of commissions and warrants, the receipt of fees for them, and the posting and movement of officers are in **ADM 2/1394–1445**. Those about officers on half pay, 1816–46, are in **ADM 2/1446–1455**. Admiralty out-letters, 1840–9, to or about engineer officers and boys are in **ADM 2/1128–1132**. All of the above mentioned documents in the **ADM 2** series contain surname indexes.

2.12.6 Marriage certificates

Officers' marriage certificates sent with claims for widows' pensions between 1801 and 1818 are in **ADM 30/57**, which also provides husband's name, rank and date of death.

Marriage certificates, often accompanied by letters from officers, are in **ADM 13/70** (for 1806–61), **ADM 13/71** (for 1862–66) and **ADM 13/186–192** (for 1866–1902), which are arranged in alphabetical name and year order. A nominal card index to **ADM 13/70–71** is located in the Research Enquiries Room, and both of these documents include surname indexes. Boatswains', gunners' and carpenters' marriage certificates dating from around 1891 to 1902 can be found in **ADM 13/191–192**.

From January 1862 officers who wished their wives to be eligible for widows' pensions were required to place copies of their marriage certificates on file. The *Navy List* for 1862 has more information about this.

2.12.7 Oaths of allegiance and association

A roll containing the names of all the officers and men in the king's fleet who took the oaths of allegiance to Charles II in July 1660 is in **C 215/6**.

The following are document references for oaths of association signed by officers who subscribed to the 'Solemn Association' in support of William III in 1696, after an attempt on his life had been made by the Jacobites:

- **C 213/385** officers of the fleet and of Chatham (with ranks)
- **C 213/386** officers of the fleet who had returned from the Straits (with ranks)
- **C 213/387** officers of HM bomb vessels who had returned from the Straits (with ranks)
- **C 213/388** officers and men of HM yacht *William and Mary*
- **C 213/389** officers of HM yacht *Monmouth* (with ranks)

2.12.8 Resignations

In **ADM 105/39** there is a list dated 1 February 1849 of assistant surgeons who had resigned since 1846.

2.12.9 Unfit for service

Lists, covering the period 21 May 1804 to 25 May 1813, of lieutenants considered unfit for duty can be found in **ADM 6/173**, which includes addresses and a surname index. **ADM 105/38–39** contains various lists, ranging from 1838 to 1857, of surgeons and assistant surgeons considered unfit for service due to age, infirmity or illness.

2.13 Case study of a commissioned officer

The case study that follows illustrates how to use some of the documents and printed sources mentioned in this chapter to trace the career and family background of Sir Fleetwood Broughton Reynolds Pellew (1789–1861), a commissioned officer who served in the Royal Navy. Many of the sources referred to in this case study can be used to find similar information about warrant officers.

2.13.1 Printed sources

As explained in 2.1, before searching original documents it is advisable to check whether there is any mention of the officer in biographical sources (see 2.2). The main advantages of doing this are that it is likely to save time and that any information

Figure 12 Line drawing of Sir Fleetwood Broughton Reynolds Pellew, 1806 (© National Maritime Museum, ref: PW3592)

found can be used as a framework for searching documents that are numerous and varied in content. However, the biographical sources described in 2.2 cover specific periods of time and do not cover all the officer ranks, so you may need to look at relevant volumes of the *Navy List* (see 2.1) too.

From these printed sources it is worth noting key facts such as date of entry to the service and dates of seniority, promotion and retirement, so that they can be cross-checked against information contained in documentary sources. This is particularly useful when the officer's name is a common one.

References to the subject of the present case study were found in the *Dictionary of National Biography*, *Commissioned Officers of the Royal Navy 1660–1815*, *Marshall's Naval Biography* and *O'Byrne's* (see 2.2.1 and 2.2.2). An overview of his life and career obtained from these printed sources follows. (In addition, because he came from a family with a long naval tradition, these sources also afforded information about relatives who served in the navy.)

Sir Fleetwood Broughton Reynolds Pellew

- **13 December 1789:** Born, second son of Admiral Edward Pellew, first Viscount Exmouth, by Susannah, second daughter of James Frowde of Knowle, Wiltshire.
- **March 1799:** Pellew begins his naval career on board *Impetueux*, as a volunteer first class and then as a midshipman. Serves on *Tonnant* as midshipman in the Channel and Mediterranean stations, **until May 1804**.
- **April 1805:** Serves on *Culloden* in the East Indies station.
- **8 September 1805:** Promoted to lieutenant of the *Sceptre*. Returns to *Culloden*, then placed in command of *Rattlesnake* (**25 July 1806**), then *Terpsichore* (**18 September 1806**) and *Psyche* (**30 March 1806**). As an acting captain, distinguishes himself in action against Malay pirate boats (**27 November 1806**) and with the capture of Dutch shipping in the Batvia Roads (**30 March 1807**).
- **31 August 1807:** *Marshall's Naval Biography* contains a copy of Pellew's official letter reporting the capture of a Dutch corvette and Indiaman near Samarang while serving on the *Psyche*.
- **12 October 1807:** Promoted to commander. Meanwhile, appointed acting captain of *Powerful*, then *Cornwallis* and *Phaeton*.
- **11 December 1807:** As acting captain of *Powerful*, is present at Griesse when the stores and all the men of war belonging to Holland are destroyed. **15 December 1807:** *Marshall's Naval Biography* contains a transcript of a letter from Pellew, serving on *Culloden*, which gives a detailed account of the destruction of the Dutch naval force in the Indian seas.
- **14 October 1808:** Promoted to captain, serving on *Phaeton*. Takes part in the reduction of Mauritius (**1810**) and Java (**1811**). **August 1812:** *Phaeton* returns to England with large convoy of Indiamen; Pellew receives 500 guineas reward from the East India Company.
- **23 October 1812:** Posted to *Iphigenia* in the Mediterranean.
- **20 January 1813:** Posted to *Resistance*. **5 October 1813:** *Resistance* involved in action against Port D'Anzo (Anzio) batteries and capture of French vessels. **February 1814:** *Resistance* returns home and is paid off because of a mutiny on board; several men condemned to death and flogged, but sentences quashed.
- **4 June 1815:** Nominated Companion of the Bath.
- **5 June 1816:** Marries Harriet, daughter of Sir Godfrey Webster. (Their daughter would become the wife of Lord Walpole, eldest son of the Earl of Orford.)
- **25 August 1818 to 15 June 1822:** Commands the *Revolutionnaire*.
- **1822–52:** Spends 30 years on half pay.
- **January 1836:** Knighted. Also becomes Knight Commander of Hanover.
- **4 July 1842:** Appointed naval aide-de-camp to the Queen.
- **9 November 1846:** Promoted to rear admiral of the blue.
- **20 March 1848:** Promoted to rear admiral of the white.
- **1849:** Pellew's first wife, Harriet, dies.
- **1851:** Marries Cecile, daughter of Count Edouard De Melfont.
- **December 1852:** Appointed commander-in-chief of the East India and China station.

- **April 1853:** Hoists flag on *Winchester* and sails to Hong Kong.
- **22 April 1853:** Attains rank of vice admiral.
- **September 1853:** Men ask for leave; Pellew refuses, possibly due to risk of disease. Men mutiny. When the mutiny is quelled, Pellew is recalled home.
- **13 February 1858:** Becomes admiral. No further service.
- **1859:** Divorces Cecile.
- **28 July 1861:** Dies in Marseilles.

2.13.2 Service records

After printed sources, the next most important source to check would be service records, particularly if no mention of the officer could be found in printed naval biographical sources. The easiest series of officers' service records to search are those in **ADM 196**. These records are available on microfilm in the Microfilm Reading Room, and a partial personal-name card index to them is held in the same room. (As mentioned in 2.3.1, if you cannot find an officer in the personal-name card index, then it is worth checking the **ADM 196** series list in case there are relevant documents not covered by the card index.)

A search of the card index revealed two references to Pellew: **ADM 196/5** p528 and **ADM 196/37** p1050. These two documents proved a useful supplement to the information about Pellew found in the printed sources.

ADM 196/5 p528 (see p25) revealed that Pellew served on the following ships:

- *Indefatigable* from 18 February 1796 to 28 February 1799 (as a volunteer)
- *Impetueux* from 1 March 1799 to 14 October 1800 and from 1 May 1801 to 15 April 1802
- *Tonnant* from 17 March 1802 to 8 May 1804 (midshipman)
- *Culloden* from 9 May 1804 to 23 July 1806 (acting sub-lieutenant and lieutenant)
- *Rattlesnake* from 25 July to 19 September 1806 (acting commander)
- *Terpsichore* from 20 September 1806 to 1 June 1807 (acting captain)
- *Psyche* from 2 June to 11 October 1807 (acting captain)
- *Powerful* from 12 October 1807 to 18 February 1808 (acting captain)
- *Cornwallis* (afterwards *Akbar*) from 19 February to 5 July 1808 (acting captain)
- *Phaeton* 6 July 1808 to 15 August 1812 (captain)
- *Iphigenia* from 11 November 1812 to 31 January 1813 (captain)
- *Resistance* from 1 February 1813 to 7 February 1814 (captain)
- *Revolutionnaire* from 25 August 1818 to 5 August 1822 (captain)

ADM 196/37 p1050 confirmed the dates of Pellew's promotions to captain, rear admiral, vice admiral and admiral, and his date of death. It added that the date of his appointment as commander-in-chief of the East India station was 6 December 1852; that on 14 December 1852 Pellew hoisted his flag on board *Neptune* at Portsmouth; and that on 16 February 1853 was ordered to haul down his flag.

As mentioned in 2.3.1, there are also service records relating to officers in **ADM 6**, **10**, **11**, **29**, **73**, **104** and **105**. However, none of these would be relevant to Pellew, as they either refer to warrant officers or cover dates outside his period of service.

2.13.3 Surveys of officers' service

After service records, the next records to search are the surveys of officers' service, such as the ones carried out in 1817, 1828 and 1846. However, although the surveys were meant to cover all retired and serving officers, unfortunately the returns are incomplete and not always reliable (see 2.4). When using these records, it is helpful to know which rank the officer held at the time of the survey, because not all of the officer ranks are covered by these records (see table in 2.4).

Surveys of commissioned officers' service are to be found primarily in **ADM 9**, which is surname-indexed by **ADM 10/1–7**, while others that might be relevant are in **ADM 6** and **ADM 11** (see table in 2.4). A search through **ADM 10/1–5** confirmed the dates of some of Pellew's promotions. Also, alongside his name the number 450 appears. This number was cross-referenced with the **ADM 9** series list, so that the document reference relating to Pellew's 1817 survey could be identified. In this case the reference is to **ADM 9/3** p450 (see p35), which bears Pellew's signature and confirms many of the details of his commissions, though with some differences in dates of appointment and discharge. Moreover, the account of Pellew's career given in his return to the 1817 survey reveals that from March 1799 to May 1804 he served under his father, Captain Edward Pellew, in the Channel and Mediterranean stations. In addition, he mentions that between June 1804 and October 1805 he served under Sir Christopher Cole and from September 1805 to July 1806 under Captain Joseph Bingham, before returning to serve again with his father from November 1805 to July 1806. Also, that from April 1804 to August 1812 he saw service in the East Indies and India stations, and from October 1812 to June 1822 in the Mediterranean and Channel.

Although some of the returns to the 1817 surveys are located in **ADM 6/66** and **ADM 11/35–37**, these were not searched, as Pellew's return to the 1817 survey had already been found in **ADM 9/3**.

Because Pellew was still serving in 1846, a search of the indexes to the 1846 surveys was carried out. These indexes, in **ADM 10/6–7**, include an entry for Pellew (number 3161) which, using the **ADM 9** series list, was converted to **ADM 9/48** p3161. **ADM 10/6** also revealed that the survey form was sent to Pellew on 28 March, addressed to 7 Grafton Street, Bond Street, and that the Admiralty received it back from him on 8 April.

Pellew's return to the 1846 survey (**ADM 9/48** p3161), which bears his signature, confirmed much of the information already found. His age on 1 January 1846 is given as 56. His address is still 7 Grafton Street, Bond Street (useful for a census search, see 5.2). No details of any injuries received are given, nor is there any indication of Pellew receiving a pension. The columns where the officer could state whether he had passed through the *Excellent* and studied for steam are also blank. In addition, the account of

Pellew's career given in the 1846 survey fleshes out some of the information already obtained, as it includes details of despatches by superior officers and other officials in which good service is reported. Here details are given of Pellew's command of the East India squadron that captured and destroyed enemy ships of war and merchant ships in the Batvia Roads in 1806 – an action that led to him being awarded post rank by the Admiralty. Moreover, reference is made to other actions in which Pellew was involved. It is noted that in November 1807, as captain of the *Terpsichore*, he participated in the destruction and capture of Malay pirate boats; and details are given of his capture of the *Scipio* and 150 men off the coast of Java. It is also stated that in 1807 Pellew was present at the destruction of three enemy battle ships and the capture of the batteries of Griesse Island, off Java, and that he was made prisoner when the commander-in-chief sent him to the French commandant with a flag of truce. In 1808, Pellew sailed to Japan as captain of the *Phaeton* and, while in the admiral's barge, was fired upon by Chinese war junks during the occupation of Macao. Serving on the *Phaeton* against the Isle of France (Mauritius), Pellew led a division of light dragoons under Captain Thorpe. Pellew also served in the whole expedition against Java in 1811: he had charge of a division of the army from India to Java, assisted in landing the army near Batvia (Jakarta) and commanded the gunboats. He served at the storming of the fort and town of Madura (an island off the coast of Java), with Captain George Harris, on HMS *Drake*. He brought home a large convoy, consisting of 18 sail, from Bengal to the Downs in 1812, for which he received 500 guineas from the East India Company. He captained the *Resistance* in 1813, which was involved in an action off Naples and also in the capture of the Port D'Anzo (Anzio) batteries and a convoy of French vessels. In the engagement with the batteries the main mast of his ship was shot off, and he had to return to Mahon. In 1821 he commanded the *Revolutionnaire*, which destroyed some pirate boats.

2.13.4 Other documentary sources

The printed sources, service records and surveys of service mentioned above provided a great deal of information about Pellew's career and background. But other documentary sources can be searched, too, to add further details about an officer or help establish an overview of his career when service records are incomplete or have not survived. Many of the documents described in sections 2.6 to 2.12 were searched to discover more about Pellew, but for the purposes of this case study only those that yielded information about him will be described. When conducting your own research, depending on factors such as the dates when an officer entered or left the navy, you may decide that there is no point in looking at certain records – either because they do not cover the relevant years or because they duplicate material already found elsewhere.

After service records and surveys of service, the next sources to be searched for information about a commissioned officer will usually be passing certificates (see 2.6) and full and half pay records (see 2.8.1 and 2.8.2). Pellew was promoted to lieutenant on 8 September 1805. Passing certificates for this date are located in **ADM 6/103** and **117–118** and **ADM 107/32–33** and **67**. No passing certificate for Pellew could be found in these documents. However, **ADM 1/176** contains a despatch (S 40) from Edward Pellew, dated 29 April 1805, requesting confirmation of the appointment of his son Fleetwood to the rank of acting lieutenant because of the purchase of additional ships for HM fleet. Edward Pellew states that he is aware that this appointment 'is not one which falls under my patronage and therefore Mr Pellew with several others so appointed must depend on their Lordships' confirmation and I trust that he will become an officer deserving their favour and protection.' The **ADM 1/176** reference was obtained by converting a reference found in **ADM 12/114** for 1805, using the method described in Chapter 7.

Full pay records for Pellew were found on page 139 of **ADM 24/6**, which is indexed by **ADM 24/11**. These confirm details of the ships he served on and give rates of pay for the period 25 July 1806 to 7 February 1814. **ADM 24/85** gives similar information for 7 April 1807 to 7 February 1814.

Half pay records for Pellew were found in sampled documents for 1822–36 in **ADM 25/201–256**, which give rates of pay and details of the person to whom it was sent (in Pellew's case this was usually his agent, Mr J.P. Maspratt). Similar information for 1836–8 was found in **PMG 15/1–3** and **5**. **PMG 15/12, 18, 24, 30, 35, 40, 45** and **50** give the same information, as well as confirming Pellew's address between 1840 and 1861 as 7 Grafton Street. **PMG 15/50** makes reference to Pellew's death and provides details of his will.

In **PMG 73/2** Pellew's name appears in a list dated 1837 of 150 captains receiving 12 shillings and 6 pence per diem, and his address is given as 7 Grafton Street, Bond Street.

Analyses of officers' service records (see 2.4) also make reference to Pellew. **ADM 11/10** gives Pellew's age as of 1 July 1847 as 57 years and 7 months; **ADM 11/64** (see p36) states that Pellew's rank was captain, seniority 14 October 1808, date of first entry 1 March 1799, seniority as lieutenant 8 September 1805, commander 12 October 1807, and that his age as of 1 April 1844 was 54 years 4 months. Entry 289 in **ADM 11/1** (see 2.11.3) confirms his dates of seniority and how Pellew distinguished himself at the Batvia Roads, Samarang and French fortresses, etc. No mention of Pellew's marriages could be found in **ADM 13/70** (see 2.12.6).

Reference to Pellew was also found in leave books (see 2.12.4). For example, **ADM 6/203** records that starting on 2 November 1812 Pellew took seven days' leave from HMS *Iphigenia*, stationed in Portsmouth; **ADM 6/204** states that Pellew took leave from HMS *Revolutionnaire*, stationed in Portsmouth, commencing on 26 January 1819; and **ADM 6/208** reveals that he took 12 months' leave from 13 August 1816 to visit the Continent.

References to Pellew were found in succession books (see 2.10.1), too. **ADM 11/60** mentions that Pellew is serving on the *Resistance*. In **ADM 11/61** Pellew's seniority is given as 14 October 1808, and the date of his appointment to HMS *Revolutionnaire* as 25 August 1818. **ADM 11/74** confirms Pellew's date of death as 28 July 1861.

The next step was to search the census returns (see 5.2) for 7 Grafton Street, Bond Street, St George Hanover Square, London, for 1841, 1851 and 1861. The 1841 return, which is to be found in **HO 107/734** (book 1, folio 39, page 24), gives the following details:

- **Sir F. Pellew:** Age: 50. Profession/trade: Royal Navy. Whether born in this county: no.

- **Lady Pellew:** Age: 45. Profession/trade: independent. Born: Italy.

- **Miss Pellew:** Age: 20. Profession/trade: independent. Born: Malta.

But there was no trace of the Pellew family at that address in the 1851 and 1861 census returns.

The date of Pellew's death is confirmed in **ADM 6/445** (see 4.8), but no mention of his will could be found in the records described in 5.3. However, the probate register in **PMG 50/3** contains an entry for Pellew's death and will, which was proved on 26 October 1861 (the executors being Messrs Brabant and Mugford, and the value of his estate given as £18,000). The date of probate was subsequently used for a search of the National Probate Indexes (see 5.3.7), which confirmed many of the details mentioned. Also, a death duty entry (see 5.3.8) for Pellew was found on page 1169 of **IR 26/2265**.

The court martial record concerning the mutiny alleged to have taken place on HMS *Resistance* while Pellew was captain can be found in **ADM 1/5437** (see 4.5.1 and 4.5.2). The proceedings are dated 22 July 1813.

Other documents available for research include the captain's log (see 4.2.4) of HMS *Phaeton* covering 9 February 1812 to 29 October 1819, in **ADM 51/2643**; that of HMS *Revolutionnaire* for 5 November 1812 to 31 August 1819, in **ADM 51/2780**; and an admiral's journal (see 4.2.4) in **ADM 50/261**, covering 7 December 1852 to 15 April 1854, when Pellew was commander-in-chief of the East India and China station.

Finally, it is very likely that a variety of despatches and letters from or about Pellew would be found in **ADM 1** (see Chapter 7), and there must be station records (see 4.2.6) containing references to him. However, these would be too numerous to mention here.

3 Ratings

As explained in 1.3, before attempting to search for information about an ancestor who served in the Royal Navy it is important to establish whether the person you are interested in was an officer or a rating. In many instances this will be obvious – but not always. The following list of some of the numerous ratings used by the navy may help you identify which of these two categories applies. For information about the various ratings, see 1.3.3 and 3.1; for descriptions of the officer ranks, see 1.3.1 and 1.3.2.

Figure 13 Photograph of ratings cleaning the deck of a ship, *Illustrated London News*, 1916. (ZPER 34/148)

3.1 Types of rating

Able seaman	Gunner's crew, mate or yeoman
Airman (CPO)*	Gunroom cook
Barber	Gunroom steward
Boatswain's mate (CPO)*	King's letter boys
Boatswain's yeoman	Landsman
Boy (first, second or third class)	Leading seaman
Captain of the afterguard	Leading telegrapher
Captain of the forecastle	Midshipman's servant
Captain of the foretop	Ordinary seaman
Captain of the head	Petty officers
Captain of the hold	Poulterer
Captain of the maintop	Purser's steward
Captain of the mast	Purser's storekeeper
Captain of the mizentop	Purser's yeoman
Captain's cook	Quarter gunner
Captain's coxswain	Quarter master
Captain's steward	Sailmaker's crew
Carpenter's crew, mate or yeoman	Sailmaker's mate
Caulker's mate	Schoolmaster (CPO)*
Chief air artificer	Ship's corporal
Chief armourer	Ship's steward
Chief electrical engineer	Sick berth attendant (CPO)*
Chief engine room artificer	Steward's mate
Chief mechanician	Stoker
Chief ordnance artificer	Tailor
Chief shipwright	Telegraphist (CPO)*
Chief stoker	Volunteer
Chief yeoman of signals	Volunteer (first or second class from
Cook (CPO)*	1824)
Cook's mate	Ward cook
Cooper	Ward steward
Cooper's crew or mate	Wardmaster
Coxswain of the launch	Writer (CPO)*
Coxswain of the pinnace	Yeoman of the powder room
Engine room artificer	Yeoman of the signals

* CPO = Chief Petty Officer

3.2 Sources for ratings before 1853

Before 1853 the Royal Navy employed ratings on a hire-and-fire basis depending on its manpower needs, which were always more acute in times of war. For example, in 1814 there were 713 ships on active war service, with up to 145,000 men serving on them; by 1817 this figure had shrunk to 19,000 as the navy was placed on a peacetime footing. Only 134 ships were on active service in 1820. Tens of thousands of men were usually laid off at the end of a war, with no guarantee that they would be re-employed by the Royal Navy. As a result, seamen alternated between serving in the Royal Navy and working in the merchant navy or a privateering capacity.

In peacetime the required manning levels of the navy were met by volunteers attracted by the prospect of going to sea and the popularity of certain officers or by the provision of food and clothes, the chance of advancement, prize money, and pensions for some forms of injury. However, during times of war the number of volunteers was rarely sufficient to meet the total needed to man the larger fleets. In such national emergencies the navy had to recruit men quickly; in the seventeenth century, for example, during the Anglo-Dutch Wars 20,000 men were required in addition to the volunteers. The government had to resort to 'impressment': the forcible recruitment by press gangs of men to serve in the fleet. These gangs, commanded by officers, usually operated in seaports (often near pubs), but also in towns where they might be able to press into service seamen living there or visiting. Men were sometimes taken under protest and in violent circumstances. They were entered on a ship's pay list as pressed men or landsmen, and were paid lower wages than volunteers. The impress service also operated at sea. Homeward-bound merchant ships were stopped by naval vessels and a number of crew exchanged for men from the 'pressing' ship. This exchange, known as 'men in lieu', allowed the navy to swap untrained or unwanted men for fully trained and experienced merchant seamen. Although the Royal Navy used impressment for the last time during the Napoleonic Wars, the right to press men was retained in Britain beyond those dates.

Sometimes impressment was not enough to secure the numbers of men needed to serve in the navy when war was imminent. Bounty money was used to attract volunteers, which varied in value according to the person being recruited and the need for men. In the early 1700s the bounties for able seamen and ordinary seamen were 30 and 25 shillings respectively, and by the end of the eighteenth century they had reached £5. Two Quota Acts passed in 1795 stipulated that each county and borough had to provide a quota of men to serve in the navy. As a result, undesirables such as criminals, tramps and vagabonds were often drafted into the navy to fill the quotas. Men recruited under the Quota Acts also qualified for the bounty paid to volunteers, which by this time could be as much as £70.

Given the uncertain nature of ratings' careers and conditions of employment, until the mid nineteenth century the Admiralty did not need to maintain service records for every man in the navy. For this reason, it can be difficult to search for information about a rating who served before 1853, unless you have the name of a ship that he served on or it is known, for example, that he was in receipt of a pension or killed in action.

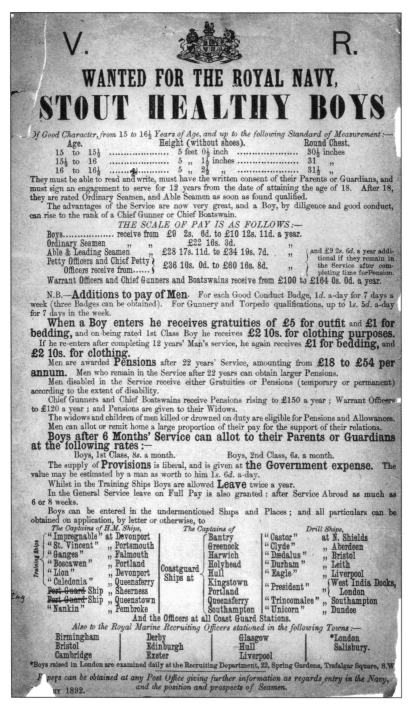

Figure 14 Royal Navy recruitment poster, 1892. (ADM 76/16 pt. 1, p151)

Many different sources may have to be searched in order to piece together the details of a rating's background and career prior to 1853, but the most appropriate starting point for such a search will generally be the ships' pay books and musters in **ADM 31–39, 41, 115** and **117**, which range in date from 1667 to 1884 (see 4.1.1). These provide information such as age (from around 1761), place of birth (from 1761), date of death, remittance of wages to next of kin (from around 1758), whether the rating went into hospital, what ship he had previously served on and, possibly, what ship he went on to join. To search these records, it is necessary to know the name of a ship the rating served on and the dates when he served on it. If you have this information, a search of the PRO's online catalogue (accessible in the PRO reading rooms and via the website www.pro.gov.uk) is recommended.

If you do not have the name of any of the ships a rating served on, then the easiest way to trace his career may be through certificates of service created for special purposes. For example, the applications for Greenwich Hospital pensions in **ADM 73/1–35** (see 3.2.2), which cover the years 1790–1865, are normally accompanied by certificates of service. Others, dating from 1802–94, are to be found in **ADM 29** (see 3.2.1), accompanying claims by ratings for pensions and medals, applications for admittance to Greenwich Hospital, and assessments of deceased ratings' children for entry to Greenwich Hospital School. As well as original certificates of service, the school's admission papers (1728–1870) in **ADM 73/154–389**, which are arranged alphabetically by applicant's name, often include documents such as marriage and death certificates and children's baptismal certificates.

If it is known which ship a rating served on and when, then it is worth searching sources such as the allotment registers for 1795–1852 in **ADM 27**, the remittance ledgers for 1795–1851 in **ADM 26**, and the remittance registers for 1758–1839 in **ADM 26** and **ADM 174**. These records refer to the payments of part of ratings' wages to their wives or next of kin (see 3.2.3 and 3.2.4).

Further guidance and hints on how to track down information about ratings who served in the navy before 1853 are given in the case study in 3.4.

3.2.1 Ratings' service records 1802–94 (ADM 29)

If it is known that a rating (or warrant officer) received a pension, search the records in **ADM 29/1–96**, which are available on microfilm in the Microfilm Reading Room. These were compiled from ships' musters on behalf of ratings (and warrant officers) who applied for a pension, medal or gratuity and when applications were made for the removal of 'run' (signifying desertion) from a ship's muster, or for admission of orphaned children to Greenwich Hospital Lower School (also known as the Royal Naval Asylum). Some of these applications, such as the ones involving orphaned children, would have been made on behalf of ratings who were deceased. It is also worth noting that **ADM 29/1–96** are arranged by date of application, which could be many years after the applicant had left the service.

ADM 29/1–96 are name-indexed by **ADM 29/97–100** for 1802–68, and by **ADM 29/101–104** for 1868–94. Entries in the indexes in **ADM 29/97–104** have to be converted to **ADM 29** document references. A typical index entry would be '**Allen, Charles 84 226**'. The 84 denotes the piece reference within the **ADM 29** series, while 226 is the number of the page where Charles Allen's service history will be found. In other words, the reference is to **ADM 29/84** p226. Alongside the numbers, some index entries have a ship's name and a date. These are the name of the last ship on which the rating served and the date when he was granted a pension.

The records in **ADM 29/1–96** (see p91 for example) usually list name, place of birth, age on entry to the navy, rating or rank, dates of entry and discharge from each named ship served on – useful for searching ships' pay books and musters (see 3.4 and 4.1.1) – and total time served. From 1834 these documents may provide ships' pay book numbers and state whether the rating volunteered or was pressed into service. From about 1858 they include character references, from 1869 the number of good conduct medals awarded, and from 1870 place and date of birth.

The certificates of service that feature in **ADM 29/17, 19, 25, 34, 43, 50, 59, 70** and **80–96** were used to support applications for the admission of ratings' and warrant officers' orphaned children to Greenwich Hospital Lower School (see 4.10). The applications themselves, which often provide information about the children and next of kin, can be found in **ADM 73/154–389** (see 4.10.1).

In instances where official and continuous service (CS) numbers are the only details that appear in **ADM 29/1–96**, these can be used to find a fuller service record in either **ADM 139** or **ADM 188**, as explained in sections 3.3.1 and 3.3.2.

Successful applications for pensions are noted in **ADM 29/1–96** by the presence of a date at the bottom of the service record preceded by either 'A' or 'Admiralty'. This date can be useful in tracing applications for pensions (see 4.9.2 and 4.9.5), as shown in the case study in 3.4, which offers further hints about using **ADM 29/1–104**.

3.2.2 Applications for admittance to Greenwich Hospital 1790–1865 (ADM 73)

ADM 73/1–35 consist of applications by ratings for admission to Greenwich Hospital as in-pensioners. Although these applications date from 1790 onwards, they can contain details of service 40 years or more before the application was made. The records in **ADM 73/1–35**, which are arranged by initial letter of surname and date of application, contain pensioners' admission papers and proof of service – normally consisting of extracts of service records, details of character, name of last ship served on, age at time of entry and discharge from the navy, and total amount of time served. The applications are sometimes annotated with the date of admittance to Greenwich Hospital. You will find that not all of the records under each letter of the alphabet commence in 1790, nor do they all end in 1865.

3.2.3 Allotment registers 1795–1852

Admiralty records relating to ratings rarely provide details of next of kin. But these details do appear in the registers that record allotments by a rating (or warrant officer) of part of his pay for the maintenance of his wife or mother or other dependants under the provisions of the 1795 Naval Act. However, because of the way the allotment registers are arranged, it may be easier to search the remittance ledgers and registers (see 3.2.4). The names of ratings (and warrant officers) who allotted part of their pay are given in ships' musters and pay books (see 4.1.1).

The allotment registers for 1795–1812 and 1830–52 are located in **ADM 27**. Up to 1812 they are arranged by ship's name and, in addition to supplying the first names of next of kin, give the number of children and their town of residence. From 1830 the registers are arranged by allotment declaration number, to which there is no index; but there is a ship index for 1830–40 available in the Research Enquiries Room. Information about whoever was to receive the allotted pay becomes more detailed from 1830. If it was to be the rating's wife, date and place of marriage are given; full addresses are provided; and for children, place of baptism, as well as names.

Allotment declarations made on promotion can be found in **ADM 27/114–120** for 1837–52. These declarations are arranged by ship's name and provide the following information: the rating's name, rank and ship's pay book number, his signature or mark, the name, address and relationship of the person to whom the allotment is to be paid, and the date of allotment. If the allotment was to be paid to the rating's wife, her name and the date and place of marriage are included; if to a child, the child's name and place of baptism are given.

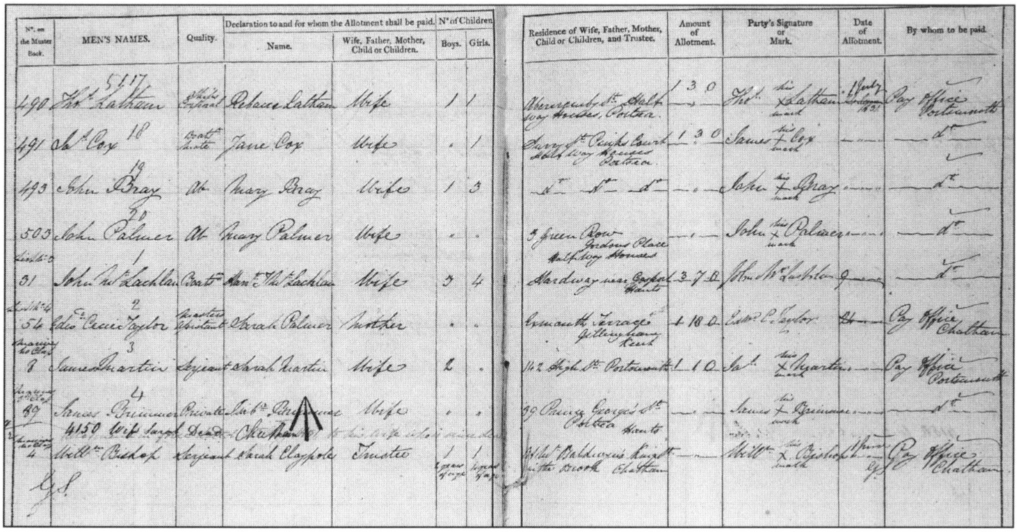

Figure 15 Extract of the allotment register for HMS *Donegal* for 1 July 1831, with an entry for John Bray (see p96). (ADM 27/27)

3.2.4 Remittance ledgers and registers 1758–1851

These records are also a useful source if you need information about a rating's next of kin. Some of them are indexed by the rating's name and so are easier to search than the allotment registers (see 3.2.3).

The remittance ledgers for 1795–1824 in **ADM 26/28–38** record payments to named next of kin from wages and prize money due to ratings serving on ships in home waters. They are arranged in date order and contain surname indexes.

Similar ledgers relating to ratings serving on ships in foreign waters, for the years 1838–51, can be found in **ADM 26/39–54**. Arranged by ship's name, these records often give the name and address of the person receiving the remittance and include the rating's signature, consenting to the payment to be sent.

Remittance registers kept by the Navy Pay Office listing payments made to next of kin by ratings from ships at Plymouth during 1758–98 are located in **ADM 174/291–293**. Further registers arranged by name, which in many instances provide the name and address of next of kin, can be found in **ADM 26/1–20**; these cover the years 1795–1839 and are partially name-indexed by **ADM 26/21–27**.

3.2.5 Merchant navy

When not employed by the Royal Navy, many ratings served in the merchant navy. In times of war, the Royal Navy recruited thousands of men who would previously have served on merchant ships, colliers, barges and fishing vessels. Because of the problems of manning naval fleets for war and reluctance to use the unpopular method of impressment (see 3.2), the government created registers of all merchant and naval seamen who could be called upon in the event of a national emergency. These registers, which cover the years 1835–6 (**BT 120**), 1835–44 (**BT 112**) and 1853–7 (**BT 116**), are name-indexed by **BT 119**. For each seaman, they give name, age and place of birth, plus names of ships served in and details of voyages. By 1839 there were 175,000 names recorded in the registers, though the total had dropped to 150,000 by 1852. *Records of Merchant Shipping and Seamen* by K. Smith, C.T. Watts and M.J. Watts (PRO, 1998) is an excellent guide to these and associated records.

3.2.6 Miscellaneous sources for ratings before 1853

Some of the miscellaneous documents listed in the following table may prove useful in researching details of a rating's background and career prior to 1853.

PRO reference	Remarks
ADM 30/17	Bounty recall lists paid at Deptford, 1674.
ADM 30/8–16	Lists of able and ordinary seamen who volunteered for service on HM ships as declared in HM proclamations of 1690–1, 1701–8 and 1741–2.
ADM 30/63/5	List of men raised at Greenock, 1790. Gives age, place and county where born.
ADM 30/63/11	List of men raised at Falmouth, 1792–1800. Provides name, date of entry, whether volunteered or prest, and the name of the ship joined.
ADM 30/18	Unusual cases and precedents relating to the payment of bounty to volunteers, 1793–5. Contains lists of names.
ADM 30/63/8	List of volunteers under the Quota Acts from the Isle of Wight, 1795. Gives volunteer's name, name of parish serving and residing in, age, height, physical description, and sums paid.
ADM 7/361–362	Nominal lists of men raised at the port of London in 1795 and in Essex in 1796–7. May give trade, place of birth or settlement, rating, and sum of bounty paid.
ADM 30/63/10	List of men raised at Londonderry, 1803.
ADM 30/53–54	Appointments of ratings to signal stations, 1810–14.
ADM 1/5123/25	List of smugglers pressed into the navy, 1824.
ADM 29/107	List of stokers joining the navy, 1834–6. Contains a surname index.
ADM 6/99	Lists of ratings appointed as coastguard boatmen, 1831–50.
ADM 29/106	Services of engineer boys, 1839–53. Contains a surname index.

3.3 Ratings' service records from 1853

As already mentioned, before 1853 the Admiralty employed ratings on a casual basis – usually for no longer than a ship's commission (which generally lasted four to five years). In wartime, ratings tended to serve for longer periods. However, when continuous service engagements were introduced by the Admiralty on 14 June 1853, ratings serving in the navy and recruits aged 18 or over were given the choice of 'signing on' for an initial period – seven years for existing ratings and 10 years for those about to join. They were also given the opportunity, after completing this initial period, of signing further engagements with a view to serving continuously for 20 years (the period required for a long-service pension). This meant that for the first time in British naval history there was a standing navy, and men who opted to commit themselves to continuous service were guaranteed a secure career. Not all ratings chose to opt for continuous service engagements (indeed some ratings were not allowed to), but the records of those that did can be found in **ADM 139**.

It is worth noting that many of the records mentioned in sections 3.2.1 to 3.2.5 overlap the service records described below and can be used to supplement information found in them.

3.3.1 Continuous service engagement books 1853–72 (ADM 139)

ADM 139 is arranged by continuous service (CS) numbers. These were assigned to serving ratings who opted for continuous service engagements and to men who joined the navy when continuous service was introduced. Surname indexes giving each individual's CS number are available on microfilm, in **ADM 139/1019–1027**, in the Microfilm Reading Room. For details, see the table below.

Document reference	Surnames	Date range	Content
ADM 139/1019	A–D	1853–62	Name, ledger number, page number.
ADM 139/1020	E–J	1853–62	Name, ledger number, page number.
ADM 139/1021	K–R	1853–62	Name, ledger number, page number.
ADM 139/1022	S–Z	1853–62	Name, ledger number, page number.
ADM 139/1023	A–D	1863–72	Includes name, year of birth, number of CS engagement, ship in which engagement was signed, and ships previously served in. In the last column, former CS numbers are given and the letters 'FE' are to be found (FE signifying first entry).
ADM 139/1024	E–J	1863–72	Ditto.
ADM 139/1025	K–R	1863–72	Ditto.
ADM 139/1026	S–Z	1863–72	Ditto.
ADM 139/1027			Official number index for men serving before 1873. This index covers CS numbers 40101–79950 and some (but not all) of the numbers between 80934 and 112377.

3.3.1.1 Finding a rating's service record 1853–72

To obtain the document reference for a rating's service record, you will need to know his CS number. For the period 1853–62, which is covered by the name indexes in **ADM 139/1019–1022**, this number will be found in the 'page number' column (the numbers in the 'ledger number' column relate to the rating's year of birth).

For the period 1863–72, covered by the name indexes in **ADM 139/1023–1026**, the CS number is given in the 'number of continuous service engagement' column. Additionally, these indexes sometimes record the name of the ship in which the rating was serving when he signed his first continuous service engagement.

When using the name indexes in **ADM 139/1019–1026**, make sure you note down the rating's CS number accurately – because three sets of CS numbers were used, which are only distinguished by the letters A and B. If you take a quick look at some of these indexes, it may appear that a rating has a straight forward CS number, but on

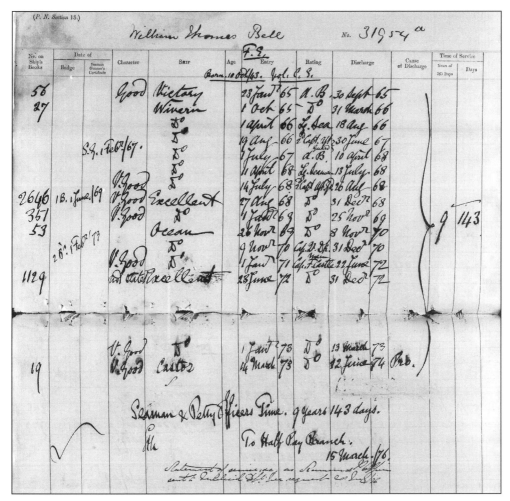

Figure 16 Part of the rating's continuous service record of William Thomas Bell, CS number 31954A. (ADM 139/720)

closer inspection you will find that the number falls within the A or B series. The three sets of numbers are as follows:

- CS numbers 1–40,000 were issued from 1853 to 1858. The service records of ratings with these numbers are in **ADM 139/1–400**.
- CS numbers 1A–40,000A were issued from 1859 to 1866. The service records of ratings with these numbers are in **ADM 139/401–800**.
- CS numbers 1B–21,800B were issued from 1867 to 1872. The service records of ratings with these numbers are in **ADM 139/801–1018.**

Because ratings could now sign on for further engagements, you will find that some ratings had more than one CS number during their naval career.

Once you know the CS number (having found it in the surname index, or perhaps having obtained it from some other source, such as a medal roll or muster), you need to identify the document containing the service record, which is done in the following way.

To find the service record of James Gorman, for example, whose CS number is 27060, the first step is to look at the **ADM 139** series list, available in the Microfilm Reading Room. The **ADM 139** series list is arranged in CS number order and, as can be seen from the following example, the CS numbers appear on the right-hand side of the list:

ADM 139/270	CS numbers 26901–27000
ADM 139/271	CS numbers 27001–27100
ADM 139/272	CS numbers 27101–27200

Since James Gorman's CS number is 27060, his service record will be found in **ADM 139/271**. The service records themselves are arranged by CS number.

Some of the **ADM 139** service records (currently those in **ADM 139/1–220**) are available on microfilm in the Microfilm Reading Room.

3.3.1.2 Details contained in the records

The type of information found in these service records includes date and place of birth, a physical description, date of entry into the navy, names of ships served in, together with dates of entry and discharge, ratings held, date of pension, and date of death if in service. Next of kin details are not given except in cases where parental consent was required to allow boys to join the navy.

Information contained in service records may sometimes be inaccurate. Those entering the navy sometimes used aliases or gave wrong birthplaces and, in order to be accepted, boys often lied about their age.

3.3.2 Registers of seamen's services 1873–92 (ADM 188)

From 1 January 1873 every rating serving in or joining the Royal Navy was allocated an official number. The Admiralty decided to issue numbers from 40,001, thus avoiding confusion with the CS numbers used previously (see 3.3.1). Service records of men who joined between 1873 and 1892 can be found in **ADM 188** which is available on microfilm in the Microfilm Reading Room.

Records for men with the official numbers 40,001–86,600 begin in **ADM 188/5–82**, but are continued in a series of 'continuation books' in **ADM 188/83–90**. References in service records to 'new registers' relate to these continuation books.

Service records for ratings issued with CS numbers 1–40,000, 1–40,000A and 1–21,800B, who were given official numbers in 1873, can be found in **ADM 188/1–4**.

The service registers in **ADM 188** are arranged by date of entry and official number.

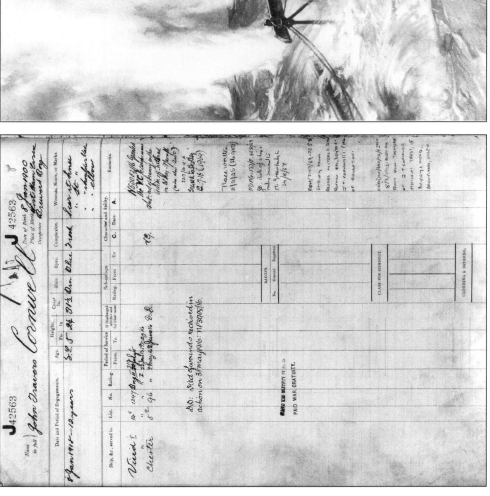

Figure 17 Service record of John Travers Cornwell, youngest naval Victoria Cross winner (ADM 188/732) official number J42563, together with a picture of him (*The Great War*, Vol 7, p461).

To locate the record of a rating who joined the navy between 1873 and 1892, it is essential to find his official number (also referred to as his service number). This can be done by searching the surname indexes in **ADM 188/245–267**, which are available on microfilm in the Microfilm Reading Room. Arranged alphabetically by initial letter of surname, though not in strict alphabetical order, they contain the following information: name, official number, continuous service number (usually annotated in red), year of birth, year of entry into the service, and place of birth.

Once you have found a rating's official number, look at the **ADM 188** series list to identify the document containing his service record. The documents themselves are arranged in official-number order. Any references in the surname indexes to continuous service (CS) numbers – usually marked in red – relate to the continuous service records in **ADM 139** (see 3.3.1.1).

The details provided in the **ADM 188** service registers mirror the type of information found in the continuous service records in **ADM 139** (see 3.3.1.2), except that no next of kin details are given.

3.3.3 Registers of seamen's services 1893–1923 (ADM 188)

The official-number system as described in 3.3.2 was used by the Royal Navy until 1 January 1894. The official numbers used (40,000–178,000) were issued sequentially, regardless of whether the rating was a seaman, stoker, artificer, etc. On 1 January 1894 the Admiralty decided to alter this system. Six batches of official numbers (see left-hand column of table below) were introduced to identify which branch of the service a rating was from. By 1907 there was a risk that these groups of numbers would overlap, so on 1 January 1908 new numbers (see right-hand column of table below) prefixed by J, K, L or M were introduced to help further identify types of rating.

1894–1907	Type of rating	1908–1923
178001–240500	Seamen and communications ratings	J1–J110000
268001–273000	Engine room artificers	M1–M38000
276001–313000	Stokers	K1–K63500
340001–348000	Artisans and miscellaneous	M1–M38000
350001–352000	Sick berth staff and ship's police	M1–M38000
353001–366450	Officers' stewards, officers' cooks and boy servants/stewards	L1–L15000

The service records for ratings who joined the navy between 1893 and 1923 are in **ADM 188/269–1131**. To identify the relevant records, you need to know the rating's service number and the year when he joined the navy. His service number can be found by searching the surname indexes in **ADM 188/1132–1154** for 1893–1912 and **ADM 188/1155–1177** for 1913–23, which are available on microfilm in the Microfilm

Reading Room. These indexes have the same format as the ones described in 3.3.2. Once you have found the service number, look at the **ADM 188** series list to obtain the microfilm document reference for the service record of the rating you are researching.

When searching the surname indexes in **ADM 188/1132–1154**, you may come across service numbers prefixed with a Y. These were given to men who enrolled under a deferred volunteer scheme, the Royal Naval Volunteer Reserve (see 6.4). Where men have both a Y number and another service number, the record of service will be found using the other service number, not the Y number. If they have a Y number only, this means that although they had volunteered to serve they were not actually called up, so no service record will be found.

In 1903 the Admiralty introduced a short-service scheme whereby men could serve for 12 years, part of which (usually either 5 or 7 years) was spent in the navy and the remainder with the Royal Fleet Reserve, which consisted of ratings pensioned from the navy after 20 years' service but still of military age. Official numbers for short-service men were introduced on 1 July 1903 (numbers SS1–SS10000 were issued to seamen, and SS10001 onwards to stokers).

The kind of information found in service records for this period is the same as described in 3.3.2.

It is important to note that these service records will only contain information about a rating's service up to 1928. So if, for example, a rating joined the navy in 1920 and served beyond 1928, the earlier part of his service will be recorded in **ADM 188**, but his post-1928 service will be in records held by the Ministry of Defence (see 3.3.4).

Service records for ratings who served in armoured cars in Russia, 1915–17, can be found in **ADM 116/1717**.

A nominal roll of officers and ratings who served in the South African campaign during 1899–1900 is located in **ADM 116/529**.

In the early 1900s it was not uncommon for ratings who served in the navy to go on to join the coastguard service, keeping their Royal Navy service number. Their naval service records will be found in **ADM 188**. To trace their coastguard service, look at the record cards in **ADM 175/82A–84B** (arranged alphabetically by surname) and the service registers in **ADM 175/85–89**. These service registers, which cover ratings with service numbers 112500–358500, are surname-indexed by **ADM 175/108**. You may also find references to them in the discharge documents (arranged by rank) in **ADM 175/91–96**, each of which contains a surname index.

Service records of engine room artificers, 1868–71, arranged by date of entry, can be found in **ADM 29/123**. Those of chief engine room artificers, 1877–88, arranged by date of promotion to that rating, are in **ADM 29/124**. Both **ADM 29/123** and **ADM 29/124** include surname indexes.

Engagement ledgers giving details of ratings who joined the Royal Navy between 1905 and 1921 are held by the Fleet Air Arm Museum (for address and contact details, see Appendix 2). These ledgers include the rating's name, date of joining, physical description, trade, details of any previous military service, and sometimes proof of birth and the rating's signature. If the entrant was a boy, there may be a consent form giving him permission to join, signed by next of kin.

3.3.4 Ratings' service records after 1928

In 1928 the Admiralty introduced new service records for ratings, known as docket books. For men who joined the Royal Navy between 1928 and 1938, these are held by the Ministry of Defence at the Navy Records Centre in Hayes, Middlesex (for address, see Appendix 2). The records of men who joined the navy in or since 1938 are held at the PPPA address given in Appendix 2.

Service records from 1928 onwards are (at the time of writing) still closed to public inspection. However, information from them can be provided to ex-servicemen or (for a fee) to next of kin, on application to the Navy Records Centre or PPPA as appropriate.

3.4 Case study of a pre-1853 naval rating

3.4.1 Which records to search?

Because ratings' service records were only kept systematically from 1853, tracing the career and family background of a rating who served in the Royal Navy before then can be laborious and time-consuming, unless you know the name of a ship on which he served, plus the dates when he served on it, or are in possession of some other pointer as to where you should start your search.

- If you know the name of a ship on which an ancestor served and the dates when he served on it, you may be able to search the ship's pay books and musters (see 4.1.1) and allotment and remittance registers (see 3.2.3 and 3.2.4).

- If you do not know the names of any of the ships on which your ancestor served but know where he was at a particular time, look at the list books in **ADM 8** (see 4.2.1). These monthly returns, ranging from 1673 to 1909, indicate the whereabouts of Royal Navy ships at home and abroad. You can therefore use them to establish which ships were near a particular place, and then search the ships' musters to see whether your ancestor was a member of the crew.

- If your ancestor was injured, wounded or killed in action, you may want to search some of the records mentioned in 4.8, 4.9.10–13 and 4.10.

- If he was in receipt of a pension, it is worth searching the sources described in 3.2.1 and 3.2.2 (see 4.9, especially 4.9.4, for further guidance).

- If none of the details mentioned above are known, you may need to search the sources mentioned in sections 4 and 5, as well as those described in 3.2, in order to discover some key facts, such as names of ships your ancestor served on (ideally, with dates).

The case study that follows uses many of the sources described so far to piece together genealogical and service information about a rating named John Bray. It is assumed that at the outset the researcher knows only that Bray was a naval pensioner in 1836 and that he was born in Portsmouth.

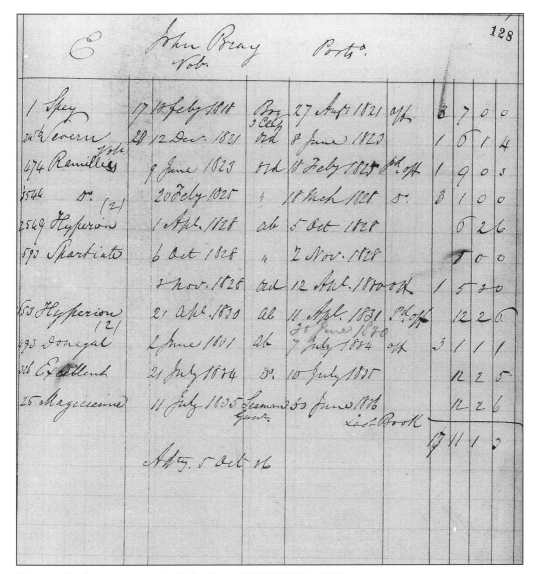

Figure 18 Service record of John Bray. (ADM 29/13 p197)

3.4.2 Searching the records

The best place to begin a search for a naval-rating ancestor who received a naval pension would probably be **ADM 29/1–96** (see 3.2.1). Given that John Bray was being paid a naval pension in 1836, he must have applied for his pension and/or been awarded it either before 1836 or during that year. The records in **ADM 29/1–96** are surname-indexed by two series of registers on microfilm covering 1802–68 and 1868–94 (see 3.2.1). Since Bray was in receipt of his pension in 1836, the register to search would be **ADM 29/97** (covering surnames beginning with B between 1802 and

1868) – where an entry for a John Bray was found, with the reference 13/197 alongside his name. Converting this to the relevant **ADM 29** document reference in the manner described in 3.2.1 led to **ADM 29/13** p197, which contains service records issued between July 1836 and January 1837.

Was this the right John Bray? Common names are likely to appear many times in the indexes. It is therefore worth looking at the dates of the various documents in the **ADM 29** series list – which may enable you to rule out some entries immediately (for example, those relating to men whose service records were issued before your ancestor joined the navy). Also, it should be borne in mind that records in **ADM 29** may have been issued many years after the rating concerned ended his service, and that they were used in applications for the admittance of orphaned children to Greenwich Hospital Lower School (see 3.2.1 and 4.10.1).

On **ADM 29/13** p197, under the name John Bray the abbreviations 'vol' (for volunteer) – as opposed to 'prest' (pressed) – and 'Ports' (for Portsmouth) appear, the place name being his place of birth. The document sets out his service history as follows:

1		2	3	4	5	6	7	8	9	10
1	*Spey*	17	13 Feb 1818	Boy 3 Class	27 Aug 1821	off	3	7	0	0
3456	*Severn*	20	12 Dec 1821	Ord	8 June 1823		1	6	1	4
474	*Ramillies*		9 June 1823	Ord	18 Feb 1825	Paid off	1	9	0	3
3544	*Ramillies* (2)		20 Feb 1825	Ord	18 March 1828	Paid off	3	1	0	0
2549	*Hyperion*		1 April 1828	Ab	5 Oct 1828			6	2	6
593	*Spartiate*		6 Oct 1828	Ab	2 Nov 1828			1	0	0
			3 Nov 1828	Ord	12 Aug 1830	off	1	5	3	0
3653	*Hyperion* (2)		21 April 1830	Ab	11 April 1831	Paid off		12	2	6
					30 June 1830					
493	*Donegal*		2 June 1831	Ab	7 July 1834	off	3	1	1	1
326	*Excellent*		21 July 1834	Ab	10 July 1835			12	2	5
25	*Magicienne*		11 July 1835	Seaman Gunner	30 June 1836 Last Book			12	2	6
			Adty 5 Oct 36				17	11	1	3

- Column 1 lists the ships John Bray served on and his ship's pay book numbers, which are useful when searching ship's pay books and musters – especially since these may contain hundreds of names, and the surname indexes that began to appear in ships' pay books from about 1760 and in ships' musters from 1797 can be unreliable.

- Column 2 gives the rating's age on joining a ship (this information is not always correct, and in this instance is given for only two of the ships).

- Column 3 gives the date when Bray joined a ship. 'Adty 5 Oct 36' at the bottom of Column 3 is the date when the Admiralty granted him a pension.

- Column 4 indicates Bray's rating ('Ord' and 'Ab' are short for ordinary seaman and able seaman).

- Column 5 gives the date when he left a ship he was serving on.

- Column 6 states the reason why.

- Columns 7–10 show the amount of time Bray served on each ship, in years, months, weeks and days, and (in the bottom line) record the total amount of time he served in the navy (17 years, 11 months, 1 week, and 3 days).

The document provides the information that John Bray was born in Portsmouth around 1801, served nearly 18 years in the navy, and was awarded a pension on 5 October 1836. More importantly, the revelation of the names of the ships Bray served on, together with dates, makes it possible to search the relevant musters and pay books and also to search pension records and the records of Greenwich Hospital School.

ADM 31–39, 41, 115 and 117 (see 4.1.1) contain a variety of ships' pay books and musters (see 4.1.1), ranging from 1667 to 1884. These records overlap, so it is possible to find more than one muster for the same ship covering the same date. Also, some of the musters have not survived. If all you have to go on is the name of a ship on which a rating served and the dates of his service on that ship, searching through these records may be the only way to trace the basic details of his naval career. In theory, these records should provide the name of the ship on which he served previously and (where relevant) the name of the ship he joined next. However, this information is not always provided – which is why searching ships' pay books and musters can be time-consuming. On the other hand, the musters can yield valuable details, such as age, place of birth, a physical description of the rating, whether he allotted his pay (useful for tracing details of next of kin in allotment and remittance registers), whether he made a will and, if he died in service, his date of death. Also, if he fell ill or was injured, they may give details such as the name of the hospital he was sent to (useful for searching hospital musters, see 4.1.5).

The dates John Bray served (13 February 1818 to 30 June 1836) rule out ADM 31, 33, 34, 36, 39, 41, 115 and 117 (see 4.1.1), as they do not contain ships' pay books or musters relevant to his period of service. So the search could be narrowed to ADM 32, 35, 37 and 38, and it transpired that pay books and musters were available for the following ships, covering the dates that Bray served on them (see table that follows).

Dates	Ship	Document reference
8 Sept 1815 to 17 Oct 1821	HMS *Spey*	**ADM 35/4291**
Feb 1818 to Oct 1821	HMS *Spey*	**ADM 37/6280–6282**
Oct 1821 to July 1822	HMS *Severn*	**ADM 37/6393–6394**
Nov 1821 to Dec 1822	HMS *Severn*	**ADM 37/6385–6391**
1 July 1822 to 8 June 1823	HMS *Severn*	**ADM 35/4270–4272**
Sept 1822 to June 1823	HMS *Ramillies*	**ADM 37/6523**
Jan 1823 to June 1823	HMS *Severn*	**ADM 37/6608–6610**
June 1823 to Dec 1825	HMS *Ramillies*	**ADM 37/6841–6855**
4 June 1823 to 31 Dec 1825	HMS *Ramillies*	**ADM 35/4242–4245**
Jan 1826 to March 1828	HMS *Ramillies*	**ADM 37/7666–7679**
1 Jan 1826 to 30 June 1828	HMS *Ramillies*	**ADM 35/4467–4471**
1 Jan 1828 to 31 Dec 1828	HMS *Hyperion*	**ADM 35/4403–4404**
1 Jan 1828 to 20 Oct 1831	HMS *Spartiate*	**ADM 35/4487**
March 1828 to Oct 1828	HMS *Hyperion*	**ADM 37/7503–7506**
July 1828 to Feb 1830	HMS *Spartiate*	**ADM 37/7727–7732**
1 Jan 1830 to 30 May 1831	HMS *Hyperion*	**ADM 35/4407–4408**
March 1830 to May 1831	HMS *Hyperion*	**ADM 37/7515–7521**
July 1830 to Oct 1834	HMS *Donegal*	**ADM 37/8031–8041**
1 Nov 1830 to 7 July 1834	HMS *Donegal*	**ADM 32/327–329**
April 1834 to Dec 1835	HMS *Excellent*	**ADM 37/9023–9024**
March 1835 to June 1842	HMS *Excellent*	**ADM 37/9036**
April 1835 to Dec 1836	HMS *Magicienne*	**ADM 37/9317–9318**
July to Sept 1838	HMS *Magicienne*	**ADM 37/9321**

A quick way of finding out whether there is a ship's pay book or muster for a given date is to search the PRO online catalogue at www.pro.gov.uk, using the ship's name as a keyword.

Although some of the details found in these records duplicated information already known, useful new facts and additional details were discovered:

- It emerged that Bray allotted part of his pay on 1 February 1822 (**ADM 35/4271**), 1 January 1824, (**ADM 35/4243**), 1 April 1825 (**ADM 37/6851**), 7 May 1828 (**ADM 37/7504–7506**), 24 May 1830 (**ADM 35/4407**), 24 June 1831 (**ADM 32/327**) and 1 August 1834 (**ADM 37/9023**).
- **ADM 35/4468**, **ADM 35/4487** and **ADM 37/7516** record promotions: to able seaman on 25 July 1826, to ordinary seaman on 3 November 1828, and to leading seaman on 12 April 1830.

- **ADM 37/9023** gives Bray's place of birth as High Street, Portsmouth.
- **ADM 37/8038** states that Bray is married, gives his place of abode as Portsmouth, and supplies details of ships he served on between 1818 and 1831. It also provides a physical description of Bray at the age of 30 (height 5 feet 4¾ inches; complexion, pale; hair, brown; eyes, blue) and mentions that he has a mark on his arm.
- HMS *Magicienne*'s muster (**ADM 37/9318**) confirmed that Bray qualified as a seaman gunner and revealed that on 17 July 1836 he was discharged sick to HMS *Malabar* for a passage to the nearest hospital in England.

ADM 37/9318 is tantalizing, in that it does not specify which hospital Bray was taken to (in some instances, the musters are more specific). However, the *Magicienne*'s ship's log for 17 July 1836 (**ADM 53/894**) shows that she was then in Cadiz, Spain, and the *Malabar*'s ship's log for 18 July 1836 (**ADM 53/897**) makes reference to having received two invalided seamen from HMS *Magicienne*. Subsequently, the *Malabar* sailed from Cadiz and arrived in Plymouth Sound on 1 August 1836. The nearest hospital to Plymouth Sound would be the naval hospital in Plymouth.

As mentioned briefly above, as well as ships' musters there are hospital musters (see 4.1.5), which are located in **ADM 102**. The Plymouth Hospital muster for August to September 1836 (**ADM 102/643**) shows that John Bray, number 24, seaman gunner, was received on 1 August 1836, suffering from pneumonia, and that in September he was no longer fit to undertake service and was to collect his wages. The Admiralty was informed on 3 September 1836 and he was discharged from the hospital on 14 September 1836, after 45 days there. As the hospital had found him unsuitable for service because of ill health, the next step was to check whether he was awarded his pension soon after being discharged. Applications submitted in 1836–7 for Greenwich Hospital pensions and other relief (see 4.9.5) are in **ADM 6/297**. The name of John Bray appears in a list of seamen and marines who have been granted pensions at the examination of 6 October 1836 (although according to his service record in **ADM 29/13** the Admiralty awarded him his pension on the previous day). The total time served by Bray is confirmed, his illness is given as consumption, and we learn that he was granted a life pension of £12 and 4 shillings per annum. There is no indication that Bray was to be admitted to Greenwich Hospital as an in-pensioner or receive any other form of relief. This suggested that he must have received an out-pension – an inference confirmed by the absence of any application from him for admission as an in-pensioner among those preserved in **ADM 73/3–4** (see 3.2.2).

The records of Greenwich Hospital's out-pension payments are mainly in **ADM 22** (see 4.9.6). **ADM 22/405** covers out-pension payments for 1835–6, and under number 6117 there is an entry for Bray confirming that his out-pension started on 6 October 1836, that the last ship he served on was the *Magicienne*, that he had served 17 years, 11 months, 1 week, 3 days, and that his annual pension was to be £12 and 4 shillings. It also states that he died on 16 January 1837.

Ships' pay books and musters revealed that Bray allotted part of his pay to dependants. Records of such payments can sometimes be found in allotment and remittance registers (see 3.2.3 and 3.2.4). The registers in **ADM 26/16** and **18–20** and in

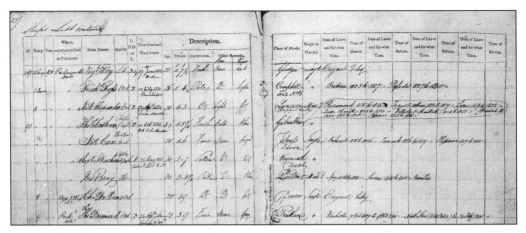

Figure 19 Copy of a page from HMS *Donegal's* description book which contains an entry for John Bray. (ADM 37/8038)

ADM 27/22–24, 28, 30–35, 37–43 and **45–46** were therefore searched for references to Bray allotting his pay – but without success. However, the allotment list for HMS *Donegal* dated 2 July 1831 in **ADM 27/27** (see p81) showed that John Bray, ship's pay book number 493, rank AB, was allotting part of his pay to his wife, Mary Bray, and four children (one boy and three girls, names not given) residing in Surry Street, Pinks Court, Half Way Houses, Portsea.

Since John Bray died leaving a wife and four children, the next step was to investigate whether his wife ever applied for any of their children to be admitted to the Greenwich Hospital School. The main source for such applications are the school's admission papers for 1728–1870 in **ADM 73/154–389**, which are arranged alphabetically by name (see 4.10.1). **ADM 73/176** includes applications received from individuals whose surnames begin with 'Bra'. However, not knowing the full names of the children meant that every application on behalf of a child named Bray had to be searched to see if mention was made of a father named John or a mother named Mary. The search proved rewarding, since an application was found relating to an Anne Amelia Bray, which, besides containing two service records for John Bray that matched those found in **ADM 29/13** (see p91), yielded the following information about his family (see p163):

- Child's name: Anne Amelia Bray.
- Names and ages of other children maintained: John Bray, aged 14 in November 1838, and Susannah Bray aged 7 in June 1838. (No mention was made of the third girl, who was presumably either older or dead.)
- Place of residence: 16 New Street, St Nicholas Deptford, Kent.
- Was the father killed in HM service? No.
- Did the father die in HM service? Died at home.
- How long served? 17 years.
- Mother dead or living? Living.

Accompanying this application are a copy of Anne Amelia Bray's birth certificate, signed by the minister of Deptford parish church, which reveals that she was born on 11 May 1829, and a marriage certificate which shows that John Bray married Mary Hurley in Hythe, in Kent, on 30 October 1823. Further confirmation is provided by another birth certificate for Anne Amelia in which Mary, widow of John Bray, declared that her daughter was born on 11 May 1829 in Portsmouth. Finally, there is a letter approving the entry of Anne Amelia Bray to the Lower School, Greenwich, between 12 and 20 September 1839.

No references to the other children were found, but the search yielded two further references to Anne Amelia Bray. **ADM 73/443** confirms her date of birth and shows she was admitted to the school on 24 September 1839, while **ADM 73/441** p54, entry number 1826, reveals that Anne Amelia Bray's application was dated 9 July 1838. It also gives the following information:

- Born: 11 May 1829.
- Baptized: 18 April 1830.
- Parents' names.
- Date of parents' marriage: 30 Oct 1823.
- Number of children to maintain: 2.
- Residence: 16 New Street, St Nicholas Deptford.
- Father's time served: 18 years, 1 month. Rank: seaman gunner. Discharged to hospital 1836, died of consumption at home 1837. Good character.
- Number of class: 5.
- When classed or admitted: Oct 1838.
- Admitted: 24 Sept 1839.

Having learned when Anne Amelia Bray was admitted to the Lower School, it was possible to determine when she left the school by searching the records mentioned in 4.10.1. **ADM 73/448**, number 125, revealed that Anne left the school on 11 April 1843 and returned to her mother's residence at 3 Flaggon's Row, Deptford. (This address could now be used to search the census returns, as described in 5.2.) Curiously, an address and instruction for Anne to be sent to Hicklescott, near Shrewsbury, and left at the post office in Church Stratton, Salop, has been crossed out.

A search of pension documents for ratings' widows and next of kin in **PMG 16/2–5** (see 4.9.10) revealed no trace of any pension being paid to Mary Bray or other relations. A search for a will or grant of administration yielded nothing, and no mention of John Bray could be found in relevant Death Duty records (see 5.3). This suggests that if he did leave a will, it may have been proved locally.

With the introduction of continuous service records in 1853 (see 3.3.1), searches for information about naval ratings become much easier. But even after 1853 many of the sources described above can play a useful role in tracing genealogical and career details, and may lead to other documents that will contribute further information.

4 Features of naval service

The records covering subjects such as pay, discipline, conduct, rewards, health and welfare described in this chapter constitute significant genealogical sources. They can be searched to discover how much those who served in the Royal Navy were paid, where they travelled to, how they were cared for while in the navy and after completing their service, and what provisions were made for their next of kin in the event of serious injury or death.

Figure 20 Photograph of some officers and ratings on board HMS *Buzzard* 1898. (COPY 1/476; photo: Alfred Ellis)

4.1 Ships' pay books and musters, record and establishment books, ships' ledgers, description books, and hospital musters

4.1.1 Ships' pay books and musters 1667–1878

These records are to be found in the following series. Many of the pre-1688 ships' musters were destroyed by fire, and most of the musters and ledgers for 1878–1909 were destroyed by enemy action in 1941.

Ships' pay books

ADM 31	Controllers' pay books, 1691–1710
ADM 32	Ships' pay books, Ticket Office, 1692–1856
ADM 33	Ships' pay books, Treasurer's Series I, 1669–1778
ADM 34	Ships' pay books, Treasurer's Series II, 1766–85
ADM 35	Ships' pay books, Treasurer's Series III, 1777–1832

Ships' musters

ADM 36	Ships' musters, Series I, 1688–1808
ADM 37	Ships' musters, Series II, 1792–1842
ADM 38	Ships' musters, Series III, 1793–1878
ADM 39	Ships' musters, Series IV, 1667–1798
ADM 41	Ships' musters, hired armed vessels, 1794–1815

Musters for ships that were not in service ('commissioned') but in reserve ('in ordinary') and stationed in dock can be found in **ADM 7, 33, 36–38, 42, 106, 108, 113** and **224**. These musters are useful in tracing information about 'standing officers' (pursers, boatswains, gunners, carpenters and cooks), who in theory were supposed to be warranted to a ship indefinitely, regardless of whether she was in service or not.

Ships' pay books and musters may play a useful role in tracing details about an officer during the earlier part of his naval career, but tend to be less useful once he has attained commissioned or warrant officer status. But if you are trying to track down information about a rating, the importance of these records cannot be stressed highly enough. As explained in Chapter 3, there are not many records dating from before the introduction of continuous service in 1853 that will help you trace the naval career or family background of a rating unless he received a pension (see 3.2.1) or allotted part of his pay to dependants (see 3.2.3 and 3.2.4).

The names of all the men (but not women) serving on board a ship were noted in the musters and pay books, since these records were used to determine the crew's wages and their consumption of victuals, which would be charged against their pay. The names of supernumeraries (men over and above the established complement) were also entered in these records, though in a separate list. Ships' pay books and musters often duplicate each other (but not entirely), so cross-checking may enable you to fill in gaps. The information they record may include:

- age, from around 1761
- place of birth, from 1761
- date of death – useful for tracing wills and associated documents (see 5.3)
- remittance of wages to dependants (see 3.2.3 and 3.2.4), from 1758
- whether anyone on board was sent to hospital – useful for searching hospital musters (see 4.1.5)
- which ship a member of the crew had served on previously, and which one he went on to join.

Surname indexes – known as 'alphabets' because they are arranged by the alphabetical order of the initial letter only – appear in ships' pay books from about 1760, and in ships' musters from 1797. You may therefore find that between 1760 and 1797 it saves time to search the pay books first.

The various musters and pay books are arranged by ship's name and cover specific periods of time, but because some have not survived there is no guarantee that you will find a ship's muster or pay book for a particular date. In order to find the relevant records, you need to have the name of a ship an officer or a rating served on and know when he served on it; once you have these details, you can search the PRO online catalogue, either in the PRO reading rooms or on the internet via www.pro.gov.uk, to find out whether there are musters or pay books for that ship for relevant dates. If you do not have a ship's name, then it may be possible to identify likely ships by searching the list books in **ADM 8** (see 3.4.1 and 4.2.1).

When searching ships' musters and pay books, the following points should be borne in mind:

- On joining a ship an officer or rating was allocated an individual pay book number, which normally remained unique to him during the ship's commission. If you come across this number during the course of your research, it is worth making a note of it, so you can use it when looking for the name of the officer or rating in a relevant muster or pay book.
- The information contained in the surviving musters and pay books was normally copied from rough musters kept by the captain and purser, so mistakes easily occurred and sometimes details were omitted altogether.
- Often, blank entries are to be interpreted as ditto.
- Especially in early ships' musters and pay books, you may find that not all of the columns have been filled in.

Also, if you are trying to establish which ship a naval ancestor served on previously or served on next, the following considerations may be relevant:

- Before 1853 ratings were normally employed for the duration of a ship's commission – which rarely lasted longer than five years (see 3.3).

- After serving on HM ships, in many instances ratings joined the merchant navy, as it offered better pay and conditions.
- Seamen often went on to join a ship commanded by a captain they had served with previously – particularly if he treated his crew well and offered a good chance of earning prize money.

Documents similar to ships' musters and pay books include:

- record and establishment books for 1857–73 in **ADM 115** (see 4.1.2)
- ships' ledgers for 1872–84 in **ADM 117** (see 4.1.3)
- hospital musters for 1740–1860 in **ADM 102** (see 4.1.5).

4.1.2 Record and establishment books 1857–73 (ADM 115)

The record and establishment books in **ADM 115** record the names of every officer and rating serving on each ship. The **ADM 115** series list is arranged by ship's name and date order. The records contain the following information: ship's pay book number, whether in continuous service, place and date of birth (given in respect of ratings only), rank/rating, badges issued, date of entry, name of last ship, and date of discharge to another ship (with cause). Where relevant, the CS number is given – which is useful for finding ratings' service records (see 3.3.1).

4.1.3 Ships' ledgers 1872–84 (ADM 117)

These were instituted on 21 September 1872, by the Admiralty's circular letter number 53. Each ship's ledger was to record the full pay and allowances of every officer, man and boy on board, together with all necessary particulars in regard to victualling. The introduction of this system rendered unnecessary the record and establishment books (see 4.1.2) and description books (see 4.1.4). The revised system was to come into operation both on ships commissioned after the date of the circular and on all other ships, except those paid off on 1 January 1873.

Ships' ledgers do not include date and place of birth, but they do contain the following details. Borne (i.e. date when assigned to ship); place, ship or list received from; and date of appearance if different from date of commencing pay. If entered from shore, last ship served in and date of discharge. If first entry, to be so stated. If continuous service men, date and period of engagement. Officers' dates of appointment, ratings, badges, and gunnery notations. Whether discharged (D), discharged dead (DD) or 'run' (R) – i.e. deserted – often with date, place, name of ship and for what cause. Details of character and allotments may be given. Ships' ledgers also contain transfer and discharge lists, lists of wills made (by whom, on what date, and in whose favour), accounts of effects left by persons who have died or deserted during the period of the ledger, and surname indexes.

Most of the ships' ledgers for 1878–1909 were destroyed by fire in 1941.

4.1.4 Description books

Description books are mainly to be found in **ADM 38**, which cover the years 1836–72. In the **ADM 38** series list, they are identified by the letter 'D' alongside a ship's name. Pre-1840 description books usually give a physical description of each man, his pay number, age, marital status, rank, and date of entry and discharge. Between 1840 and 1870 they list the following additional details: last rating; when D, DD or R (see 4.1.6); whether conduct noted on certificate; where born; address; if had smallpox or been vaccinated; previous trade; if an out-pensioner, ticket number; copy of certificate produced; ships served with; ship's pay book number and dates of entry and discharge; time served; conduct; captain's signature; if ever invalided, when, for what complaint and from what station. From 1853, they include continuous service (CS) numbers (useful for locating service records – see 3.3.1 and 3.3.2), length of service signed for, and details of long-service or good-conduct badges (see p for an example of description book). Details of the past service of warrant and subordinate officers, ratings and supernumeraries are given in description books, but they do not provide details of this kind for commissioned officers.

Early description books can be found in **ADM 36–37** and in **ADM 41**, which gives details of the crews of hired armed vessels, 1794–1815. There are no indexes to the description books in **ADM 37** and **ADM 41**, but there is one to those in the **ADM 36** series list.

4.1.5 Hospital musters 1740–1860 (ADM 102)

ADM 102 consists chiefly of musters of patients in naval hospitals at home and abroad and on stationary hospital ships. These musters are arranged alphabetically by hospital or hospital-ship name, and can be quickly searched by hospital name using the PRO online catalogue (accessible via www.pro.gov.uk). Hospital musters can include those of attached hospital ships, and vice versa. The musters of seagoing hospital ships are included with those of other HM ships in **ADM 36–37**.

Up to 1791 hospital musters generally provide the following details: current number, ship's pay book number, name of the ship on which the person was serving, person's name, received sick on shore, quality (see 4.1.6), when received on shore (date), type of disease or hurt, D, DD or R (see 4.1.6), time when, what ship returned to or how disposed of, time in cure, 'chequed charge of cloathes', conduct money, funeral (where relevant), and date of muster. From 1792 to 1860 the format mirrors that of the pre-1791 musters – except there are two extra columns, introduced in 1808, recording date and amount of allotments (also, when reported to the Navy Board) and stoppages of fourpence a day.

The musters of the Royal Naval Hospital Malta (Bighi) for 1811–79 are in **ADM 304/14–18** and **22–24**. Those of the Haslar Hospital (see 1.1.3) for 1852–95 and 1906 are in **ADM 304/36–41** and **88**.

For further records about patients in naval hospitals and their treatment, see sections 4.3.1 to 4.3.3.

4.1.6 Terms and abbreviations used in musters and pay and description books

The various types of muster reflect the detailed accounting methods used by the Royal Navy, which can be difficult to interpret and use. In addition, they contain many abbreviations and terms that can obscure information of potential use to researchers. A key to these abbreviations and terms is given below.

Abbreviations		
A, B, C, D, E, F, G, H		Method of recording when wages were paid. Found under the heading 'When paid or mustered'.
CP	= Civil Power	The civil legal authorities on land.
D	= Discharged	Normally used when an officer or rating left the ship.
DD	= Discharged Dead	Cause of death may be given; if not, assume illness is the cause.
DFQ	= Discharged Foreign Remove Ticket	Procedure used when abroad to transfer a man from one ship to another.
DS/DSQ	= Discharged Sick Quarters	Normally followed by the name of a hospital or hospital ship.
DSS	= Discharged Shore Sick	
DUS	= Discharged Unserviceable	Indicates a man unfit for service on medical grounds.
E	= Entered	
FB	= Former Book	
HH	= Haslar Hospital	May signify Haslar Hospital, depending on context.
HS	= Hospital Ship	
LO	= List of Officers	
Lt	= Lent	
LV	= Leave	
NB	= North Britain	Used in 'Place and country where born' column to indicate Scotland.
PFRT	= Per Foreign Remove Ticket	Ticket used when abroad to transfer a man from one ship to another.
PLO	= Per Lords Order	Normally used when referring to an officer's discharge.
PRQT	= Per Request	Usually used to request the transfer of a man to a different ship.
Q	= Query	Instituted by Admiralty order in 1690. Used to denote sick men put ashore. Once recovered, the men were to return to their ships to collect their wages. In cases where men did not do this, the 'Q' would be altered to 'R'.
R	= Run	Deserted (see 4.4).
SLVO	= Supernumerary List Victualling Only	
SS	= Sick on Shore	
SW	= South Wales	Used in 'Place and country where born' column.
TOL	= Turn Over Lists	Lists of men transferred to other ships.

Terms	
Instructions passed on imprest	This signifies that no deductions were to be made from individual officers' wages because their accounts were in order.
Journal and log book delivered	Master's evidence of good performance of duty.
Journal produced	Used to denote midshipmen and master's mates providing their logs to draw wages and in order to qualify for lieutenancy examination.
Men in lieu	Men persuaded to join the Royal Navy in place of departing seamen (see 3.2).
Ordinary	From the Reserve.
Petty warrants	Clerk of the Cheque's authority to pay men preparing ships for sea (see 'Under the cheque').
Purser's necessaries	A purser's supplies and stocks of victuals.
Quality	Either rank/rating or type, depending on context.
Rendezvous	Recruiting post set up by officers of the impress service.
Rigging wages	Wages paid to those who prepared the ship for sea.
Sea wages	Wages paid to the ship's complement.
Slops	Clothes.
Stragglers	Deserters.
Substitutes	See 'Men in lieu'.
Superseded	Used when an officer is replaced, reason usually given.
Truss	A surgical appliance serving for support in cases of rupture.
Under the cheque	The Clerk of the Cheque was responsible for paying the wages of men and preparing a ship for sea. Any ship in port (not in commission) was said to be 'under the cheque'.
Unserviceable	Unfit for service on medical grounds.
Victuals	Clothes, bedding, tobacco, blankets.

4.2 Operational records and ships' photographs and histories

As we have already seen, a variety of sources can be used to discover the names of the ships that an officer or rating served on. From other records it is possible to investigate where a ship sailed to, or what happened on board it day by day. Although individuals are seldom mentioned in these accounts, descriptions of events and voyages are included in records such as captains' and masters' logs.

4.2.1 Ships' movements 1648–1914

Many records relating to the movements and whereabouts of ships and convoys from the mid seventeenth century to the end of the nineteenth century can be found in **ADM 7** and **ADM 8**. If you know where a naval ancestor was on a given date but do not have the name of the ship he was serving on, you can search these records to establish which ships were nearest to that place and then check their musters (see 4.1) to see if he was on board.

ADM 7 is a miscellaneous collection of documents relating to naval administration, navigation and other maritime matters for the period 1563–1953. Details of some key documents in **ADM 7** relating to the movement and whereabouts of ships are given below.

Document references	Content
ADM 7/777–780	Miscellaneous collection of ships' logs, 1648–1707 (see section 4.2.4).
ADM 7/550A	List of ships and their stations, 1696–1714.
ADM 7/569–575	Abstracts of ships' journals, 1736–95. These abstracts list captains' and ships' names, and for every ship the number of days spent at each named port, dates of sailing, total time spent at sea or cruising, and details of any remarkable observations or accidents.
ADM 7/413–501	Muster books of ships, 1741–1804. These do not list the names of the crew, but contain such information as ship's name, home station and number of crew.
ADM 7/782–787, 789, 791–792, 794, 796, 799, 802	Registers of convoys (both home and abroad) for 1793–1815, with some gaps. The registers record master's name, description of cargo, where bound, and date of sailing.
ADM 7/233–296	Movements of and instructions to ships, April 1798 to December 1829.
ADM 7/502–538	Daily returns to the First Lord as to ships and their stations, March 1812 to December 1830, with dates of sailing and destinations (overseas included).
ADM 7/539–548	Monthly lists of ships in commission at foreign stations, 1846–55. These provide name and rate of ship, and the dates when each ship was commissioned, sailed from England, and was ordered home.

The documents known as list books, in **ADM 8**, range in date from 1673 to 1909. They consist of monthly returns entitled 'the present disposal of His/Her Majesty's ships and vessels in sea pay'. Both home and foreign stations are included. **ADM 8/135–172** all contain nominal ship indexes. If you have established that one of your ancestors served in the navy between 1673 and 1909 but do not know the names of any of the ships he served on, the list books may be a good place to start your search (see 3.4.1). However, it should be pointed out that the references in **ADM 8** to ships in foreign stations are sometimes unreliable, and that most of the information from 1815 onwards can be found more easily in the *Navy List* (see 2.1).

Other records that provide information about ships' movements during this period include those listed in the following table:

Document references	Dates	Content
SP 42/111–116	1693–1748	Records listing rate and name of ship, complement, bourne (destination), mustered and what port or where located.
ADM 174/182	1696–1712	Entry book of Admiralty and Navy Board warrants for the movement and launching of ships.
ADM 2/1097–1115	1793–1824	Admiralty and Secretariat out-letters containing orders for admirals and commanding officers in relation to convoys.
ADM 2/1473–1582	1816–59	Military Branch out-letters to home stations relating to naval operations and orders concerning HM ship activities.
ADM 2/1583–1616	1816–59	Military Branch out-letters to foreign stations relating to naval operations and orders concerning HM ship activities.
ADM 13/8–27	1859–69	Military Branch out-letters to home stations relating to naval operations and orders concerning HM ship activities.
ADM 13/28–40	1859–69	Military Branch out-letters to foreign stations relating to naval operations and orders concerning HM ship activities.

4.2.2 Ship and submarine movements 1915–39

Details of the distribution of war vessels (including submarines) in home and foreign waters and losses of British ships can be found in **ADM 186/12–15** (1915), **ADM 186/22–25** (1916), **ADM 186/43–46** (1918), **ADM 186/50–52** (1919), **ADM 186/54** (1920), **ADM 186/57** (Jan, June 1921) and **ADM 186/61** (Feb, Sept, Oct 1922).

The mobilization returns of ranks and ratings required for vessels ready for commission, 1887–1939, in **ADM 286/1–197** provide the vessels' name and type together with relevant home and foreign ports. **ADM 286/1–5** list home ports only; **ADM 286/6–197** include both foreign and home ports.

4.2.3 Ship and submarine movements: Second World War

The following table provides an overview of the key documents relating to the movements of ships and submarines during the Second World War. These can be complemented by the more detailed operational records described in 4.2.4 and 4.2.5.

Series	Dates	Content
ADM 187	1939–45	**Pink lists.** Regularly printed lists, usually compiled every three or four days, showing the stations and movements of the ships of the Royal Navy and those of Allied countries, with dates of arrival and departure. These records continue to 1975. Each volume contains a ship index.
ADM 236	1939–45	**Offices of captains of submarine flotillas.** Submarine war patrols' reports and associated records, arranged by submarines name.
ADM 208	1940–9	**Red lists.** Weekly lists of all minor vessels in home waters, including those of Allied countries, arranged by commands. Each volume contains a ship index.
ADM 210	1942–6	**Green lists.** Weekly lists of landing ships, crafts and barges in home waters and foreign stations, arranged by command. Similar details are given for US vessels in UK waters.

4.2.4 Logs and journals

Other sources for tracing ships' and submarines' movements include the various logs and journals kept by officers. Lieutenants' logs are held by the National Maritime Museum (for address, see Appendix 2). To find document references for logs and journals held by the Public Record Office, you can search the PRO online catalogue (accessible via www.pro.gov.uk) using the name of the ship or submarine as a keyword.

Series	Dates	Content
ADM 50	1702–1916	**Admirals' journals.** Arranged by admiral's name.
ADM 51	1669–1852	**Captains' logs.** These mostly derive from information contained in masters' logs, but with the addition of whatever information the captain was obliged to give by regulation or thought it useful to record. They are arranged by ship's name and normally provide details of the ship's routine duties.
ADM 52	1672–1840	**Masters' logs.** These logs, which record the ship's movements and weather conditions, were kept by the master for navigational purposes. They are arranged by ship's name.
ADM 54	1808–71	**Masters' logs (supplementary logs).** These were preserved to fill in gaps in **ADM 52**. They are arranged by ship's name and date.
ADM 53	1799–1965	**Ships' logs.** Arranged by ship's name and date, the logs in this series supersede the various other types of log in **ADM 51, ADM 52** and **ADM 54**. They are similar in content to the logs in **ADM 52** in that they contain details about weather conditions and the ship's movements and routine duties. It should be noted that HM ships did not keep war diaries and that the PRO has only a small collection of ships' logs from the Second World War (the remainder are believed not to have survived).
ADM 55	1757–1904	**Supplementary ships' logs, Series II (explorations).** Log books of ships engaged on explorations. Additional ships' log books of this type will be found in **ADM 51**, under the heading 'Explorations'.
ADM 173	1914–65	**Submarine logs.** Arranged by submarine's name and date.

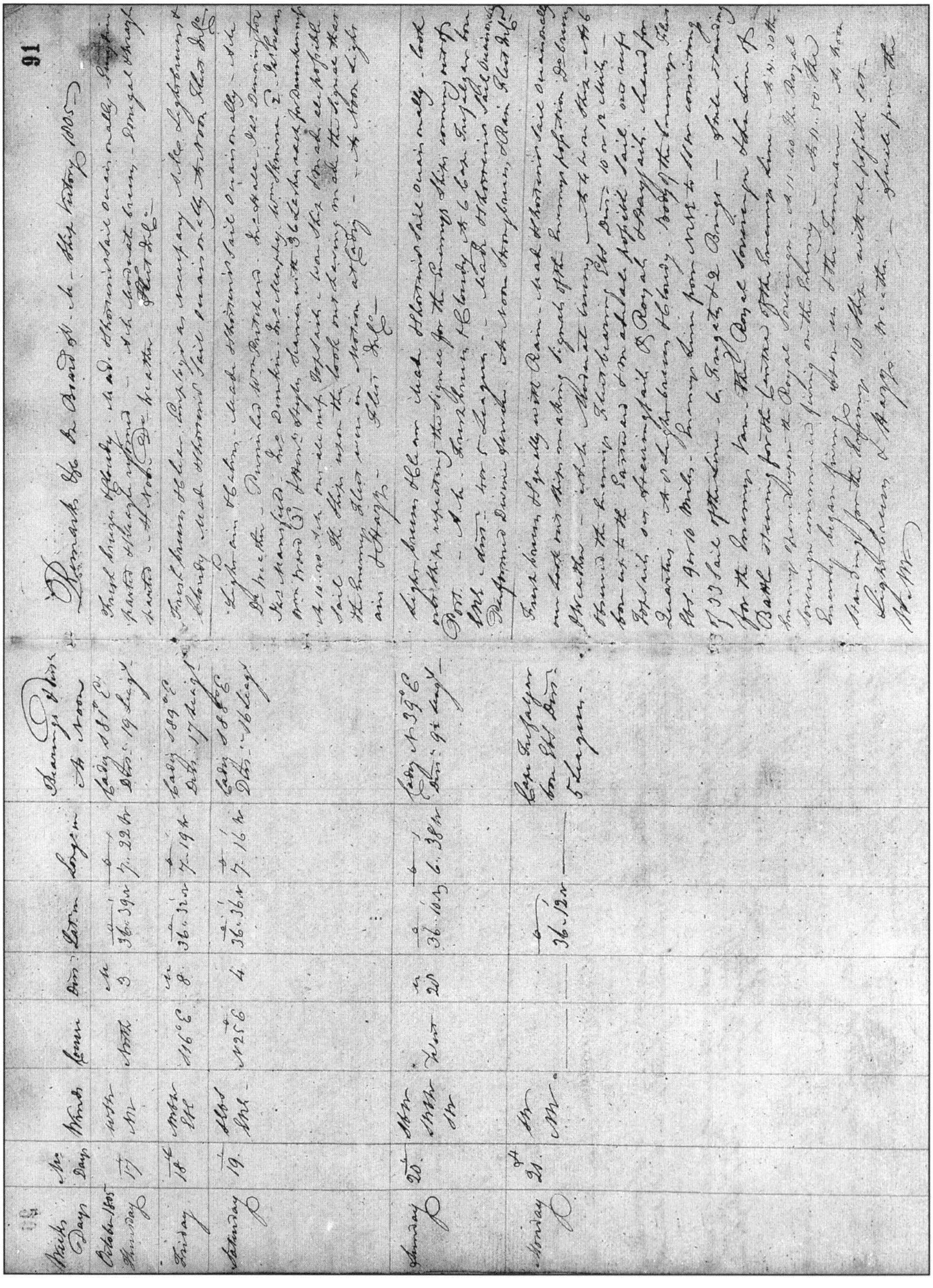

Figure 21 Extract from HMS *Victory* master's log entry for the Battle of Trafalgar, 21 October 1805. (ADM 52/3711)

4.2.5 First and Second World War operational records

4.2.5.1 First World War

Further operational records of ships for the First World War will be found among the Admiralty and Secretariat papers in **ADM 1** and **ADM 116**, and the 'packs and miscellaneous records' of the Admiralty Historical Section in **ADM 137**. The documents in **ADM 1** and **ADM 137** for this period are indexed by **ADM 12** (see 7.5).

4.2.5.2 Second World War

Operational records from the Second World War will be found among the Admiralty and Secretariat papers in **ADM 1** and **ADM 116**; the war history cases and papers in **ADM 199**; the 'offices of captains of submarine flotillas' (submarine war patrols' reports and associated records, arranged by submarine's name) in **ADM 236**; and the convoy records (case files on individual convoys) in **ADM 237**.

The finding aids in the Research Enquiries Room include card indexes of convoys (arranged by convoy number), operation code names, and ships and submarines (see Appendix 1). These indexes may help you locate documents about operations in which ships and submarines were involved.

4.2.5.3 Reference works

The following publications (all available in the PRO Library) are essential reference works for anyone interested in naval operations during the two world wars:

- **For the First World War:** *The Official History of the War* (Longman, Green & Co., 1920).

- **For the Second World War:** *The War at Sea* by S.W. Roskill (HMSO, 1954) and *The Chronology of the War at Sea, 1939–1945* by J. Rohwer and G. Hummelchen (Greenhill Books, 1972).

4.2.6 Station records

Additional information relating to naval bases and fleet and ship activities can be found in station records and correspondence.

PRO series	Station	Dates	Remarks
SP 42		1700–72	Letters and papers sent to the Secretaries of State by the naval commanders of various stations.
ADM 123	Africa	1797–1932	Includes: Cape of Good Hope; Africa (East Coast); Indian Ocean islands; Africa (West Coast) including Ascension, St Helena and Tristan da Cunha. Indexed by **ADM 124** for 1845–1918 only.
ADM 145	Atlantic Fleet	1902–10	Records of the fleet known before 1904 as the Channel Fleet (see below). Indexed by **ADM 146** for 1867–1910 only.
ADM 122	Australia	1855–96	Also includes New Guinea and Samoa.
ADM 144	Channel Fleet	1867–1907	On 14 December 1904 this fleet was renamed the Atlantic Fleet, and the Home Fleet became the Channel Fleet. Up to 1904, these records relate to the Channel Fleet, thereafter to the Home Fleet. Indexed by **ADM 146** for 1867–1910.
ADM 125	China	1828–1936	Includes East Indies, Japan, Korea, Australasia, Pacific Ocean islands, Bering Sea. Indexed by **ADM 126** for 1856–1914.
ADM 127	East Indies	1808–1930	Includes India, Ceylon Burma, Aden, Red Sea, Persian Gulf, Africa (East Coast) and Indian Ocean Islands.
ADM 148	Ireland	1821–5	Commander-in-chief entry books of orders and memoranda.
ADM 149	Ireland	1816–1912	Indexed by **ADM 150** for 1816–1912.
ADM 121	Mediterranean	1843–1968	
ADM 151	Nore	1805–39	Indexed by **ADM 152** for 1866–1901.
ADM 128	North America and West Indies	1810–1913	Covers Labrador, in the north, and Central America. Indexed by **ADM 129** for 1859–82.
ADM 172	Pacific	1843–58	Indexed by **ADM 155**. Some Pacific station records are on permanent loan to the government of British Columbia.
ADM 130	Plymouth	1859–1928	Commander-in-chief entry books of orders and memoranda.
ADM 131	Plymouth	1842–1926	Indexed by **ADM 143** for 1876–1912.
ADM 179	Portsmouth	1880–1948	
ADM 147	Southeast America	1871–1904	Includes Brazil and Patagonia.
ADM 217	Western Approaches	1942–5	

4.2.7 Ships' photographs 1854–1945 (ADM 176)

Photographs of a variety of vessels are to be found in **ADM 176**. Searching this series might therefore lead you to a photograph of a ship on which a naval ancestor served. The series can be searched by ship's name using the PRO online catalogue, either in the PRO reading rooms or on the internet, via www.pro.gov.uk.

Figure 22 Photograph of HMS *Monmouth* launched in 1901. (ADM 176/457)

4.2.8 Ships' histories

4.2.8.1 Construction, maintenance and related subjects

Key records relating to the construction, repair, maintenance and disposal of HM ships can be found in the following series:

Series	Content
ADM 180	Navy Board and Admiralty progress and dimension books, 1620–1912.
ADM 135–136	Ship's books, Series I–II, 1807–1962.
ADM 83, 87, 91–95	Correspondence to and from the Office of the Surveyor of Ships, 1688–1959.

The records in **ADM 95/23–62** consist of documents dating from 1742 to 1847, arranged by ship's name, relating to the sailing qualities of various ships.

4.2.8.2 Reference works

For those who want to find out more about the history of a ship on which an ancestor served, *Ships of the Royal Navy* by J.J. Colledge (David & Charles, 1969) and *The Sailing Navy List – All the ships of the Royal Navy built, purchased and captured, 1688–1860* by D. Lyon (Conway Maritime Press, 1993), both available in the PRO Library, are essential reference works.

4.3   Medical records

If you know, or discover in the course of your research, that an officer or rating fell ill or sustained an injury as a result of an accident or was wounded in battle, you may find that details about him figure in medical records held by the PRO.

4.3.1   Medical officers' journals 1785–1963 (ADM 101)

The journals compiled by naval surgeons who served in HM naval, convict and emigrant ships, hospitals, naval brigades and shore parties offer a fascinating insight into the methods and medicines used to treat the sick and injured, and also include personal details about them. Only a proportion of these journals survive, and those that do are often overlooked by family historians. Nevertheless, they constitute an important source of genealogical information.

Up to the end of 1915 the journals in **ADM 101** are mainly arranged by ship's name; then from 1916 they are arranged by year, with each document covering a range of ships. The journals provide detailed accounts of medical cases treated, including the patient's name, age and rank. They also give the date when the patient was discharged to duty or sent to hospital and, if the illness or injury proved fatal, date of death. From 1837 sick lists may be found in these journals, in which are recorded the names of men treated for illness during a ship's commission, together with dates of illness and details of the disease or wound. A card index of ships' names in **ADM 101** is located in the Research Enquiries Room. The **ADM 101** series list contains a ship index to **ADM 101/128–293**.

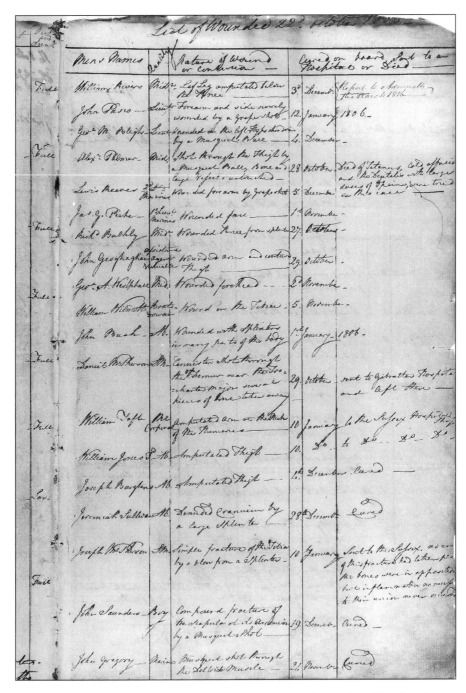

Figure 23 Extract from the medical journal of HMS *Victory* dated 22 October 1805, one day after the Battle of Trafalgar. (ADM 101/125/1)

Further medical officers' journals for convict ships, covering 1858–67, can be found in **MT 32**. A card index to ships' names in **MT 32** is located in the Research Enquiries Room.

Second World War medical officers' journals may make reference to medical reports compiled for the Medical Director of the Navy. Many of these have not survived, but an example is the report compiled for HMS *Ithuriel* in November 1942, which can be found in **ADM 1/27769**.

If the medical journals mention that a patient is being transferred to a naval hospital, it may be worth searching relevant hospital musters (see 4.1.5) to find out what details they contain.

Further reading

Those interested in the history and development of the naval medical profession and its practices are recommended to read *Medicine and the Navy, 1200–1900* by J.J. Keevil *et al.* (Livingstone, 1957), a copy of which is available in the PRO Library.

4.3.2 First World War medical records

During and immediately after the First World War, the Medical Research Council and the British Museum collected together diverse medical records for a statistical study of the treatment given for injuries sustained and diseases contracted by British troops. The results were published in 1931, in the *History of the Great War based on Official Documents: Medical Services and Medical Statistics of the Great War* by T.J. Mitchell and G.M. Smith. A sample of the original collection has been preserved in **MH 106**, which contains records of Royal Navy, Royal Naval Division and Royal Naval Air Service casualties treated by 149 Field Ambulance, 3, 11, 31, 34 Casualty Clearing Stations, 2, 18–19, 28, 85 General Hospitals, 4 Stationary Hospital, and HM hospital ship *Assaye*. War diaries for these medical units can be found in **WO 95**. The locations of medical units in the First World War are listed in **MH 106/2386** and **2389** and in **WO 95/5494**.

The records in **MH 106** mainly consist of hospital admission/discharge registers and Medical Board reports. The registers and reports include details such as service number, rank, name, age, time served, nature of illness or wound, dates of admission and discharge, dates and details of transfers to other hospitals, religion, details of operations carried out and, in fatal cases, cause and date of death. **MH 106** also contains operation books and X-ray registers; Women's Royal Naval Service medical sheets (**MH 106/2207**); medical sheets arranged by disease, gunshot and other wounds; and records relating to Napsbury, Queen Alexandra's, Catterick and Craiglockhart hospitals.

4.3.3 Miscellaneous health and sickness returns

As well as the series described in 4.3.1 and 4.3.2, the PRO holds a variety of other records relating to the health of those who served in the navy. These are listed in the following table.

Document references	Date range	Remarks
ADM 1/4280–4281	1718–1816	Letters from the Barber-Surgeons' Company, Surgeons' Company and Royal College of Surgeons for England. These contain medical certificates of officers examined for superannuation or pensions for wounds. There are also similar letters from the Royal Colleges of Surgeons in Scotland and Ireland; petitions from bodies of naval surgeons; and letters from the Watermen's Company and Apothecaries' Company.
ADM 30/6	1739–42	Sick quarters arrears list. Payments made to sick men quartered in Plymouth and Gosport.
ADM 30/51	1757	Sick quarters pay lists for Rochester, Plymouth, Deal, Woolwich and Deptford.
ADM 30/52	1758	Sick quarters pay lists for Plymouth, Deal, Rochester and Woolwich.
ADM 1/5117/16	1772	A return of the sick in Halifax Hospital.
ADM 105/31	1779–1848	Copies of reports made to the Admiralty concerning wounded officers. Name, rank, age, care (nature of wound, treatment given, and opinion as to condition). Contains surname index.
ADM 106/3514	1781–1822	Nominations and applications for admittance to Christ's Hospital.
ADM 305/67–70	1787, 1792	Haslar Hospital prescription book (wards 9, 10 and 102). These records list date of entry, ship, person's name, rank, nature of disorder, medicine given, and details of diet.
ADM 1/5120/19	1792	Lists of men discharged unfit for service from Haslar Hospital.
ADM 1/3533–3541	1793–1839	Reports from physicians in charge of Haslar and Stonehouse naval hospitals on the health of individual officers.
ADM 304/21–24	1804–40	Bighi Hospital (Royal Naval Hospital, Malta), entry book of patients. Gives ship, name, rank, disease or hurt (nature of), date of entry and discharge (to which ship), date of death, and observations.
ADM 6/67	1812–15	List of men discharged unfit from Plymouth.
ADM 105/28	1812–32	Reports on individual cases of lunacy.
ADM 305/35	1813–17	List of lunatics at Haslar Hospital (names and when admitted).
ADM 100/3	1817–22	Accounts of sick seamen at Rockingham House.
ADM 97/42–84	1817–32	Correspondence about patients from medical officers serving in hospitals, hospital ships and sick quarters, both at home and abroad.

ADM 304/25	1829–38	Bighi Hospital post-mortem examinations.
ADM 305/102	1830–42	Haslar Hospital's lunatic-asylum journal. Arranged by date of entry. Gives name, rank, ship, age, and case listing. In addition, contains detailed case studies of some of the inmates.
ADM 105/4	6 Sept 1824	Returns of patients in Haslar Hospital. Name, age, rank, date of admission, disease, present state, remarks.
ADM 105/4	Sept 1824	Returns of lunatics in Haslar Hospital. Name, age, rank, date of entry, period insane before admission, form of disease, treatment summary.
ADM 105/5	15 and 17 Sept 1825	Returns of patients in Plymouth Hospital. Name, age, rank, date of admission, disease, present state, remarks.
ADM 105/6	7 Sept 1827, Aug 1828	Returns of patients in Plymouth Hospital. Name, age, rank, date of admission, disease, present state, remarks.
ADM 105/6	13 Sept 1828	Returns of patients in Haslar Hospital. Name, age, rank, date of admission, disease, present state, remarks.
ADM 304/14–18, 36–41	April 1836 to 1895	Bighi Hospital admission and discharge registers (muster books). Details include from which ship, name, quality, date received, disease or hurt, discharged, date of death, run, date of discharge, to what ship.
ADM 105/33–35	1847–63	Medical director general's comments on officers invalided from abroad. Date of report, name, age, rank, when invalided (nature and dates of sickness, which ship serving on). Sometimes officers' addresses are given. Each document contains a surname index.
ADM 304/33	1857–9	Bighi Hospital in-patients. Age, name, duration of symptoms, and treatment given.
ADM 305/87	1861	Haywards Heath Hospital muster of lunatics.
ADM 305/87	1863	Haslar Hospital muster of lunatics.
ADM 105/79	1867–96	Register of important medical cases treated at the Royal Naval Dockyard, Sheerness, by R.J.C Scott, staff surgeon.
ADM 305/84–85	1887–8, 1897–8	Haslar Hospital, surgeon's admission books. Patient's name, rank, ship's name, nature of illness, financial position, address.
ADM 305/88	1906	Haslar Hospital muster book, arranged alphabetically by surname.

ADM 104/150–151	1911–20	Admiralty Medical Department notation books. Although general in nature, these contain medical details in relation to officers and ratings. They include indexes of surnames, ships and stations.
ADM 261/1	1939–45	Reports from medical officers of treatment given to casualties and survivors from the ships *Achilles, Adventure, Ajax, Bengairn, Berwick, Bittern, Bonaventure, Calcutta, Cambrian, Cornwall, Cromarty, Dido, Dorsetshire, Dunedin, Eagle, Enterprise, Erebus, Exeter, Fiji, Gallant, Gipsy, Glonus, Gloucester, Grenville, Greyhound, Hermes, Hollyhock, Illustrious, Jackal, Jervis Bay, Jewel, Juno, Kashmir, Kelly, Lively, Medway, Mishobra, Norfolk, Palomeres, Phoebe, Prince of Wales, Punjabi, Repulse, Saumarez, Sheffield, St Fagen, Tenedos, Uganda, Undaunted, Vampire, Vansittart, Warspite, Wishart, York, Zaafaren.*

4.4 Desertion

During the Seven Years' War (1756–63), some 36,000–40,000 men are estimated to have 'run' (deserted) from the Royal Navy. This figure fell during the nineteenth century – between 1850 and 1860, for example, it is estimated that 2,000–2,500 men a year deserted. If a man 'ran' from the navy, he would lose all rights to pay, prize money and medals, and to any possessions he left on board his ship. The Naval Discipline Act 1860 defined desertion as unauthorized absence from a ship for more than 21 days.

The main sources for tracing details about a naval deserter are ships' pay books and musters (see 4.1). In the pay books and musters an 'R' was noted alongside the name of a deserter, to indicate 'Run'; and in musters there are sometimes lists of men who had deserted during a ship's commission. Information about naval deserters may also be found in **ADM 12** (see Chapter 7) and in court martial records (see 4.5.2).

Rewards were offered for the capture of deserters. Payments of such rewards may be found in the 'King's Rembrancer Receivers' Accounts of Land and Assessed Taxes' in **E 182**, which extend from 1689 to 1830. There is a personal-name card index relating to these documents in the Research Enquiries Room.

After 1875 lists of deserters from HM ships, together with details of rewards for their capture, can be found in the *Police Gazette*. These give name of ship deserted from, date of desertion, rating, age, where born, a physical description, and details of ships previously served on. Copies of the *Police Gazette* from 1877 onwards are held by the British Library Newspaper Library (for address, see Appendix 2). Some issues include photographs of deserters.

4.5 Courts martial

Before 1652 there was no uniform system for enforcing discipline on board ships at sea. Disciplinary offences were punished in accordance with a captain's own code of conduct or the ancient maritime laws that feature in the Black Book of the Admiralty of 1336.

In 1652 the Admiralty introduced a naval code of conduct, the Articles of War, with the aim of preventing indiscipline and cowardice and to establish a disciplinary code that was not dependent on the whims of individual captains and which could be applied consistently and fairly.

Enforced by courts martial, the Articles of War made provision for certain offences to be punished by fixed punishments, whilst more serious offences could result in a death sentence. The Articles of War applied during 'peacetime' as well as wartime. Subsequently they were used as a framework for the naval disciplinary Acts passed by Parliament in 1661, 1749 and 1886.

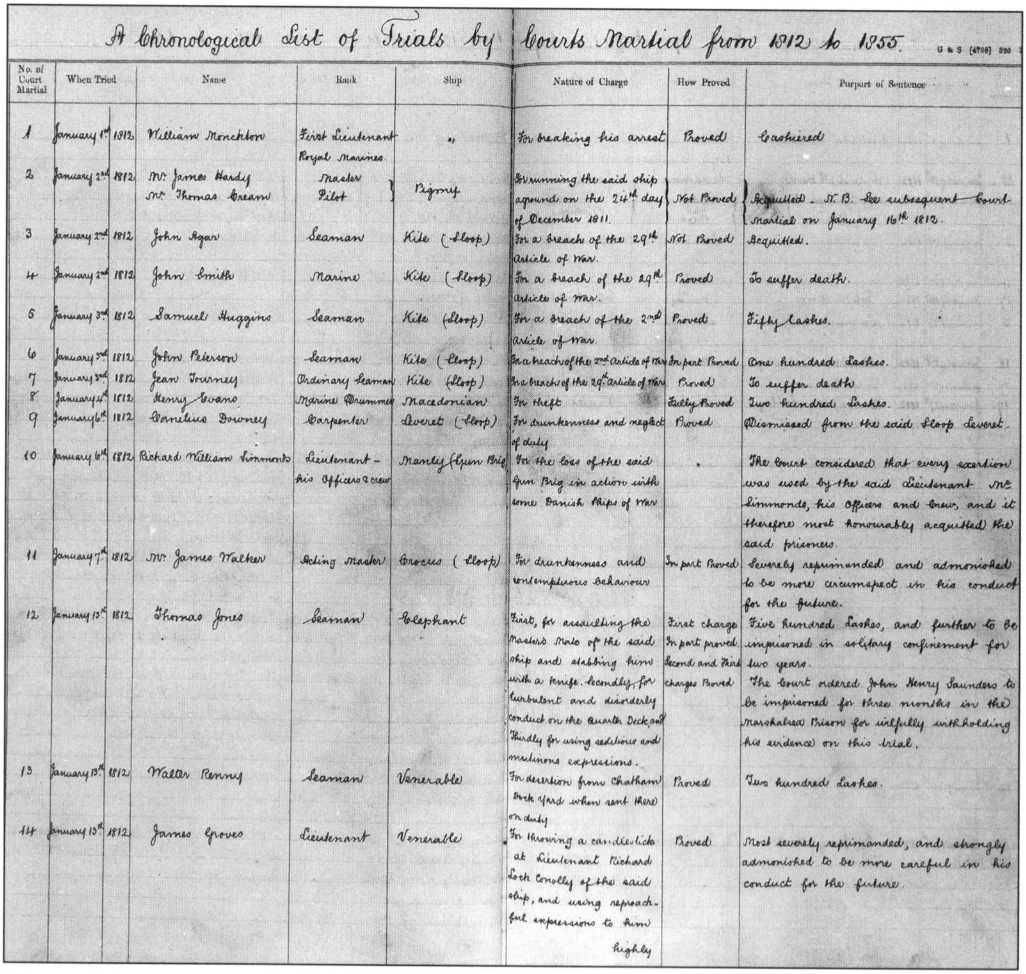

A Chronological List of Trials by Courts Martial from 1812 to 1855. G & S [4708] 320

No. of Court Martial	When Tried		Name	Rank	Ship	Nature of Charge	How Proved	Purport of Sentence
1	January 1st	1812	William Monckton	First Lieutenant Royal Marines	"	For breaking his arrest	Proved	Cashiered
2	January 2nd	1812	Mr James Hardy Mr Thomas Cream	Master Pilot	Pigmy	For running the said ship aground on the 24th day of December 1811.	Not Proved	Acquitted. N. B. See subsequent Court Martial on January 16th 1812.
3	January 2nd	1812	John Agar	Seaman	Kite (Sloop)	For a breach of the 29th Article of War.	Not Proved	Acquitted.
4	January 2nd	1812	John Smith	Marine	Kite (Sloop)	For a breach of the 29th Article of War.	Proved	To suffer death.
5	January 3rd	1812	Samuel Huggins	Seaman	Kite (Sloop)	For a breach of the 2nd Article of War.	Proved	Fifty Lashes.
6	January 3rd	1812	John Peterson	Seaman	Kite (Sloop)	For a breach of the 2nd Article of War	In part Proved	One hundred Lashes.
7	January 3rd	1812	Jean Journey	Ordinary Seaman	Kite (Sloop)	For a breach of the 29th Article of War	Proved	To suffer death
8	January 4th	1812	Henry Evans	Marine Drummer	Macedonian	For theft	Fully Proved	Two hundred Lashes.
9	January 6th	1812	Cornelius Downey	Carpenter	Leveret (Sloop)	For drunkenness and neglect of duty	Proved	Dismissed from the said Sloop Leveret.
10	January 6th	1812	Richard William Simmonds	Lieutenant – his Officers & crew	Manly (Gun Brig)	For the loss of the said Gun Brig in action with some Danish Ships of War	.	The Court considered that every exertion was used by the said Lieutenant Mr Simmonds, his Officers and Crew, and it therefore most honourably acquitted the said prisoners.
11	January 7th	1812	Mr James Walker	Acting Master	Crocus (Sloop)	For drunkenness and contemptuous behaviour	In part Proved	Severely reprimanded and admonished to be more circumspect in his conduct for the future.
12	January 13th	1812	Thomas Jones	Seaman	Elephant	First, for assaulting the Master's Mate of the said ship and stabbing him with a knife. Secondly, for turbulent and disorderly conduct on the Quarter Deck, and Thirdly for using seditious and mutinous expressions.	First charge In part proved. Second and Third charges Proved	Five hundred Lashes, and further to be imprisoned in solitary confinement for two years. The Court ordered John Henry Saunders to be imprisoned for three months in the Marshalsea Prison for wilfully withholding his evidence on this trial.
13	January 13th	1812	Walter Renny	Seaman	Venerable	For desertion from Chatham Dock Yard when sent there on duty	Proved	Two hundred Lashes.
14	January 13th	1812	James Groves	Lieutenant	Venerable	For throwing a candlestick at Lieutenant Richard Loch Conolly of the said ship, and using reproachful expressions to him highly	Proved	Most severely reprimanded, and strongly admonished to be more careful in his conduct for the future.

Figure 24 Part of the courts martial register index for 1812–55. (ADM 194/42)

At a court martial, a panel consisting of a minimum of five and a maximum of 13 officers would question an individual or individuals charged with committing an offence contrary to the Articles of War or naval disciplinary Acts and decide whether the charge was proven and what punishment, if any, would be imposed. The decision as to whether or not a court martial would be held was taken by the commander-in-chief of the station in which the alleged offence had taken place.

4.5.1 Indexes to court martial records

To find a record of court martial proceedings, you need to know the date when the court martial took place (which could be some time after the alleged offence occurred). If you already know this, you may be able to go straight to the court martial records (see 4.5.2). If you do not have the date, using the person's name as a keyword to search the PRO online catalogue (accessible via www.pro.gov.uk) may provide you with a court martial reference; otherwise, try the **ADM 12** registers (see below).

You can find the date of a court martial by ordering and searching the **ADM 12** registers, which act as indexes to the Admiralty and Secretariat papers in **ADM 1** (see Chapter 7). Arranged by year, they extend from 1793 to 1958. There are two types of register in **ADM 12**: one arranged by initial letter of surname or ship's name, the other by digest number referring to a subject. The digest number relating to courts martial is 28. In these registers, the letters CM were entered alongside a person's name to indicate that he had been court-martialled.

Once you have established the date of the proceedings, you can use it to find a document reference for the court martial record. The majority of court martial records are in **ADM 1** (see 4.5.2), although some of these have not survived (for example, there are none for 1840–4). However, sometimes court martial records that no longer survive in **ADM 1** were cross-referenced and summarized in the **ADM 12** registers, under the digest heading number 28. Although the court martial records themselves are usually closed for 75 years, by using the **ADM 12** registers you can find information concerning courts martial up to 1958. For guidance on how to use **ADM 12**, including examples, see Chapter 7.

Under the Articles of War, if a Royal Naval ship was lost there had to be a court martial. *The Lost Ships of the Royal Navy 1793–1900* by W.P. Gosset (New York, 1986), available in the PRO Library, provides details and dates of courts martial relating to such losses, plus PRO document references.

There are many other indexes that can provide the date of a court martial, along with information about the officer or rating charged, details of the charges, and the outcome of the proceedings. These indexes are listed in the following table.

Document references	Dates	Nature of index
ADM 1	1680–1701	Nominal card index to naval courts martial, held in the Research Enquiries Room. Arranged both by surname and by ship's name.
ADM 12/28A	1750–1803	Four-part index relating to officers tried by court martial 1750–92 and 1793–1803 and to ships lost during 1750–92 and 1793–1803. The entries are arranged by date of trial and provide name, rank and charge. No information about the sentence is given.
ADM 12/21–26	1755–1806	Analysis and digest of officers' court martial convictions, arranged by offence. Each document contains a name index, arranged by rank, that gives the entry number found in the volume in question. The entries provide the date of the court martial and a brief summary of the charge and sentence.
ADM 13/103	1803–56	Index and register of courts martial arranged by initial letter of surname and then by date of court martial. Officer's name, rank, ship served on, charge and sentence are given.
ADM 12/35	1806	Index of officers and ratings tried by court martial in 1806 and ships lost during that year. Arranged by initial letter of surname and by date of court martial. Name, rank, charge and sentence are given. The index covers all charges, not just those relating to ships lost.
ADM 12/27A	1810–16	Alphabetical digest of convictions of officers at courts martial, grouped together by initial letter of surname. For each officer, it records name, rank, ship, date of court martial, charge and sentence.
ADM 12/27F	1812–55	Index and digest of court martial verdicts, 1812–55. Includes a surname index, and indexes of convictions, sentences and ships lost. It also contains a chronological list of courts martial for both officers and ratings, giving date of trial, name, rank, ship, nature of charge, how proved, and sentence. There are also copies of this document in **ADM 194/42** and **ADM 13/104**.
ADM 194/43–45	1857–1913	Registers of courts martial of officers arranged by initial letter of surname and then by date of court martial. They provide name, rank, ship's name, charge and sentence. **ADM 194/45** also contains an index of ships lost, arranged by initial letter of ship's name and then by date of court martial. This index includes the date when the ship was lost, the charge, sentence and names of those sentenced.

4.5.2 Court martial records

As explained in 4.5.1, before searching for a court martial record you need to know when it took place, as the records are usually arranged by date.

Court martial records from 1680 vary from full formal transcripts and proceedings to brief summaries of the case and sentence. From the 1850s onwards, annexed to transcripts of trials you may find officers' and ratings' service records, casualty lists, copies of ships' logs, pursers' accounts, and other formal documents submitted as evidence. As mentioned earlier, not all court martial records have survived. Most notably, from the middle of the nineteenth century until the twentieth they appear to have been kept only in cases that set legal precedents.

Regarding the earlier court martial records, there is a miscellaneous batch for 1679–1714 in **ADM 106/3074**.

Records of courts martial for 1680–1839 are to be found in **ADM 1/5253–5494**. Those for 1845–1910 are in **ADM 1**, arranged in year order (no court martial records for 1840–4 survive in **ADM 1**).

Further court martial records and board of enquiry reports for 1892–1951 are in **ADM 178**. Overlapping records of courts martial for 1911–65 are in **ADM 156**. However, some of the records in **ADM 178** and **ADM 156** are subject to a 75-year closure rule.

References to court martial and board of enquiry records concerning the loss of HM ships after 1910 can be found in the **ADM 1** and **ADM 116** series lists, under the code number 28. Some court martial and board of enquiry records for 1964–71 are in **ADM 330**.

Entry books (i.e. registers) of reports and returns of courts martial held on the Nore station between 1848–63 are in **ADM 153/1–2**. There are reports and papers relating to discipline and courts martial in the Mediterranean station for 1863–74 in **ADM 121/68**. Similar records for the Channel squadron and Fleet station from July 1903 to December 1906 can be found in **ADM 144/23**.

HCA 55/1–3 contain records ranging from 1802 to 1856 (with some gaps) of warrants, issued by the commissioners exercising the office of lord high admiral, relating to the arrest and imprisonment of officers and ratings for breaches of naval or criminal law and the execution, suspension and respite of sentences. A warrant entry book kept by the Lords Commissioners of the Admiralty concerned with the execution of sentences imposed by courts martial between 1811 and 1857 is to be found in **HCA 38/79**, which contains a surname index. Letters, ranging from 1781 to 1816, from the Lords Commissioners of the Admiralty ordering and empowering senior officers in home waters to hold courts martial are in **ADM 2/1116–1126**.

Records relating to the court martial of Admiral John Byng in 1756–7 have been preserved in **ADM 7/946** and **ADM 1/5296**, while those relating to the trial of Arthur, Earl of Torrington (July/August 1690) are in **ADM 7/831**. An account of Admiral Keppel's trial of 7 January 1779 is in **ADM 7/947**.

4.5.3 *Black Books of the Admiralty*

These record the names of officers who were not to be employed by the Admiralty, having been charged with misconduct. The 'Black Books' for 1741–1815 can be found in **ADM 12/27B–27D**, which is indexed by **ADM 12/27E**. Arranged by initial letter of officer's surname, they provide date of court martial, summary of charge, and sentence. A Black Book for 1741–1815, relating to warrant officers, is in **ADM 11/39**.

ADM 11/27–29 contain lists of clerks (1833–42) and midshipmen (1833–48) discharged for misconduct. Similar lists relating to engineers (1834–42) can be found under the letter 'X' in **ADM 11/49**, which includes a surname index. Another list of officers charged with misconduct, mostly at courts martial held between 1842 and 1871, is located in **ADM 6/445**.

4.6 Prisoners of war

Information about prisoners of war (POWs) is scattered throughout a variety of records held by the PRO. For the period 1760–1919 the records are sparse and sometimes of a general nature, so not easily searched. However, if it is known when and where an officer or rating was captured, a search of the records may be straightforward.

4.6.1 *Prisoners of war: sources before 1793*

Documents held by the PRO relating to British troops captured during the American Revolutionary War and in earlier military and naval actions in North America can be identified from *Guide to the Materials for American History to 1783 in the Public Record Office of Great Britain* by C.M. Andrews (Washington, DC, 1912–14) and the *Alphabetical Guide to the War Office and other Military Records* (List and Index Society, volume LIII), both available in the Research Enquiries Room. The List and Index Society volume is also useful for tracing later material concerning POWs. General files regarding POWs may be found in **SP 42** (for example, **SP 42/142** contains papers about the exchange of prisoners with Spain in 1742). Nominal lists of British POWs held in various French towns during 1779–80 can be found in **ADM 103/134**.

4.6.2 *Prisoners of war: sources for 1793–1815*

The main sources of records relating to British POWs for 1793–1815 are **ADM 103/171, 441, 466–472, 474–477, 479–481, 506–507, 629–632, 648, ADM 105/47–51, 55–57, ADM 30/63/12–15, 17, ADM 97/128/2** and **ADM 108/29**. As well as nominal lists of POWs (both officers and ratings in receipt of pay) and of those who died in captivity, there are lists of released POWs and of those exchanged for enemy prisoners of war. The lists usually provide such details as name of POW, rank, name of ship captured from, date of capture and, in some cases, place of birth. The table below gives details of some of the key sources to be found among these documents. It should be noted that many of the documents in **ADM 103** are written in French.

Document references	Dates	Content
ADM 103/630–632	1794–1815	Deaths of British POWs in France, arranged by initial letter of surname. These records give prisoner's name, rank, ship or corps, place of birth, age, when taken, date of death, disorder, places of parole or prison.
ADM 105/55	1799–1800	Lists of applications for British POWs in France to be returned home. Name, rank, ship or corps.
ADM 105/57	1799–1810	Requests for information concerning British prisoners in enemy hands. Name, rank, whereabouts of POWs, and details of information supplied. Contains own surname index.
ADM 105/56	1801	Lists of applications for British POWs in France to be returned home. Name, rank, ship or corps, date of discharge.
ADM 97/128/2	1804	Lists of POWs held in Guadeloupe.
ADM 97/128/2	1804	List of British POWs discharged from Martinique.
ADM 97/128/2	29 Nov 1805 to 20 Feb 1806	List of British POWs received in Barbados from the French government.
ADM 97/128/2	1806	List of British POWs received in Guadeloupe. Includes details such as name, rank, and which vessel captured from.
ADM 30/63/12	1806	Pay lists of British POWs in Givet, in France. They list name, rank, sum, and signatures of officers and ratings receiving pay.
ADM 30/63/14	1806	Pay lists of British POWs in Valenciennes, in France.
ADM 30/63/15	1806	Pay lists of British POWs in Arras, in France.
ADM 30/63/13	1806–7	Pay lists of British POWs in Verdun, in France.
ADM 105/47	1810–14	Entry book of enquiries for British POWs. Arranged by date of request. Lists name of POW, ship, assumed whereabouts, name of prison and, where relevant, dates of death. Contains own surname index.

ADM 103/466	1812	Lists of British POWs captured by the United States and held in America. These give name, rank, to what ship belonging, by which ship captured, when and where captured, where held, and when and how disposed of. Contains 15,508 entries.
ADM 103/472	1812–15	List of British POWs held in France. Arranged alphabetically by initial letter of surname. Gives name, rank, ship or corps, from what place or prison, date of capture and by what vessel.
ADM 103/171	19 Aug 1812 to 12 April 1815	Lists of British POWs exchanged for American POWs. These give date of capture, name, rank, ship or corps (ship's name given), by whom captured (name of ship), and date of exchange.
ADM 103/468	1813	Contains many records, among them a complete list of British POWs held in France.
ADM 105/48	1814–17	Entry book of enquiries concerning British prisoners. Arranged by date of request, it includes POW's name, rank, ship or corps, name and address of applicant, information from the applicant, result of search, and remarks. Contains own surname index.
ADM 105/49–51	1814–24	Entry books of enquiries concerning British POWs. Arranged by date of request and initial letter of surname. They include POW's name, rank, ship or corps, applicant's name and address, information from the applicant, and result of search.
ADM 30/63/17	1815	Pay lists of British POWs in Bitche, in France.

4.6.3 Prisoners of war: 1793–1913 (general sources)

The correspondence of the Sick and Hurt Board – responsible for POWs until 1795 – and the Transport Board, which took over this responsibility from 1796, can be found in **ADM 105/44–57** and **59–66**. Medical and Prisoners of War Department in-letters for this period are in **ADM 97/98–259**; those from 1832–62 are indexed by registers in **ADM 132–133**. Out-letter books of the Transport Board and Victualling Board concerning POWs can be found in **ADM 98**. Transport Board minutes relating to prisoners are in **ADM 99/92–263**, with an index in **ADM 99/264–265**; and there are various accounts in **ADM 100/4–5** and **ADM 10/14**.

A further important source of information regarding POWs, both for this period and later years, is to be found in **ADM 12** under code 79.21 and code 79.22 (see Chapter 7).

4.6.4 Prisoners of war: First World War

The PRO does not have a single unified list of British POWs for the First World War. However, a very useful guide to this topic, *Researching British and Commonwealth Prisoners of War, World War One* by Alan Bowgen, is available at the Research Enquiries Room desk.

ADM 1/8420/124 provides a list of British and Dominion POWs, mainly from the crews of HMS *Maori* and HMS *Crusader*, taken prisoner in May 1915 and held in Gressen POW camp. The list gives service number, rating, name and address of next of kin, where captured and where held.

Lists of POWs held in Germany, Turkey and Switzerland in 1916 – which usually list name, rank, name of ship or submarine, place of internment, and in some instances dates of birth and addresses – can be found in **AIR 1/892/204/5/696–698**.

There are reports of interviews with liberated British officers in **WO 161/96**. The *Navy List* for 1917 contains a nominal list of Royal Naval Air Service officers held as POWs.

Records of deaths of POWs in military and non-military hospitals and in enemy hands are sometimes to be found in **RG 35**. These are indexed by **RG 43**.

A useful publication entitled *List of British Officers taken prisoner in the Various Theatres of war between August 1914 and November 1918*, compiled by the military agents Cox & Co., is available in the PRO Library. This lists officers from the Royal Naval Division, Royal Naval Air Service and the Royal Naval Reserve taken prisoner. It includes a name index and gives rank, date of capture, where the officer was imprisoned, date of repatriation, and date of death if he died in captivity.

FO 383/307 contains a list of Royal Navy, Royal Naval Reserve and Royal Naval Volunteer Reserve officers held as POWs between 10 October 1914 and 28 July 1917. It provides name, rank, camp where held, date of capture, and name of service.

The Archives Division of the International Council of the Red Cross holds a list of all known POWs for the First World War. They will carry out a search, for a fee, in response to a written application (for address, see Appendix 2).

4.6.5 Prisoners of war: First World War (general sources)

The correspondence of the Prisoners of War and Aliens Department of the Foreign Office, in **FO 383**, contains much information about British POWs. Material relating to POWs is also to be found in the general political correspondence of the Foreign Office in **FO 371**, which can be searched by a card index, arranged by year, held in the Research Enquiries Room. In **FO 506/1837–1874** there are Prisoners and Aliens Registers for 1915–19, arranged by country; however, much of the correspondence referred to in these registers has not survived.

Further information concerning First World War POWs may be found in **ADM 1**, **ADM 116** and **ADM 137**, and in **ADM 12** under code 79 (see Chapter 7).

4.6.6 Prisoners of war: Second World War

The PRO does not hold a unified single list of British POWs for the Second World War. However, you will find a useful printed source in the PRO Library entitled *Prisoners of War Naval and Air Forces of Great Britain and the Empire 1939–1945* (Hayward, 1990). As well as the names of RN, RNVR, RNR and WRNS officers and ratings who were captured, this lists their service number, rank/rating and POW number, and gives the name of the camp in which they were held.

The Archives Division of the International Council of the Red Cross holds a list of all known POWs for the Second World War. They will carry out a search, for a fee, in response to a written application (for address, see Appendix 2).

FO 916/179 and **FO 916/189** contain lists of POWs held in France in 1941. Alphabetical lists of POWs held in Germany or German-occupied territory, for September 1944, can be found in **WO 392/7**. These are split between officers and ratings, and provide details such as where held, camp number, POW's number, rank and service number. Similar lists of POWs in Italy for September 1944 are in **WO 392/21**.

The nominal lists in **WO 392/23–26** of POWs held in Japan or Japanese-occupied territory give rank, service number, date of capture and liberation, where held, and remarks such as whether died. Series **WO 345** consists of Japanese index cards in regards to POWs. These cards (which contain entries in Japanese) provide details of camps, name of POW, nationality, rank, place and date of capture, father's name, place of origin, destination of report, POW camp number, date of birth, service number, mother's name, occupation, and sometimes medical details. Further records of POWs held in Japanese camps are in **WO 208/4283–4290**. Arranged by place, these records provide details such as POW number, rank, service number, next of kin and, where relevant, date of death and place of burial. Some of these records are closed for 75 years.

A list of RNR officers held as POWs during the Second World War can be found in **BT 164/23**, which includes a surname index.

POW escape reports for 1940–5 have been preserved in **WO 208/3298–3327**. These provide rank, ship's name, where and when captured, where and when escaped, date and place of arrival in the UK, peacetime occupation, private address, date of birth and date of entry into the service, plus detailed accounts of capture and escape. There is a name card index to these records in the Research Enquiries Room. POW reports of escapes via Switzerland during 1943–4 can be found in **WO 208/4238–4276** and **4368–4371**. Arranged alphabetically by surname, they give service number, rank, nationality, name, unit, date and place of capture, date and place of final escape, date of arrival in Switzerland, brief circumstances of capture, where imprisoned (camp number), how employed, details of escapes attempted (dates and brief details), details of final escape and subsequent journey, names and addresses of any helpers, and type of help given.

POW liberation reports are located in **WO 208/3328–3340**. They give name, rank, unit, where and when captured, date of birth, date of entry into service, where and when escaped, peacetime occupation, private address, and details of capture and escape. Miscellaneous interrogation reports of returning POWs for 1945 can be found in **WO 208/3343–3345**.

4.6.7 Prisoners of war: Second World War (general sources)

There are reports on Allied POWs in the War Office registered files in **WO 32** (under code 91) and Military Headquarters papers in **WO 219/1448–1474**. Medical reports on conditions in POW camps, with some reports on escapes, feature among the Medical Historian's papers in **WO 222/1352–1393**.

The indexes to the general correspondence of the Foreign Office, 1920–51, available in the Reference Room, include many entries relating to POWs. Where the correspondence itself has been preserved, it is most likely to be found in **FO 371**.

The Prisoners of War and Internment files in the Admiralty and Secretariat papers in **ADM 1** (Series I, code 79), **ADM 1** (Series II, code 79) and **ADM 116** (code 79) contain numerous documents concerning the Royal Navy's involvement with and policy on POWs.

4.7 Medals and awards

Before the introduction of Britain's first official naval campaign medal, the China Medal of 1842, men who had served in significant naval actions were rewarded in various ways. One of the oldest forms of reward was prize money. This was distributed among the crew of ships that had captured enemy vessels, with officers taking a greater share than ratings (some prize money lists, ranging from 1803 to 1937 and giving name, rank/rating, sum paid, date of payment and to whom, can be found in **ADM 238**). It was considerably cheaper for the navy to make use of captured ships rather than build new ones – so, besides acting as an incentive, the payment of prize money represented a saving. Another reward was the promotion of those who distinguished themselves in action. Although this reward tended to be given to commissioned officers, it offered a chance of advancement to junior officers who did not have the backing of powerful patrons and also to ratings. To many, prize money and promotion were the main attractions of a naval career.

Sometimes these rewards were supplemented by more personal forms of acknowledgement, such as decorative medallions, for example which were awarded in 1650 to celebrate naval victories over the Dutch. However, it was not until 1794, with the institution of the King's Naval Gold Medal by George III, that the practice became established on a regular basis. Even so, this was usually awarded to admirals and captains, and only for the most important actions of the Napoleonic Wars. Service in naval actions was also acknowledged by the award of presentation swords, the most notable being those presented to officers by the City of London and Lloyd's Patriotic Fund.

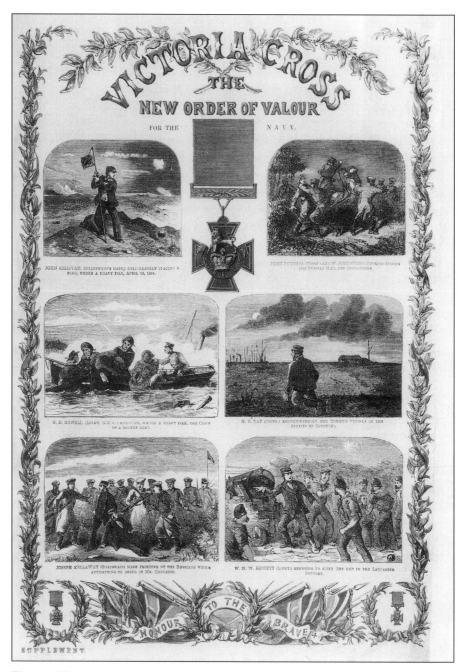

Figure 25 Line drawings of early Victoria Cross naval winners from the *Illustrated London News*, 1857. (ZPER 34/30, p622)

In 1784 the East India Company began to award general service medals to its army and naval personnel. Not longer after, Nelson's prize agent, Alexander Davison, and Matthew Boulton, a Birmingham industrialist, presented medals to all those who had fought in the Battle of the Nile (1798) and at Trafalgar (1805).

In 1842 the East India Company awarded a medal to all its forces that had taken part in the first China War (1840–2). These forces had been helped by a number of regular units from the army and navy, to whom the Government decided to issue the China War Medal. When this medal was issued, many people pointed out the anomaly that men who had participated in a relatively minor war were being rewarded, while the thousands who had served in the French Revolutionary and Napoleonic Wars were not. This provoked a public outcry, with debates in Parliament, which resulted in the introduction in 1847 of the Naval General Service Medal, with special clasps denoting service in 231 selected actions, of varying importance, between 1793 and 1840.

4.7.1 Naval General Service Medal and campaign medals 1793–1913

The Naval General Service Medal and campaign medal rolls for this period are to be found in **ADM 171**, which is available on microfilm in the Microfilm Reading Room. To search them, you need to know the date of the naval action and, ideally, the name of the ship on which the recipient of the medal served. The details given in medal rolls vary, but they normally include ship's names – important for tracing a rating's career prior to 1853 (see 3.2).

Further reading

The following publications (all available in the PRO Library) may be of help if you are trying to trace details of an ancestor who was awarded a naval medal during the eighteenth or nineteenth centuries:

- *The Naval General Service Medal Roll 1793–1840* by K. Douglas-Morris (London, 1982) lists the recipients of this medal under name of action, together with rank, ship's name, and in some cases date of death.

- *The Naval General Service Medal 1793–1840* by Commander W.B. Rowbotham (manuscript, located among Research Enquiries Room supplementary finding aids) gives the names of ships for which claims have been proved and actions for which the medal was awarded, together with a list of officers present in fleet and squadron medal actions between 1794 and 1811.

- *Naval Medals 1793–1856* (London, 1987) and *Naval Medals 1857–1880* (London, 1994), both by K. Douglas-Morris, contain much useful information relating to naval medals, including numerous nominal lists.

4.7.2 First and Second World War campaign medal rolls

First World War campaign medal rolls for officers who served in the Royal Navy, RNVR or RNAS are to be found in **ADM 171/89–91**, while those for officers who served in the RNR are in **ADM 171/92–93**. These medal rolls are arranged alphabetically by name.

Similar medal rolls are located in **ADM 171/94–119** for ratings who served in the Royal Navy or RNAS; in **ADM 171/120–124** for ratings who served in the RNR; and in **ADM 171/125–129** for those who served in the RNVR. These medal rolls are in typescript and are arranged in alphabetical order by name, making them easy to search. What is more, they provide each man's service number – essential for locating a rating's service record and well worth noting, since the nominal indexes relating to ratings' service records in **ADM 139** and **ADM 188** are not in strict alphabetical order by name (see 3.3.1 and 3.3.2) and some of them are missing or incomplete (see 6.4.2).

A number of campaign medal rolls for the interwar years 1920–37 are held by the PRO, in **ADM 171**.

Information from Second World War and postwar campaign medal rolls can be given only to the person awarded the medal or to next of kin. These medal rolls are held by the Naval Medal Office of the Ministry of Defence (for address, see Appendix 2).

4.7.3 Naval long-service and good-conduct medals

Introduced in 1830, these medals are awarded to petty officers and ratings who have served for 15 years with good character. No Admiralty medal rolls for their award prior to 1912 are known to have survived, but the service records in **ADM 29, ADM 139** and **ADM 188** (see 3.2.1 and 3.3) should indicate whether a rating or petty officer was a recipient of these medals. *Naval Long Service Medals, 1830–1900* by K. Douglas-Morris (London, 1991), available in the PRO Library, provides an excellent guide for researchers interested in their history and the regulations governing their award; it also includes nominal lists of those awarded long-service medals between 1830 and 1973. Document references for relevant medal rolls held by the PRO are given in the table below.

Document references	Date range	Content
ADM 171/73	1912–19	Royal Navy Good Conduct Medal (receipt numbers 10930–50974). Includes date of claim, date received and sent for trace, date of ordering medal, name, rating, ship, date medal sent and to whom, and receipt number.
ADM 171/140–145	1920–47	Royal Navy Long Service and Good Conduct Medal issue books. Arranged by initial letter of surname. Official number, name, number of medal, rank or rating, Royal Navy, date medal issued and to whom.

ADM 171/156–159	1925–69	Royal Navy Long Service and Good Conduct Medal register index. Name, rating and folio. This document is not reliable as an index.
ADM 171/149–155	1925–70	Royal Navy Long Service and Good Conduct Medal application book. Claim number, date received, name, rating, official number, ship or division, award schedule number, authority for payment of gratuity.
ADM 171/160–163	1935–72	Royal Fleet Reserve Long Service and Good Conduct Medal claim books and indexes. Claim number, name, Royal Fleet Reserve number, port or marine division, registrar informed, remarks.
ADM 171/146–147	1921–42	Royal Fleet Reserve Long Service Medal roll. Arranged alphabetically. Official number, RFR number, medal number, rank, rating, Royal Navy or Royal Marine, date medal issued and to whom.
ADM 171/70–72	1909–49	Royal Naval Reserve Long Service and Good Conduct Medal roll, arranged by name. Service number, medal number, rank/rating, date medal issued and to whom. From 1919, men who had served 12 years in the Royal Naval Auxiliary Sick Berth Reserve could also qualify for the medal.
ADM 171/70–72	1909–49	Royal Naval Volunteer Reserve Long Service and Good Conduct Medal roll. Official number, RNVR number, number of medal, rank or rating, Royal Navy or Royal Marine, date medal issued and to whom.

4.7.4 Naval Good Shooting Medal

Introduced by King Edward VII in August 1903, this medal was awarded annually to seamen who achieved a high ratio of hits in target practice during fleet exercises. Initially the medal was awarded without a bar; but if a seaman requalified for the medal, he received a bar inscribed with the name of his ship, type of gun fired, and the year. The Naval Good Shooting Medal roll for 1903–14 in **ADM 171/57** provides official or regimental number, name, number of medal, rank or rating, gun, ship, and when delivered or sent.

4.7.5 Gallantry awards

The most important document for those researching a gallantry award is the citation, which provides details about the act of bravery that led to the award being made. However, citations do not always survive and searching for relevant information can prove time-consuming, particularly if you do not know which medal was awarded nor the date of its award. The best starting point for this type of search is the *London Gazette*, copies of which are held in **ZJ 1** (see below). You will then need to search some of the documents and printed sources listed in sections 4.7.7 to 4.7.20, and possibly the records in **ADM 12** (see Chapter 7) as well. For further sources relating to First and Second World War gallantry awards, see 4.7.18.

Further reading

British Gallantry Awards by P.E. Abbott and J.M.A. Tamplin (Nimrod Dix & Co., London, 1981), which is available in the PRO Library, gives detailed information about the history of gallantry awards and the regulations concerning them.

4.7.6 *The* London Gazette

Details of gallantry awards, along with appointments and promotions of naval officers, were usually announced in the *London Gazette*, the Crown's official newspaper, founded in 1665. The PRO holds copies of the *London Gazette* from 1665 to 1986, in **ZJ 1**. Up to 1914 it is possible to find citations in the *London Gazette*; but First and Second World War citations are rare, owing to the sheer number of awards that were made. The PRO's copies of the *London Gazette* are mainly arranged in monthly order by year, and from 1790 these have integral name indexes. The **ZJ 1** series list indicates which of the *London Gazette* volumes contain such indexes. This is useful to note, as these indexes were normally published on a quarterly, half-yearly and annual basis – for example, the volume containing the June 1944 issue of the *London Gazette* (**ZJ 1/985**) includes the name index covering April–June 1944. Up to January 1942 the names of naval personnel awarded gallantry medals appear in the 'State Intelligence' section of these indexes, arranged alphabetically by gallantry medal and then by person's name; from 1942 they are listed under 'Honours, Awards and Decorations', in alphabetical order.

Most of the issues of the *London Gazette* in **ZJ 1** are ordered and produced as original documents – except for 1914–19 (**ZJ 1/613–681**) and 1939–46 (**ZJ 1/920–1015**), which are available in the Microfilm Reading Room, on microfilm, along with printed copies of the name indexes for 1914–21 and 1940–46.

To search the *London Gazette* name indexes effectively, it is useful to know name, service number and rank, the type of award (pre-1942), and when it was awarded. A typical name-index entry has a page number alongside the person's name. For example, the entry '**Harvey, A.W. 2112**' appears under the heading 'Honours, Decorations and Medals' in the index volume for 1943. To identify the document reference for the 1943 issue of the *London Gazette* that includes page number 2112, you will need to consult the **ZJ 1** series list (*London Gazette* page numbers appear in the right-hand margin of the list). In this example, the announcement relating to A.W. Harvey is to be found in **ZJ 1/972**, on page 2112. The information presented in it is typical of the announcements published in the *London Gazette* during the two world wars:

> The King has been graciously pleased to give orders for the following Appointments to the Distinguished Service Order and to approve the following rewards and awards:
> For courage, skill and devotion to duty in action in North African waters, The Distinguished Service Medal, Petty Officer Arthur Walter Harvey, C/J 110286.

The *London Gazette* for January 1914 to December 1920 and January 1939 to December 1948 can also be searched online at www.gazettes-online.co.uk.

4.7.7 Albert Medal

The Albert Medal was instituted by royal warrant in 1866. Initially it was awarded for acts of gallantry in saving life at sea, but from 1867 it was also awarded for saving life on land. The names of those who received this medal between 1866 and 1941 are to be found under the heading 'State Intelligence' in the *London Gazette* (see 4.7.6), in **ZJ 1**.

BT 97/1 is a register of awards of the Albert Medal between 1866 and 1913 (from 1891, this register lists awards to civilians only). **BT 97/2** is a photograph album of recipients of the Albert Medal, 1866–79.

ADM 171/65–66, which cover Albert Medal awards between 1866 and 1948, provide name of recipient, rank, ship and, in some cases, citations. **ADM 171/61**, which covers 1929–66, gives number and date of gazette, name, rank or rating, service number, ship's pay book number, ship's name, reason for the issue of the medal, and date of issue.

Files with citations relating to the award or non-award of the Albert Medal can be found in **HO 45** and **HO 144**, under the heading 'Albert Medal'. Similar files can be found under the heading 'Awards' in **MT 9**.

Further reading

Honours and Awards Army, Navy and Air Force 1914–1920 (Hayward, 1979), held in the PRO Library, contains a list of RN and RNR officers and ratings awarded the Albert Medal between 1867 and 1919.

4.7.8 Conspicuous Gallantry Medal

This medal was introduced specifically for the Crimean War (1854–6). At the end of the Ashanti War (1873–4), it was reintroduced to reward petty officers and seamen who distinguished themselves by acts of bravery. No awards appear to be gazetted in **ZJ 1** between 1874 and 1894 (see 4.7.6).

Recipients of the CGM are noted in the *Navy List*. Between 1875 and 1920, nominal lists of surviving recipients are to be found both in the *Navy List* (see 2.1) and in the Admiralty Fleet Orders in **ADM 182**.

ADM 171/75 is an index to the Conspicuous Gallantry Medal rolls, 1914–18. It gives the name and service number of the recipient and the number of the medal.

The Conspicuous Gallantry Medal roll for 1914–29 in **ADM 171/61** lists service number, name, number of medal, rank or rating, ship's pay book number, when delivered or sent, reason for award, and date of announcement in *London Gazette*.

Further reading

The following publications, both available in the PRO Library, are helpful when researching recipients of the CGM:

- *For Conspicuous Gallantry – The Register of the Conspicuous Gallantry Medal, 1855–1992* by P. McDermott (Naval and Military Press, 1998).

- *Honours and Awards Army, Navy and Air Force 1914–1920* (Hayward, 1979), which lists the names of petty officers and men, with rank and year of award, who were awarded the CGM between 1874 and 1918.

4.7.9 *Conspicuous Service Cross and Distinguished Service Cross*

In 1914 the Conspicuous Service Cross was renamed the Distinguished Service Cross. Names of recipients of the CSC from 1901 to 1913 are to be found under the heading 'Conspicuous Service Cross' in the naval promotions section of the *London Gazette* indexes in **ZJ 1** (see 4.7.6), but no citations are given. From October 1901 lists of recipients can be found in the *Navy List* (see 2.1); from 1914 onwards all awards are listed in the *London Gazette*, in **ZJ 1**.

The Distinguished Service Cross medal rolls for 1942–72 in **ADM 171/164–165** are arranged alphabetically. They list the name and official number of the recipient, the award, and the *London Gazette* number and date.

BT 164/23 records Distinguished Service Cross awards to RNR officers between 1939 and 1946. It contains a surname index and lists *London Gazette* date, name, rank, number and ship.

Further reading

The following publications, all available in the PRO Library, are helpful when researching the DSC:

- *The Distinguished Service Cross 1901–1938* by W.H. Fevyer (London Stamp Exchange, 1991) contains a surname index and lists of recipients that give rank, date of announcement in the *London Gazette* and, in some cases, reason for award.

- *Fringes of the Fleet and the Distinguished Service Cross* by R.C. Witte (Dix Noonan Webb, 1997) is especially useful for First World War awards of the DSC.

- *Honours and Awards Army, Navy and Air Force 1914–1920* (Hayward, 1979) lists the names of RN, RNR, RNVR and RNAS officers awarded the DSC between 1 July

1901 and 17 March 1919, including date of announcement in the *London Gazette* and rank at the time of the act for which the medal was awarded.

4.7.10 Distinguished Service Medal

From 1915 to 1920 lists of DSM awards were published in the *Navy List* (see 2.1). From 1920 onwards they appear in the Admiralty Fleet Orders in **ADM 182**.

In **ADM 171/75** there is a Distinguished Service Medal index for 1914–18, which gives the name and official number of recipients and the number of the medal.

Distinguished Service Medal rolls for 1914–37 are to be found in **ADM 171/61**. These list name and official number of recipient, ship's pay book number, name of ship, and when delivered or sent.

The Distinguished Service medal rolls for 1942–72 in **ADM 171/164–165**, which are arranged alphabetically, list name and official number, award, and *London Gazette* number and date.

Further reading

The following publications, available in the PRO Library, are helpful when researching the DSM:

- *The Distinguished Service Medal 1914–1920* by W.H. Fevyer (Hayward, 1982) contains a surname index and a list of recipients that gives rank, official number, *London Gazette* date and, in some cases, reason for award.

- *The Distinguished Service Medal 1939–1946* by W.H. Fevyer (Hayward, 1981) includes a surname index and a list of recipients that gives official number, name of ship, and reason for award.

- *Honours and Awards Army, Navy and Air Force 1914–1920* (Hayward, 1979) lists the names of men awarded the DSM between 1914 and 1919 who served in the RN, RNR or RNVR. It gives their rank at the time of the award and the year when the award was made.

4.7.11 Distinguished Service Order

Information about awards of the DSO between 1886 and 1945 can be found in **WO 390**, which is available on microfilm in the Microfilm Reading Room.

Further reading

The following publications are helpful when researching the DSM (both available in the PRO Library):

- *The Distinguished Service Order 1886–1923* by Sir O'Moore Creagh VC, GCB, GCSI and E.M. Humphries (Hayward, 1979) provides a complete record of the recipients of the DSO from 1886 to 12 June 1923, with details of the deeds and service for which the award was given. It includes many biographical and career details, and in some instances photographs of the recipients.

- *Honours and Awards Army, Navy and Air Force 1914–1920* (Hayward, 1979) lists the names of all RN, RNR and RNVR officers awarded the DSO between 1887 and 1919, with rank and date of award.

4.7.12 George Cross

The George Cross was introduced by royal warrant in 1940. Lists of surviving recipients up to 1960 appear in *Whitaker's Almanac*, copies of which are available in the PRO Library. Details of the award of this medal since 1960 can be found in the *London Gazette* (see 4.7.6). Also, numerous recommendations for the GC are to be found in **AIR 2** (under code 30).

   ADM 1/23187 contains a list of George Cross awards to naval personnel in 1940–6, which gives name and rank of recipient, ship's name, and the dates of the act of bravery and the announcement in the *London Gazette*.

Further reading

The Story of the George Cross by the Right Hon. Sir John Smyth, Bt, VC, MC (Arthur Baker, 1968), which is available in the PRO Library, is helpful when researching the GC.

4.7.13 George Medal

Details of the award of this medal from its introduction in 1940 can be found in the *London Gazette* (see 4.7.6). From 1941 the announcements sometimes include the home town of recipients (in rare cases addresses are given), but this practice ceased at the end of the war.

   ADM 171/164–165 list awards of the George Medal between 1942 and 1972. Arranged alphabetically, the lists give name and service number, the award, and the *London Gazette* number and date.

4.7.14 Meritorious Service Medal

ADM 171/61 lists Meritorious Service Medal awards for 1919–20. It gives name and service number of recipient, number of medal, rank, ship's pay book number, clasp (if relevant), and when delivered or sent.

Further reading

The following publications, available in the PRO Library, are helpful when researching the MSM:

- *The Meritorious Service Medal, the immediate awards, 1916–1928* by I. McInnes (Naval and Military Press, 1992) lists recipients' names, together with date of *London Gazette* announcement.

- *Honours and Awards Army, Navy and Air Force 1914–1920* (Hayward, 1979) lists the names of men awarded the MSM in 1919, with rank.

4.7.15 Military Medal

The Military Medal was introduced by a Royal Warrant of 25 March 1916.

From 1917 the recipient's home town was included in the *London Gazette* announcement (see 4.7.6), but this procedure ceased at the end of the First World War. It was revived in June 1941, but not followed consistently.

ADM 171/61, which lists Military Medal awards for 1917–21, gives name and service number, *London Gazette* date, number of medal, rank, ship's pay book number, clasp (if relevant), and when delivered or sent.

ADM 171/164–165 list MM awards from 1942 to 1972. Arranged alphabetically, they give name and service number, award, and *London Gazette* number and date.

4.7.16 Victoria Cross

Lists of those awarded the Victoria Cross between 1856 and 1951, including citation and *London Gazette* date, can be found in the Victoria Cross binder held in the PRO Library.

Citations for the Victoria Cross are often included in the *London Gazette* (see 4.7.6) **ADM 1/23187** contains a list of awards to naval personnel between 1854 and 1945. **CAB 106/312** lists recipients of the VC between 1939 and 1946, together with citations.

Further reading

The following publications, available in the PRO Library, are helpful when researching the VC:

- *The Victoria Cross at Sea* by J. Winton provides much biographical information for Royal Navy personnel awarded the Victoria Cross.

- *The Register of the Victoria Cross* (Cheltenham, This England Books, 1981) includes many photographs and pictures of Victoria Cross winners.

- *Honours and Awards Army, Navy and Air Force 1914–1920* (Hayward, 1979) contains a list of officers and men of the RN, RNR and RNVR awarded the Victoria Cross

C O P Y

T H E   V I C T O R I A   C R O S S

P/JX.139070 Acting Leading Seaman Jack Foreman Mantle,

H.M.S. Foylebank.
- - - - - - - - -

Leading Seaman Jack Mantle was in charge of the Starboard pom-pom
when Foylebank was attacked by enemy aircraft on the 4th of July, 1940.

Early in the action his left leg was shattered by a bomb, but he
stood fast at his gun and went on firing with hand-gear only; for the
ship's electric power had failed.   Almost at once he was wounded again
in many places.

Between his bursts of fire he had time to reflect on the grievous
injuries of which he was soon to die; but his great courage bore him up
till the end of the fight, when he fell by the gun he had so valiantly
served.

Figure 26 Copy of the citation for the Victoria Cross won by Jack Foreman Mantle during the Second World War. (CAB 106/312; image of Mantle, INF 3/414)

between 21 May 1884 and 17 March 1919, including name and rank, place where the act of gallantry was performed, the date of the act of gallantry and rank at that time, and the *London Gazette* date.

● *Victoria Cross Bibliography* by J. Mulholland and A. Jordan (Spink, 1999).

4.7.17 Mentions in despatches

This procedure was used to bring the services of deserving officers and men to higher authority. These despatches were often used for the basis of awards or promotion. The format of the mention was sometimes a list of names and sometimes a detailed description of the service performed, resembling a citation. In 1902 the Inter-departmental Rewards Committee recommended that to constitute a mention publication in the *London Gazette* (see 4.7.6) should be regarded as essential.

Prior to 1916 there are no indexes of names mentioned in naval despatches published in the *London Gazette*. Before 1916, it is necessary to identify the appropriate despatch by date and then search for the name. Sometimes lists of names can be found at the end of a despatch, or in an additional listing which may not have been published at the same time as the despatch itself. From 1916 to 1941 names appear under the heading 'State Intelligence' in the indexes to the *London Gazette*. After 1941, up to 1960, the names are listed in a nominal section under the heading 'Mentions in Despatches and Commendations', and all you will find under the heading 'State Intelligence' are page references for the various awards.

Details concerning recommendations and mentions in despatches during the Second World War may be found in **ADM 1** (under code 85), **ADM 116** (code 85), and **ADM 1/29358–30077** and **30098–30984**. The PRO online catalogue can be used to search these documents, either by person's name or name of ship, or they can be accessed via **ADM 12** (see Chapter 7). As well as giving details of mentions in despatches, they contain operational records that provide much additional information about the events leading to the mention.

A card index to Royal Navy personnel mentioned in despatches between 1914 and 1919 is available in the Microfilm Reading Room.

A mentions in despatch roll for August 1921 to 11 September 1941 is in **ADM 171/63**.

In **BT 164/23** there is a roll listing RNR officers mentioned in despatches between 1939 and 1946. This includes a surname index and lists the *London Gazette* date, name, rank, number and ship.

4.7.18 Gallantry awards: First and Second World Wars

A useful source for tracing details of gallantry medals awarded to officers during the First World War are the honour sheets in **ADM 171/78–88**. These record name, rank or seniority, ship, recommended by, nature of service, gazette despatch or report, and award if any. The 'nature of service' column often describes the incident or act of gallantry for which the recommendation was made. Other potentially useful finding aids are the 'Royal Navy service book index applications and recommendations, 1914–19' and 'Royal Navy miscellaneous medal recommendations, 1914–19' card indexes, both available in the Microfilm Reading Room.

ADM 1/29358–30077 and **30098–30984** contain numerous Second World War citations for gallantry medal awards, together with operational records that provide information about the events leading to the awards. You can use the PRO online catalogue to search these documents by person's name or name of ship. Alternatively, they can be accessed via **ADM 12** (see Chapter 7).

Further information about gallantry medals awarded during the Second World War may be found in **ADM 1** (code 85) and **ADM 116** (code 85).

Seedie's Submarine List 1939–1945, available in the PRO Library, is a guide to all officers and men who served in submarines and received gallantry awards, orders or foreign awards. It gives name and rank, award, and date of gazette.

Records of naval gallantry awards from the outbreak of the Second World War are held by the Admin Support section of the Naval Secretary's Department (for address, see Appendix 2). Information concerning these awards is usually supplied only to the recipient of the award or to next of kin (in some instances, a fee may be charged).

4.7.19 Foreign awards

The Treaty Department of the Foreign Office dealt with the issue of foreign honours and awards to British nationals. Records for 1745–1905 relating to this aspect of the Treaty Department's work can be found in **FO 83**, which is indexed by **FO 605** (available on microfilm in the Microfilm Reading Room) for 1808–90.

From 1906 records relating to foreign awards to British nationals are to be found in **FO 372**, which is partially indexed by the Foreign Office general correspondence indexes available in the Research Enquiries Room (in card index form for 1906–19, and in printed form for 1920–53 and 1959).

Honours and Awards Army, Navy and Air Force 1914–1920 (Hayward, 1979), in the PRO Library, includes a list of officers authorized to wear foreign orders that covers the years 1883–1919. It gives name and rank, order or decoration, class or grade, country, and date of bestowal.

ADM 171/61 contains various lists of foreign awards to RN, RNR and RNVR personnel, including medals from Denmark, France, Greece, Italy, the Netherlands, Norway, the USA and the USSR – among them a medal given for services relating to the 1908 Messina earthquake, the US Gold Medal (1920) and the Greek Cross (1929).

ADM 171/172 is a list of foreign decorations awarded to RN officers between 1905 and 1922. It contains a surname index and records name, rank and date, plus ship in which serving or service for which the honour was awarded.

A nominal card index to Royal Naval personnel who received Russian honours and awards during 1914–19 can be found in the Microfilm Reading Room.

4.7.20 Miscellaneous documents concerning campaign and gallantry medals and mentions in despatches

Below is a list of miscellaneous documents held by the PRO that may be of interest to those researching medals.

Document reference	Dates	Content
ADM 7/706	1793–1807	Register of distinguished naval actions and services. Contains own surname index. Officer's name, ship, date of action, reference to despatch, remarks, and nature of action.
ADM 105/38	March 1842	List of all officers who served at the siege of St Jean d'Acre, in Syria.
ADM 105/38	6 Dec 1842	List of assistant surgeons who served in China and were gazetted for their service.
ADM 73/94	1848–9	Alphabetical list of Greenwich Hospital in-pensioners claiming the Naval General Service Medal.
ADM 7/913	1854–99	Abstract of war services and recommendations for campaign and gallantry awards for officers and ratings relating to services in the Crimean War during 1854 to the civil war in Samoa in 1899.
ADM 7/914	1884–5	List of officers mentioned in despatches for services in the Nile, Red Sea, Suakin, Berber and Burma expeditions. Contains surname index.
ADM 116/1102	1909–12	Lists of officers and men awarded diplomas, honours and medals by the King of Italy for services relating to the 1908 Messina earthquake.

4.8 Casualty and wound records

Information about officers and ratings killed or wounded while serving in the Royal Navy can be found in a variety of documents, such as service records, ships' logs and musters, succession books, court martial records (when a ship has sunk), pension records, and hospital musters. The following sections (4.8.1 to 4.8.4.3) aim to identify the PRO records most likely to provide dates of death or wounding.

4.8.1 Casualty and wound records up to 1913

Widows of commissioned and warrant officers or ratings who had been killed in action or who had died as a result of wounds were entitled to the Royal Bounty, which was equal to 12 months' pay, the amount depending on the rank or rating their husband held. If they had children, each child was entitled to one-third of 12 months' pay. Widowed mothers – and sometimes widowed fathers – of officers and ratings could also claim the bounty, provided that they were aged 50 or over and their son had died unmarried. Initially the bounty was paid to widows and children of men killed on board HM ships and other vessels of war when fighting the enemy. This was extended in 1706 to those killed in action on tenders and boats or on shore.

Applications from next of kin claiming the bounty in respect of officers and ratings killed in action can be found in **ADM 106/3021–3035**, which extend from 1675 to 1821. These applications are often accompanied by baptismal and marriage certificates, together with a letter giving the applicant's address, the name of the ship that the officer or rating was serving on when he was killed, and his date of death. A personal-name index to **ADM 106/3021–3034** is available in the Research Enquiries Room.

ADM 106/3018–3020 contain bills made out for the payment of bounty to widows, mothers or children of officers and ratings killed in action between 1739 and 1787 (name indexes are included in **ADM 106/3018–3019**). These bills record the name of the person having the right to the bounty, relationship to the deceased, the deceased's name, rank, ship and date of death (and sometimes the number of children), the amount of money paid, and the address of the person receiving the bounty. Similar records for 1793–1832 can be found in **ADM 30/20**.

Claims from next of kin for the payment of bounty in respect of ratings killed in action between 1743 and 1780 are in **ADM 106/3017**. These claims provide the name of the rating, which ship he served on, date of death, name and parish of next of kin, and number of children (whose ages may be given).

Nominal lists of seamen who died at Haslar Hospital between 1755 and 1765, giving the names of the ships they served on and dates of death, are located in **ADM 102/374**.

ADM 80/4–5 are registers of deceased ratings' wages for 1787–1809. Arranged by initial letter of surname, they list ratings' and ships' names. **ADM 80/4** does not provide dates of death, whereas **ADM 80/5** does. Similar registers for 1798–1831 can be found in **ADM 80/6–12**, arranged by the date that the unpaid wages reached the Navy Pay Office (**ADM 80/9** is further subdivided by port). These registers record the amount of wages to be paid, the deceased's name, the name of the ship he was serving on, and when and to whom the unpaid wages were paid (this was often to next of kin, and the relationship may be stated).

In **ADM 103/633** there are various lists relating to deaths of British POWs in France, the French colonies and Spain during 1793–1816. Most of these lists provide the deceased's name, rank/rating, name of ship and dates of death. Some also give place of birth, age, place where captured, place where imprisoned, and place of death.

The death certificates of officers and ratings who died in Plymouth Hospital during 1809–15 have been preserved in **ADM 102/842**.

ADM 104/3 contains monthly statements, from June 1817 to October 1820, of expenses attending the victualling, quartering and burying of officers and ratings from the Royal Marine Infirmary in Woolwich. These records list officers' and ratings' names, which ship they last served on, rank/rating, cost of victualling, funeral expenses, and dates of death.

Letters concerning deaths of officers and ratings on board HM ships and in hospitals during 1823–32 can be found in **ADM 105/29**. A post-mortem register for the Royal Naval Hospital Malta, covering the period January 1829 to May 1838, is in **ADM 304/25**. Case books from the Royal Naval Hospital Bermuda for 1832–83 (with some gaps) are located in **ADM 104/98–101**. These list officers' and ratings' names, dates of entry to the hospital, ship discharged from, details of disease and treatment, and in some instances date of discharge or death. **ADM 104/101** contains a surname index.

Miscellaneous letters and reports to the Board of Admiralty concerning wounded officers can be found in **ADM 105/30–32**. These range from 1799 to 1855 and include surname indexes.

A list of medical officers who died on the coast of Africa between 1836 and 1838 is in **ADM 105/38**.

ADM 11/51–52 contain obituary books for commissioned and warrant officers who died between 1833 and 1846. These record name and rank, date when officer was placed on the half pay list, and date of death.

Commissioned officers who died between 1842 and 1871 are listed in **ADM 6/445**. These lists indicate where notification of death came from (from next of kin, fellow officers or *The Times* newspaper, for example). Similar records for 1903–33, located in **ADM 10/16**, also include warrant officers and RNR and RNVR officers. Microfilm copies of *The Times* from January 1790 to August 1999 are available in the Microfilm Reading Room.

ADM 80/107 provides a record of gratuities paid to the widows of ratings who were killed in action or drowned, covering 1863–5. It lists rating's name, name of ship serving on, cause and date of death, amount paid, widow's name and address, and when and how paid.

Details of officers and ratings killed or wounded as a result of the naval engagement with the forts at Kagoshima on 15 August 1863 are recorded in **ZJ 1/323**. Those who were killed or wounded during the Battle of Tel-El-Kebir on 13 October 1882 are listed in **ZJ 1/406**. Lists of ratings wounded in the expedition to Vitu on 25–26 November 1891 can be found in **ZJ 1/448**. Lists of officers and ratings killed and officers wounded in the expedition against the Sofas on 26 March 1894 are in **ZJ 1/464**.

Similar lists of officers and ratings killed in the second Boer War are located in **ADM 116/529**. These cover the years 1899–1900, and include cause and place of death.

For further records relating to officers and ratings killed or wounded during 1854–1913, see 4.8.4.

4.8.2 First World War casualties

In the Research Enquiries Room there is a name card index (**ADM 242/1–5**) of commissioned and warrant officers who died between 1914 and 1920. This card index gives the following information for each officer: rank, branch of service (RN, RNR, RNVR, RNAS, RND), ship serving on, place of death, place of burial, date of death, and sometimes name and address of next of kin. The records to which this card index refers are not known to have survived.

NAME (Surname first)	Decorations (if any)	Rating	Official No. and Post Division	Branch of Service	Ship or Unit	Date and place of birth	Date of Death	Cause of Death	Name and Address of Cemetery	Plot	Row	Grave No.	Relatives notified and their address	Remarks
CORNISH, Zaccariah,	-	Hired Mooring Hand.	N.K.	M.&M.R.	Traveler H.M.S. "Devanha".	1887. N.K.	31.10.18.	3.	Dunkerque Town Cem. (Brit.) Dunkerque,France.	1.	D.	16.	Widow, Rose, 2 Dunn's Alley, Radnor Street, Folkestone.	
CORNOCK, Ralph Ernest,	-	P.O. (C.O. A.B.)	142185 (Dev.)	R.N.	H.M.S. "Monmouth".	24.6.71. Wotton-under-Edge, Glos.	1.11.14.	1.	Ø	-	-	-	Wife, Rosina, Potter Pond, Wotton-under-Edge, Gloucestershire	
CORNWALL, William,	-	Ord. Smn.	J.48249 (Po)	R.N.	H.M.S. "Victory".	2.1.97. Chorley, Lancs.	16.2.16.	3.	St. Mary's R.C. Cemetery Buxton, Nr. Chorley, Lancs.	-	-	1.	Father, R, Daisy Hill, Buxton, Nr. Chorley, Lancs.	
CORNWELL, Albert,	-	A.B.	189092 (R.F.R.,Po. B.2109) (Po)	R.N.	H.M.S. "Alcantara".	9.4.79. Burwash, Sussex.	29.2.16.	1.	Ø	-	-	-	Widow, Mary, 2 Hollyhurst Cottages, Burwash Common, Sussex.	
CORNWELL, John Travers,	-	V.C. Boy I.	J.42563	R.N.	H.M.S. "Chester".	8.1.00. West Ham, Essex.	2.6.16.	1.	Manor Park Cem. Sebert Road, Forest Gate, London, E.7	Sq. 18	-	13.	Administrator of Parent's Estate, Mr. P.C.McCormack "Parrogh!" Park Avenue 5th Northampton.	Mentioned in Despatches
CORPES, Ernest Edward,	-	P.O.	228816 (Po)	R.N.	H.M.S. "Princess Irene".	1.3.67. Stoke, Surrey.	27.5.15.	2.	Ø	-	-	-	Widow, Edith E, 8 Trinity Gdns, Fareham,Hants.	
CORR, John,	-	Engine-man.	1781 E.S. (Dev.)	R.N.R.	H.M.Drifter "Alices".	10.12.87. Drogheda.	5.10.18.	3.	Seafield Cem. Leith, Scotland.	Lair W.75.	-	-	Friend, Mrs. Coxon, 86 Poulton Rd, Fleetwood, Lancs	
CORRAN, Arthur,	-	Cook.	949773. (Dev.)	M.&M.R.	H.M.S. "Otranto".	N.K.	6.10.18.	2.	Ø	-	-	-	Widow, Nellie, 25 Olivedale Rd, Moseley Hill, Liverpool.	
CORRIGAN, Martin,	-	Sto. 1st.	299997. (Ch)	R.N.	H.M.S. "Ettrick".	7.11.83. Sale, Cheshire.	7.7.17.	1.	Ø	-	-	-	Widow, Clara, 6 Woodsend Rd, Flixton, Manchester.	
CORRIGAN, Patrick,	-	Pte.	PO/6775 (S)	R.M.L.I, 2nd. R.M. Battn. R.N.D.	-	3.9.95. Liverpool Lancs	17.11.18.	3.	Berlin South Western Cemetery, Province of Mecklenburg Germany. *Schindorf Germany*	N	A	W	Aunt, Mrs. Mary Riok, 15 Norfolk St, Liverpool.	

Figure 27 Extract from First World War ratings' casualty roll with an entry for John Travers Cornwell, the youngest naval Victoria Cross winner. (ADM 242/7)

A war graves roll for RN, RNR, RNVR, RNAS and RND ratings who died during the First World War is to be found in **ADM 242/7–10**. Arranged in strict alphabetical order by name, it lists awards of medals, rating, service number, branch of service, ship or unit, date and place of birth, cause of death (given in code form, but an index to codes is included in each volume), name and address of cemetery, where buried, plot, row and grave number (the symbol 0 means body not recovered for funeral, X means no information as to location of grave), plus name and address of relative notified. The content of **ADM 242/7–10** is as follows:

Document reference	Names
ADM 242/7	Abbas–Cutmore
ADM 242/8	Dabbs–Knowles
ADM 242/9	Labram–Quinton
ADM 242/10	Quintrell–Zeithing

Parts II and IV of *The Cross of Sacrifice* by S.D. and D.B. Jarvis (Roberts, 1993) – available in the PRO Library – consist of lists, arranged in name order, of RN, RNR, RNVR, and RNAS officers and ratings who died during the First World War, identifying where they died and where they are commemorated, together with their rank, service, ship's name, division, battalion, and date of death.

The *Navy List* of July 1915 (available under the document reference **ADM 177/5** in the Microfilm Reading Room) lists all officers and ratings killed in action up to 18 June 1915. The *Navy List* is an important source for tracing an officer's date of death (see 2.1). Each edition of the *Navy List* has a contents list that will tell you on which page the obituary section starts.

The General Register Office (GRO) indexes listing naval war deaths between 1914 and 1921 are available on microfiche in the Microfilm Reading Room. The registers to which these indexes refer are held by the GRO in Southport and are not open to the public. However, copies of death certificates can be ordered **by post** from the General Register Office for England and Wales or **in person** at the Family Records Centre (FRC) in London (for addresses, contact details and websites, see Appendix 2). For details of the fees charged by the General Register Office and the Family Records Centre and for further information about how to order certificates, either visit their websites or consult the publications mentioned in 5.1.

Another important resource for tracing information about officers and ratings who died in the First World War is the Commonwealth War Graves Commission's 'Debt of Honour' database, which can be searched by name on their website (www.cwgc.org).

Further records relating to First World War casualties are described in 4.8.4.

4.8.3 Second World War casualties

Registers of reports of deaths relating to Royal Navy and reserve ratings for September 1939 to June 1948 can be found in **ADM 104/127–139**. Arranged alphabetically by surname, these registers list name, service numbers, branch of service, rating, ship's name, date and place of birth, cause and place of death. The cause of death is given in general terms.

A list of RNR officers killed or wounded during 1939–46 is held in **BT 164/23**, which contains a surname index. This list provides rank, number, ship, date of death or casualty. The cause and dates of death in respect of RN and RNVR medical officers who were killed or who died while on active service during the war can be found in **ADM 261/1**.

The PRO also holds copies of the General Register Office's registers of naval officers' and ratings' war deaths for 1939–48 on microfiche. For more about these registers, see 4.8.2.

Another important resource for tracing information about officers and ratings who died in the Second World War is the Commonwealth War Graves Commission's 'Debt of Honour' database, which can be searched by name on their website (www.cwgc.org).

For further records relating to Second World War casualties, see 4.8.4.

4.8.4 Casualty and wound records in ADM 104

Because the following documents cross-reference each other and form discrete sets of records in their own right, they are grouped together here for convenience and ease of use.

4.8.4.1 Indexes (ADM 104/102–108) and reports (ADM 104/109–118) of deaths on ships of officers and ratings from causes other than enemy action, 1893–1950

The indexes in **ADM 104/102–108** (which list name, rank, ship, report page, and year of death) relate to the registers of reports in **ADM 104/109–118**. Once you have found the entry you require in one of the index volumes, you can use the year of death and page number to identify the relevant register. For example, the entry for 'Aitkins C, Stoker, *Pembroke,* **page 380, 1893**' in **ADM 104/102** indicates that the report of his death will be found on page 380 of **ADM 104/109**, which is the register that covers the years 1893–1909.

4.8.4.2 Registers of reports of ratings' deaths by enemy action between 1900 and October 1941 (ADM 104/122–126)

Arranged by ranges of years, these registers provide the following information: date report received, name, rating, service number, ship serving on, date of death, date of notification of death, relative informed, and in some instances address of next of kin.

4.8.4.3 Registers of officers and ratings killed and wounded in action between 1854 and 1929 (ADM 104/144–149)

Also arranged in ranges of years, these registers include name, ship serving on, age (not always given), rank, date of injury or death, place or station, where died, injury, result of injury, how disposed of, and remarks (name of action and whether wounded, killed in action or died of wounds). Each of these registers contains its own index (the type of index is indicated in the table below).

In addition, **ADM 104/145–149** are name-indexed by **ADM 104/140–143**, using the method of cross-referencing described in 4.8.4.1.

Document reference	Date range	Type of index
ADM 104/144	1854–1911	Surname and ship index.
ADM 104/145	Aug 1914 to July 1915	Surname and ship index.
ADM 104/146	May 1915 to May 1916	Ship index.
ADM 104/147	1916–17	Ship index.
ADM 104/148	March 1917 to June 1918	Ship index.
ADM 104/149	1918–29	Ship index.

4.9 Pensions

The next part of this chapter focuses on the many different types of naval pension, including their background and the various conditions that governed the granting of them to officers, ratings and next of kin.

4.9.1 Officers' pensions

Between the seventeenth century and the mid nineteenth century no general system existed for retiring naval officers once they reached a pensionable age or after serving a fixed number of years. When they were not employed, officers were paid a retainer – 'half pay' (see 2.8.2) – for their services, irrespective of age, until they died. In cases where officers remained unemployed for a long time, half pay could be viewed as a form of pension.

Since the Admiralty had no method of retiring its officers (see 1.1.4), it was continually faced with the unacceptable situation of having very elderly officers who were unsuitable for promotion or employment but could not be officially retired. In 1672 it was decided that a fixed number of senior warrant officers should be entitled to pensions, and the 30 most senior lieutenants were granted a similar entitlement in 1737. In addition, the Admiralty promoted a number of officers – so they would

Figure 28 Drawing of a Greenwich hospital pensioner. (ADM 6/322)

receive a higher rate of half pay – on the understanding that they would no longer be required for service. In 1747, some captains at the top of their seniority lists had been there since 1713.

In 1747 the Admiralty ruled that captains whose turn it was to be promoted to flag officer rank and who were not suitable for employment should be promoted to and receive the half pay of a rear admiral, without the Admiralty specifying any squadron or 'division of colour used in the fleet'. This meant that there was no post for these particular rear admirals, and that they were in effect retired. Officially these officers were regarded as superannuated rear admirals, but they were commonly known as 'yellow admirals'. However, this did not completely solve the problem – because, rather than compelling its captains to retire, the Admiralty simply offered them the opportunity of promotion to rear admiral with the reward of higher half pay, and some turned down the Admiralty's offer in the hope of a real promotion. This system of retiring officers continued to be used in relation to captains and lieutenants until the mid nineteenth century, when the Admiralty finally established a proper method of retiring officers based on seniority and on having served a fixed number of years.

Before 1830 the Admiralty granted pensions to deserving individuals or officers, under the authority of orders in council. From 1673 it paid pensions to widows of commissioned officers killed in action or as a result of duty; and from 1809 grants and pensions were paid from the Compassionate Fund (later the Compassionate List) to next of kin of officers killed in action. From 1830 warrant officers' widows qualified for Admiralty pensions, and around 1885 their dependants became eligible for support from the Compassionate List. Widows of warrant officers killed in action or on service were also paid pensions from the Chatham Chest, founded in 1581. Management of the Chatham Chest was taken over by the Royal Greenwich Hospital in 1803 (it ceased to be an independent fund in 1814), its pensions being amalgamated with those of Greenwich Hospital.

The Charity for the Payment of Pensions to the Widows of Sea Officers, an independent body established in 1732, paid pensions to widows who could not support themselves financially. Its income was based on parliamentary grants and threepence in the pound from officers' wages. The entitlement to a widow's pension, unless the officer was killed in action, was taken from warrant officers' widows in 1830 and reintroduced in 1864. In 1836 the administration of officers' widows' pensions became the Admiralty's responsibility, leaving the Greenwich Hospital as the only independent body paying special or supplementary pensions.

In addition to these pensions, a lump sum equal to one year's wages, known as the Royal Bounty (see 4.8.1), was payable to the widows and children of officers and ratings killed in action or on active duty, and in cases of need to either of their parents if widowed and aged 50 or over.

Pensions were also paid by the Admiralty for wounds – to commissioned officers and masters from 1673, to surgeons from 1689, to warrant officers and engineers from 1866, and to midshipmen and cadets from 1902. Warrant officers who were permanently disabled or wounded as a result of service received similar pensions from the Chatham Chest.

Greenwich Hospital out-pensions were paid to a small number of captains, commanders and lieutenants from 1814; and from 1871 some Greenwich Hospital pensions, such as the Travers, Popeley and Canada Fund pensions, were made available for deserving commissioned and warrant officers.

In 1837, good-service pensions were introduced for flag officers and captains.

4.9.2 Ratings' pensions

It was not until 1859, when the recommendations of the 1858 Royal Commission on manning the navy were implemented by Parliament and the naval authorities, that pensions for service were granted automatically to all ratings. In their report, the Commission recommended that pensions be paid to ratings after 20 years' continuous service.

Up to 1859 there was no guarantee that a rating would receive a pension for service. Before then, virtually the only pensions awarded to ratings were those granted to seamen who had been wounded or hurt in action or on duty. These were paid by either the Board of Commissioners for the Sick and Wounded (commonly known as the Sick and Hurt Board), the Chatham Chest or Greenwich Hospital. Established in 1653 and wound up in 1806, the Board of Commissioners for the Sick and Wounded had the authority to grant gratuities and annual pensions to wounded men. The Chatham Chest – a charity founded in 1581, supported by the monthly deduction of sixpence from officers' and ratings' pay – also paid pensions either for life or a limited period or as one-off payments to ratings hurt or wounded in naval service.

Founded in 1694 as a home for pensioned seamen, the Royal Greenwich Hospital admitted its first pensioners in January 1705. It was supported by sixpence a month deducted from the wages of naval and merchant seamen, augmented by unclaimed prize money and the rents of estates forfeited following the Jacobite rebellion of 1715. In addition to providing care for resident in-pensioners, from 1763 the hospital paid out-pensions to deserving applicants who had served in the navy, and it also provided pensions and allowances for widows and orphans of seamen. In 1832 the direction of Greenwich Hospital passed to the Admiralty. In 1869 the hospital ceased to house in-pensioners, and in 1873 part of the building was taken over by the Royal Naval College.

Both in-pensions and out-pensions were available by application, but there was no limit to the latter, other than the hospital's income, and the number of recipients was very high. To obtain an out-pension, claimants had to show proof of former service in the navy, though there was no bar to them holding other employment, as the pensions were scarcely sufficient to live on. Many out-pensioners were still young men and it was possible for both in-pensioners and out-pensioners to re-enter the navy, at which point their pension lapsed until their discharge. After the introduction of continuous service in 1853, the majority of ratings would sign their first engagement at 18 – often having entered the navy as boys – and would therefore retire at 38, or at 43 if they signed on for a 'fifth five'. This left a man with much of his working life remaining, and many naval pensioners held other jobs. Such pensioners were often employed in dockyards and naval establishments. Few records of pension payments to ratings survive, but it is possible to tell who received service pensions from the continuous service engagement books (see 3.3.1 and 3.3.1.2) and service registers (see 3.3.2).

4.9.3 Administration of pensions after 1835

In 1835 the Paymaster General's duties – originally confined to the pay of the armed services – were extended to cover pensions payable to officers and their widows and dependants.

It was during the second Boer War (1899–1902) that the state first assumed responsibility for the support of dependants of servicemen killed or disabled in war. Previously, since the Crimean War (1854–5), the Royal Patriotic Fund Commission, which was funded by private subscriptions, had paid grants to disabled naval personnel and their dependants. A report presented by the Commission to Parliament in 1861 lists the names of 164 ratings' children it maintained. The report gives their father's name and rating, name of ship served on, his date and place of death, their mother's name, where the mother collected her grant, the child's age and address, and details about what happened to the child. A subsequent report, in 1871, provides details of 109 applications for grants – from dependants of deceased warrant officers and ratings who served in the Crimean War – that had been rejected by the Commission. The applicant's name is given, together with personal information about the deceased, such as name and rank, ship served on, length of service in the war, dates and details of illnesses or injury suffered, details of subsequent service and medical treatment, date of pension, date, place and cause of death, age at death, date of marriage, reasons why the application was refused and the date of refusal. The *Parliamentary Papers* for 1801–2001 are available on microfiche in the Microfilm Reading Room: these reports will be found under references **66.322–323** (1860) and **77.362–363** (1871).

In 1915 a statutory committee of the Commission was appointed to regulate the payment of supplementary pensions and allowances and the provision of medical care from the fund. Since voluntary subscriptions proved insufficient, in August 1916 the Treasury agreed to accept financial responsibility for the statutory committee's needs and to bring the Commission under parliamentary control, along with other organizations dealing with war pensions. In September 1916, a Cabinet committee recommended the formation of a pensions board under a minister of the Crown. After modification by Parliament, the committee's proposals were enacted as the Ministry of Pensions Act 1916, which provided for a single department to administer military and naval war pensions.

The Ministry of Pensions was established in December 1916, and in February 1917 it took over the Admiralty's responsibilities for the administration of naval death and disability pensions and allowances, including those arising from the First World War and those granted prior to 18 September 1914; in addition, it took over responsibility for various special pensions, the Greenwich Hospital pensions mentioned above, and service pensions held in conjunction with war disability pensions since September 1914. These arrangements continued until March 1924 and 1925 respectively.

In 1917, when the Ministry of Pensions came in to being, it was decided that the Admiralty should retain responsibility for service pensions (including those authorized under older regulations based upon disablement), gallantry and special campaign pensions, and pensions from Greenwich Hospital Funds. Also, they continued, under special arrangements, to deal with disability pensions held in conjunction with prewar service records. Subsequently, in October 1921, responsibility for peacetime death and disability pensions, allowances and special pensions was restored to the Admiralty. The Ministry of Pensions retained general control of war pensions arising from the First World War and previous wars, and from 1920 it took charge of pensions for wounded officers arising from the First World War.

4.9.4 Searching pension records

The next sections (4.9.5 to 4.9.14) describe, usually in date order, the main sources of records relating to the different types of pension paid to officers and ratings from the mid seventeenth century onwards. Owing to the variety of pensions and the lack of records for some periods, information about pensions paid to naval personnel can sometimes be difficult to find.

Before the introduction of continuous service and the amelioration of terms of service that followed it, most of the pensions provided by Greenwich Hospital were paid to ratings. So if you are searching for pension records relating to a rating, the best starting point is likely to be the applications to Greenwich Hospital for pensions or other relief described in 4.9.5. From these, it should be possible to determine whether the rating received an out-pension – which he would probably have collected from the Customs or Excise office nearest to where he lived – or whether he was an in-pensioner resident in Greenwich Hospital. The records of out-pension payments are described in 4.9.6, and those for in-pensioners in 4.9.7.

If you come across a reference to a Greenwich naval pensioner in documents such as census returns or birth, marriage or death certificates, then a search in the records described in either 4.9.6 or 4.9.7 is recommended, depending on whether he was an out-pensioner or an in-pensioner. In cases where a deceased rating's widow or next of kin applied for or received a pension or an allowance, the records in 4.9.10 should be searched, along with those mentioned in 4.9.12 and 4.9.13. For records of pensions paid to wounded ratings, see 4.9.11 and 4.9.12.

The main sources for officers' pensions (particularly, officers' superannuation and retirement pensions) are outlined in 4.9.8. Records concerning pensions and allowances paid to officers' widows and next of kin are summarized in sections 4.9.9 and 4.9.12–13, while those relating to pensions for wounded officers are described in 4.9.11 and 4.9.12.

4.9.5 Applications to Greenwich Hospital for pensions or other relief

Registers of ratings who applied between 1737 and 1763 for admission to Greenwich Hospital as in-pensioners are located in **ADM 6/223–224**. These registers include surname indexes and list name, rating, total time served, date when admitted, and address (rarely completed). **ADM 6/225–266** consist of similar registers for 1781–4 and 1816–59. Name card indexes to **ADM 6/223–247** are available in the Research Enquiries Room.

ADM 6/271–320 contain registers of applications made by ratings between 1789 and 1859 for entry (admission to the hospital as in-pensioners), out-pensions or other relief. These list name and age, time served, when discharged from the service, reason for application, and decision reached. The following abbreviations are used in the decision column of the registers:

Pr No	Pension number
P	Hospital pension
R	Rejected
A	Admitted
CP	Chatham Chest pension

Figures in the decision column indicate the annual amount of out-pension to be paid.

Applications made by ratings during 1790–1865 for admission as in-pensioners are in **ADM 73/1–35**. For details of these records, see 3.2.2.

Service records of warrant officers and ratings that accompanied pension applications made between 1801 and 1894 can be found in **ADM 29/1–96**. For more about these records, see 3.2.1.

An alphabetical register of ratings who applied for pensions or relief during 1821–30 is located in **ADM 6/322**. This includes details such as name and age, date of application, nature of answer, total time served, disease/wound, and in some instances ships served on and duration of pension.

Lists of seamen awarded Greenwich Hospital pensions during 1868–70, which provide age and address, are in **WO 23/24**.

PMG 70/1–3, 5–6, 9, 11, 13, 15, 17, 19–20, 22, 24, 26 and **28–30** are records for April 1866 to March 1891 of pensions paid to commissioned and warrant officers under the Admiralty order in council of 16 February 1866. They list details such as name and address, rank, names of authorities, attorney and assignees, date of authority for pension, date pension to begin, rate per annum, date paid, where paid (Customs), and date of death. **PMG 70/11, 15, 17, 19, 26** and **28** contain surname indexes.

4.9.6 Greenwich Hospital out-pension records

Admiralty and Secretariat out-letters for 1763–1815 concerning the nomination of persons to become out-pensioners can be found in **ADM 2/1143–1146**, which contain surname indexes.

The records in **ADM 73/95–131** of out-pension payments to ratings between 1781 and 1809 include dates of death. In some instances the records in **ADM 22/254–443** of payments to warrant officers and ratings during 1814–46 (which are arranged in date order and by initial letter of surname) list dates of death, too. Most of the records in **ADM 22/254–261**, which cover 1814, simply state when the pension was paid and how much, whereas **ADM 22/262–443** can provide details such as date of entry into the navy and in what ship the warrant officer or rating was wounded and last served.

Lists of out-pension payments to captains, commanders and lieutenants are to be found in **ADM 22/47–48** for 1815–39, in **ADM 11/70/3** for 1820–9, and in **ADM 6/270** (which contains a surname index) for 1835–7. These documents may provide dates of death.

The out-pension returns for 1842–83 in **WO 22** may be useful if you are trying to trace a service number or changes of address. They record when each pension began and whether it was permanent or temporary, and also indicate whether it ceased because of the death of the pensioner (in which case, age and date of death are given). These returns are arranged by the various districts in the UK and Channel Islands, India, the colonies and certain foreign stations to where the pension was sent.

PMG 71/1–13 are records of out-pension payments made between January 1846 and March 1921, mainly to captains, commanders, lieutenants, staff commanders, and masters (**PMG 71/3–13**). Addresses and dates of death are given.

4.9.7 Greenwich Hospital in-pension records

The rough entry book of ratings admitted to Greenwich Hospital during 1705–45 in **ADM 73/51** lists name, rating, date of entry, and either date of discharge or death or other reasons why the pension ended. Similar information, relating to both warrant officers and ratings, can be found in **ADM 73/36** (surname-indexed by **ADM 73/37**) for 1704–1803 and in **ADM 73/38** (surname-indexed by **ADM 73/39**) for 1764–1812.

Lists of ratings whose applications to enter the hospital were rejected during 1742–64 are in **ADM 6/223–224**, which include surname indexes.

Entry books of warrant officers and ratings admitted to Greenwich Hospital during 1748–1873 are located in **ADM 73/52–63.** These list date of entry, name and age, if married, number of children, where born, last place of residence (usually district, but address can be given), time served in the navy, trade, last ship served in, and if wounded (together with cause).

ADM 73/65 contains accounts of ratings admitted to the hospital between 1764 and 1802. These give date of entry, name and age, physical description, if wounded (with details), and ship last served in. In addition, they may note whether the pensioner was married, number of children (with ages), and wife's name and address. Similar accounts for 1803–65 can be found in **ADM 73/66–69**.

The register of warrant officers and ratings and their families for 1806–63 in **ADM 73/47** lists pensioner's entry date, name and age, naval service, parish or county, wounds or injuries (and in what ship), if married (when and where), wife's residence, children aged under 20, last ship served in, and cause of pension being ended. It is name-indexed by **ADM 73/48** and **ADM 73/50**.

4.9.8 Officers' Admiralty superannuation, retirement and other pensions

Bills drawn by the Treasurer of the Navy that include details of officers' superannuation and retirement pensions can be found in **ADM 18**, which is arranged in date order. You will find information relating to captains, 1666–1747, in **ADM 18/39–97**; masters, surgeons, pursers, boatswains, gunners, carpenters, cooks, 1672–1781, in **ADM 18/50–119**; lieutenants, 1737–81, in **ADM 18/92–119**; and 'yellow admirals' (see 4.9.1), for 1747–81, in **ADM 18/98–119**. **ADM 18/42–50** and **52–118** contain surname indexes. Similar information for 1689–1832 is located in **ADM 7/809–821**, which is surname-indexed by **ADM 7/823** (a copy of this index is in the Research Enquiries Room).

A register for 1761–1809 listing the names of commissioned and warrant officers who were to receive pensions can be found in **ADM 22/51**.

The following lists of retired or superannuated officers can be found in **ADM 11** (in some instances dates of retirement or discharge are given):

Document	Rank	Dates
ADM 11/70/3	Retired flag officers	1821–32
ADM 11/72/3	Retired flag officers	1833–8
ADM 11/72/3	Retired captains	1840–2
ADM 11/72/3	Superannuated commanders	1833–42
ADM 11/67/2	Lieutenants superannuated with rank of commander	1796–1803
ADM 11/69/3	Superannuated lieutenants	1812–19

Registers for 1781–1820 recording payments of superannuation and retirement pensions to flag officers, captains, commanders and lieutenants are to be found in **ADM 22/1–5** and **17–24**. These give name and rank, amounts paid, on what grounds, and in some instances details of ships served on. If an entry has been struck through, that indicates the officer has died. **ADM 22/2–5** and **17–24** contain surname indexes.

Records relating to payments of superannuation and retirement pensions to commissioned and warrant officers can be found in **ADM 22/27–30** (which are arranged by initial letter of surname and contain surname indexes) for 1820–1; in **ADM 23/22–23** for 1830–6; in **ADM 23/24** for 1870–80; in **ADM 23/161–163, 165–167** and **172** for 1899–1932; and in **ADM 22/488–522** for 1881–1934.

Lists of pensions paid to flag officers, captains, commanders and lieutenants during 1818–20, 1822–6 and 1828–32 are located in **ADM 22/31–33, 35–36** and **39–46** respectively. Records of superannuation payments to commissioned officers between October 1836 and March 1920 can be found in **PMG 15/1–3, 5–7, 9–13, 15–19, 21–25, 27–73, 79–82, 88–91, 97–100, 106–109, 115–118, 124–127, 149–164** and **170–174**. These records include name and rank, date of authority for pension, amount of payment, and date when paid. From April 1843, the pensioner's address and date of death are also given. **PMG 15/1–3** and **5–7** contain surname indexes; from **PMG 15/9** onwards the records are arranged by initial letter of surname.

ADM 104/66 contains records of pensions paid to the inspector general of hospitals, deputy inspector general of hospitals, physicians, staff surgeons and surgeons during 1805–75. They include details such as name and address, age on retirement, the date of the Board's order for retirement, cause of removal, and in some instances dates of leave.

Records of superannuation paid to warrant officers between October 1836 and March 1924 are in **PMG 16/1**, **3–6**, **8–15**, **17** and **PMG 69/1–29**. These give name, age and rank, cause of pension, time served, date of authority for pension, amount granted, date paid, and date of death. From 1872, pensioners' addresses can also be found.

Records of payments of Greenwich Hospital pensions to commissioned and warrant officers from 1871 to 1931 are located in **ADM 165/1–6**, which are arranged alphabetically; from 1 April 1951 to 1961 they are in **ADM 165/9**, which contains a surname index. Records of payments to lieutenants between October 1874 and March 1900 are in **PMG 16/18–25**.

Details of naval pensions to old and disabled captains, staff captains and staff commanders for 1878–85 and 1891–9 are in **ADM 23/83** and **ADM 23/87–88**.

Records of pensions paid to officers for good or meritorious service can be found in **ADM 23/23** for 1837–47, **PMG 16/3–5** for 1839–47, **ADM 23/23** for 1845–63, **PMG 16/6, 8–30** for 1848–1920, **ADM 23/89–93** for 1866–1900, and **ADM 23/206–207** for 1916–28.

4.9.9 Officers' widows and next of kin pensions and allowances and Charity for the Relief of Officers' Widows records*

Bills drawn by the Treasurer of the Navy include references to pensions payable on navy estimates to officers' widows and orphans. **ADM 18/53–118**, which contain these records for 1673–1780, are arranged in date order and each has a surname index.

Records of Chatham Chest pensions paid to officers' widows for 1653–1799 are described in 4.9.12.

Summary records for 1689–1832 of pensions paid to officers' widows and next of kin by the Admiralty under orders in council can be found in **ADM 7/809–821**. This is surname-indexed by **ADM 7/823**, a copy of which is in the Research Enquiries Room.

Certificates and other papers submitted by officers' widows to the Charity for the Relief of Officers Widows between 1797 and 1829 are in **ADM 6/335–384**, for which there is a name card index in the Research Enquiries Room.

Records of applications for officers' widows' pensions between 1809 and 1820 are in **ADM 22/238**. These give widow's name and maiden name; husband's name, rank, last ship served on, and date of death; date of marriage and where married. Similar information for 1818–29 can be found in **ADM 6/330**. Records of Compassionate Fund payments to officers' widows for 1809–1928 are described in 4.9.13.

An index of officers' widows' pensions relating to records for 1846–65 held in **ADM 1** can be found in Military Memorandum **MN 409**, available at the enquiry desk in the Research Enquiries Room. This index provides **ADM 1** document references, officer's name, rank and date of death, place of marriage, age at marriage, wife's name and age at marriage, and wife's address.

Widows granted pensions were entitled to them until death or remarriage. The pay books for officers' widows' pensions in **ADM 22/56–237**, which cover 1734–1835, list widow's name, husband's rank, dates of payment and to whom, and are signed by the widow. From 1744 (**ADM 22/61**), dates of widow's death, burial or remarriage and of

*The records mentioned in this section apply to both commissioned and warrant officers unless otherwise specified.

her husband's death can also be found. Some columns may not be completed. The 'to whom' column refers to the nearest Customs office.

ADM 23/55 and **ADM 23/106–107** contain lists recording widows' pension payments from 1830 to 1878. Arranged alphabetically by name, these usually provide widow's name, husband's name and rank, date of marriage, when widow was placed on pension list, and details of private income. The payment lists in **ADM 23/108–123** (1880–99) and **ADM 23/145–160 (**1899–1932) give widow's name, husband's name and rank, date of authority for pension, and dates of death.

Diverse records of payments of pensions and allowances to officers' widows and next of kin can be found in **PMG 16/2–5** and **7–14** covering 1836–70. **PMG 19/1–94** cover 1836–1929 and relate to widows only (**PMG 19/43–94** may list widows' addresses, and **PMG 19/63–94** widows' ages and details of private income). **PMG 20/1–4**, **6**, **8**, **10**, **12** and **17–18** cover October 1870 to March 1899 and provide information about pensions paid under Admiralty orders in council to widows and next of kin.

ADM 23/161–165 are records of pensions paid between 1899 and 1919 to relatives of officers who had been killed. The records in **PMG 44/8–9** of Ministry of Pensions payments made between April 1916 and March 1920 to relatives of officers killed in service provide information such as address of relative, details of private income, and age or year of birth. Further records of pensions paid to the widows and relatives of officers killed between 1916 and 1932 are in **ADM 23/168–169**.

Details of Ministry of Pensions supplementary allowances and special grants paid to officers and to officers' widows or next of kin during 1916–20 can be found in **PMG 43/1**. This document includes a surname index and provides name of next of kin, address, details of private income, and date of birth. Records of pensions paid during 1922–6 to widows, children and other dependants of engineers, masters and cooks killed in warlike operations are in **ADM 23/170**.

Registers of claims to Greenwich Hospital for maintenance of orphan daughters of boatswains, gunners and carpenters can be found in **ADM 162/1–2** and **ADM 162/9**, which range from 1882 to 1959, with a gap between 1911 and 1950. These registers, which contain surname indexes, record the child's date of birth, her parents' names, whether either of them is living (dates of death given), and the number of children under 15 dependent on the applicant. Similar registers of claims to Greenwich Hospital for the children of deceased or distressed flag officers, captains, commanders and lieutenants between July 1883 and June 1922 are in **ADM 163/1–2**, which include surname indexes.

A register of Greenwich Hospital grants made between 15 July 1907 and 2 January 1933 towards the education and maintenance of the children of flag officers, captains, commanders and lieutenants can be found in **ADM 164/1**, which contains a surname index. The register lists child's name, date of birth, father's name and rank, name and address of parent or guardian, and name of school, together with details of the grant.

4.9.10 Ratings' widows and next of kin: pensions and allowances

Records of ratings' widows receiving Chatham Chest payments for 1653–1799 are described in 4.9.12. For payments of the Royal Bounty to the wives, children and widowed parents of ratings killed in action, see 4.8.1.

ADM 22/54–55 consist of applications made by ratings' widows and next of kin during 1832–6 for pensions and allowances or arrears. These documents provide name and address of claimant, relationship to deceased, and rating's name and date of death.

Records of pensions paid under Admiralty orders in council to widows and dependants of ratings killed in service between October 1836 and September 1870 are in **PMG 16/2–5** and **7–14**.

ADM 80/107 provides details of gratuities paid to widows of men killed in action during 1863–5. It lists the rating's name, date of death, cause of death, ship's name, amount of pay, and widow's name and address.

Registers of claims to Greenwich Hospital for maintenance of orphan daughters between 1882 and 1959 (with a gap between August 1911 and 1950) are located in **ADM 162/1–2** and **ADM 162/9**, while registers of claims for maintenance of orphan boys (February 1884 to July 1959) are in **ADM 162/3–8**. These records, all of which include surname indexes, note the child's name, date of birth, parents' names, whether either of them is living, the number of children under 15 dependent on the applicant, and in some instances the father's date of death.

A register of applications made between September 1892 and August 1911 by widows and other dependants for Greenwich Hospital pensions and gratuities in respect of seamen killed in action can be found in **ADM 166/13**, which contains a surname index. This register provides the name and address of the applicant, the deceased's name, rating and ship, the cause of death, and details of the hospital's decision.

A list dated 11 October 1899 of ratings' widows who were receiving pensions is to be found in **ADM 169/320**.

In **PIN 71** there are selected case files on widows' pensions of ratings killed in service before the First World War. The files contain medical records (in some cases including X-rays), accounts of how and where illnesses or injuries occurred, and the men's own accounts of incidents they were involved in. Conduct sheets are also included, providing a physical description and recording place of birth, age, names of parents and children, religion, and marital and parental status. These files cover the period 1854–1975.

PIN 82 provides a sample of First World War (mostly army) widows' pension forms, from the Ministry of Pensions and its successors. These forms record widow's name and place of residence; particulars of deceased husband's service; date, place and cause of death or injury; details of assessment and entitlement to pension awards; amount awarded and the length of time for which the award was granted. Some forms mention the award of mourning grants and are accompanied by copies of death certificates.

The **PIN 71** and **PIN 82** series lists are arranged in name order. They can be easily searched using the PRO online catalogue (accessible on www.pro.gov.uk), entering a person's name as the keyword.

ADM 166/14, which has a surname index, contains details relating to ratings killed on duty but not during warlike operations. The information it provides – which is similar to that found in **ADM 166/13** (see above) – ranges from August 1911 to 1933 and also covers 1949.

Records of pensions paid during 1922–6 to widows, children and other dependants of ratings killed in action are in **ADM 23/170**. Details of allowances paid to rating's widows and orphans between April 1921 and March 1926 can be found in **PMG 72/1–2**. Records of similar payments to next of kin during 1922–6 are in **ADM 23/171**.

Selected files giving details of Second World War widows' pensions can be found in **PIN 80/29–34** and **PIN 91/159–160**.

4.9.11 Pensions for wounds and disability

Records of Chatham Chest payments to wounded or injured warrant officers and ratings are described in 4.9.12.

Bills drawn by the Treasurer of the Navy relating to pensions for wounds payable on the navy estimates to flag officers, captains, commanders, and lieutenants between 1673 and 1780 are located in **ADM 18/53–118** (each of these includes a surname index). **ADM 30/63/2** contains letters dating from 1757–63 from officers claiming pensions for wounds.

Records of payments of pensions for wounds to officers can also be found in the following documents:

- **ADM 22/27–30** for 1820–1 (these records contain surname indexes)
- **ADM 23/29–31** for 1834–84 (which also includes entries for ratings)
- **PMG 16/1**, **3–6**, **8–31** for October 1836 to March 1920 (officers' addresses are given in **PMG 16/17–31**)
- **ADM 23/94** for 1880–6
- **ADM 23/90–93** for 1886–1900

These records state name and rank, when pension started, dates paid, and in some instances date of death.

In **PIN 71** there are selected case files on disablement pensions paid to ratings in respect of service before the First World War. For further details about these records, see 4.9.10.

PMG 42/13–14 contain Ministry of Pensions records giving details of payments of temporary retired pay and gratuities awarded to invalided commissioned and warrant officers between April 1917 and December 1919. Arranged by initial letter of officers' surname, these documents list establishment number, name and address, rank, year of birth, start and end date of pension, rate per annum, and dates of payment.

Selected First World War disability pension award files can be found in **PIN 26**. Details of the type of award and the personal information obtainable from these files are indicated by the codes index included in the series list. Most of these files are closed for 50 years, and only three relate to officers. The cases are listed in order of date of termination of pension or death.

Ministry of Pensions special grants and supplementary allowances paid to disabled officers between 1916 and 1920 are in **PMG 43/1**. Selected Second World War disablement pension records for both officers and ratings can be found in **PIN 84/24–28** and **35** and in **PIN 91/157** and **166–167**.

4.9.12 Chatham Chest records

4.9.12.1 Pension payment records

The ledgers in **ADM 82/1–2, 14–35** and **37–119** provide a record ranging from 1653 to 1799 (with gaps for 1658–87 and 1690–4) of pensions payments to the widows of midshipmen, masters, surgeons, boatswains, gunners, carpenters, cooks and ratings who were either killed in action or permanently disabled as a result of injuries sustained in action or on duty. A search through successive ledgers may reveal the date of death of a warrant officer, rating or widow in receipt of the pension. By 1786 the ledger entries are grouped by initial letter of surname.

4.9.12.2 Compensation for wounds: lump-sum payment records

There are also ledgers recording one-off payments to midshipmen, masters, surgeons, boatswains, gunners, carpenters, cooks and ratings as compensation for wounds or injuries sustained in action or while on duty. These are arranged by date of payment, which could be some time after compensation was agreed. The earliest ledgers in **ADM 82/1–2**, which cover 1653–7, give name, type of injury and amount of compensation paid. Further ledgers can be found in **ADM 82/12** (1675–93), **ADM 82/16–36** (1689–1713), **ADM 82/38–58** (1714–37), **ADM 82/60–116** (1739–96) and **ADM 82/124** (1749–92). These usually give name, type of injury, ship's name, date of wound, and amount of relief paid.

ADM 82/126, which is dated 1763, contains the signatures of officers approving the claim; the details it provides are of a similar kind to those found in **ADM 82/1–2** (see above). Also dated 1763, **ADM 82/127** consists of hurt certificates issued for Chatham Chest purposes, which give the same information as **ADM 82/126**. A surname index to **ADM 82/126–127** is available in the Research Enquiries Room.

ADM 82/115–116 consist of monthly lists extending from November 1794 to July 1807. In addition to providing details of a similar kind to those found in **ADM 82/1–2**, from 4 December 1803 it gives the date when the pensioner was examined, age, place of birth, a physical description, and parents' first names.

4.9.12.3 Payment records indexes

The payment records indexes in **ADM 82/122** (1695–1779), **ADM 82/121** (1705–66), **ADM 82/120** (1744–56) and **ADM 82/123** (1779 to around 1797) usually provide pensioner's name, date and type of injury, ship served on, and date when the pension commenced or compensation was paid. These indexes do not appear to tie in with **ADM 82/1–2** and **14–119**, but the date when the pension began or compensation was paid can be used as a starting point for a search.

4.9.13 The Compassionate Fund and Compassionate List

The Compassionate Fund (later Compassionate List) was established by a parliamentary grant in 1809 in order to provide support for dependants of commissioned and warrant officers who were killed or died in service. Payments continued until an officer's widow remarried or died, or when an orphan reached the age when payments had to end.

Applications made by officer's widows and orphans to the Compassionate Fund between 1809 and 1836 are located in **ADM 6/323–328**, each of which includes a surname index. These applications give the name, age and address of the widow or orphan; date of application and by whom made; officer's name and rank, date of death, length of service, in what ship or division last served, and when and where married; reason for the applicant not being granted a regular pension; and details of the Admiralty's decision about the case. If the application was made by a widow, further details about children and private income are included. Details of the assessments of the applications received by the Fund during 1810–36 can be found in **ADM 22/239–250**.

Admiralty out-letters regarding applications made (mainly by or on behalf of orphans) between 1809 and 1845 are in **ADM 2/1085–1089**, each of which contains a surname index. Many of the applications have the applicant's address on them.

ADM 22/251–252 are Compassionate Fund indexes for 1809–51, which provide information such as when individuals were placed on the Fund's list, their age, the sum allowed, when the allowance ceased, and the reason why. Similar information can be found in **ADM 23/45**, which covers 1809–78.

Records of allowances paid from the Fund during 1829–32 are in **ADM 22/253**, while those for 1839–1921 are in **PMG 18/1–38**. In these records, the age and address of the person sent the allowance are sometimes given. Details of payments made between October 1877 and March 1920 can be found in **PMG 16/19–30**.

ADM 23/206–207 contains records of compassionate allowances paid to officers between 1916 and 1928, arranged in alphabetical order.

4.9.14 Victoria Cross and conspicuous bravery pensions

Records of payments of Victoria Cross and conspicuous bravery pensions can be found in **ADM 23/32** (May 1855 to October 1862), **ADM 23/89–93** (1866–1900), **PMG 16/13–17** (1866–74, Victoria Cross only), **PMG 16/18–30** (1874–1920) and **ADM 23/206–207** (1916–28). These records give details such as when the pension was granted, how much, where the pension was sent (address sometimes given), and date of death.

4.10 Greenwich Hospital School and the Royal Naval Asylum

The original charter of the Royal Greenwich Hospital (see 4.9.2), granted by William and Mary on 25 October 1694, outlined several aims, which were defined as 'the maintenance and education of the children of seamen happening to be slain in the service of the Crown at sea', 'further relief and encouragement of seamen' and the 'improvement of navigation and supplying of the Royal Navy with a competent number of able mariners and seamen'. Following the granting of this charter, various Acts of Parliament were passed in order to meet these objectives and to define the categories of people entitled to the benefits of the hospital school.

In 1712 the Greenwich Hospital commissioners passed a resolution stipulating that when the hospital had sufficient funds a charity school should be established to take in up to 100 children of seamen killed in action, not younger than 14 years of age, for the purpose of providing instruction in writing, arithmetic and navigation. It was envisaged that children would not be kept in the school after they had reached the age of 18. The date of this resolution, 30 December 1712, is often regarded as the founding date of the school, although it was some years before there were sufficient funds for the commissioners' plans to be put into effect.

In 1719 the number of boys to be admitted to the school was set at 10, and they had to be sons of pensioners or other poor seamen. In 1731 regulations concerning the entry of poor boys to the Royal Hospital and their maintenance and education fixed the number of boys attending the school at 60. By 1803 the number had risen to 200.

The British National Endeavour, founded in 1798, was maintained by private subscriptions until 1805. In that year it was granted parliamentary support and a royal charter, becoming the Royal Naval Asylum, and moved to Greenwich. The Royal Naval Asylum maintained and educated children of warrant officers, petty officers and seamen. Preference was given to orphans and to the children of disabled men and motherless children whose fathers were serving in distant stations. Boys were admitted between the ages of 5 and 12, and were taught reading, writing and the first four rules of arithmetic to a level that would qualify them for the duties of a seaman or other occupations. Girls were admitted between the ages of 5 and 10, and were taught writing, sewing and knitting, with a view to obtaining jobs as 'servants' or 'other female employment'.

In 1821 Greenwich Hospital School and the Royal Naval Asylum – which at this date jointly maintained and educated 800 boys and 200 girls – were amalgamated, and the name Royal Naval Asylum was used for the merged schools. But by 1830 they had been renamed, becoming Greenwich Hospital Upper and Lower School (the Upper School being the older Greenwich Hospital School).

The girls' lower class proved unsuccessful and was abolished in 1841. From then on, assistance for the education of daughters of naval officers and men was given in the way of money grants or maintenance in homes at the expense of Greenwich Hospital.

In 1861 the Lower and Upper Schools were amalgamated. Between 1861 and 1949 commissioned officers' sons were no longer admitted to the school, and in 1933 the Greenwich Hospital School moved from Greenwich to new premises at Holbrook, in Suffolk.

4.10.1 Nomination, admission, entry and leaver records

The most important series of documents relating to the entry of officers' and ratings' children into the school are the original application papers, which are often accompanied by service records, marriage and death certificates, and children's baptismal certificates. These application papers are arranged alphabetically by applicant's surname and can be found in **ADM 73/154–389**, which cover 1728–1870.

Service records of warrant officers and ratings whose children were admitted to the school can be found in **ADM 29/1–96** (see 3.2.1).

Further records relating to children who entered or left Greenwich Hospital School between 1730 and 1932 can be found in **ADM 65/68**, **ADM 66/68–79**, **ADM 67/237–242** and **254**, **ADM 73/90, 339, 390–398, 400–425, 440–443** and **448–449**, **ADM 161/1–19**, and **ADM 169/1, 25** and **230**. A Military Memorandum (**MN 437**) providing a detailed overview of these records is available at the enquiry desk in the Research Enquiries Room.

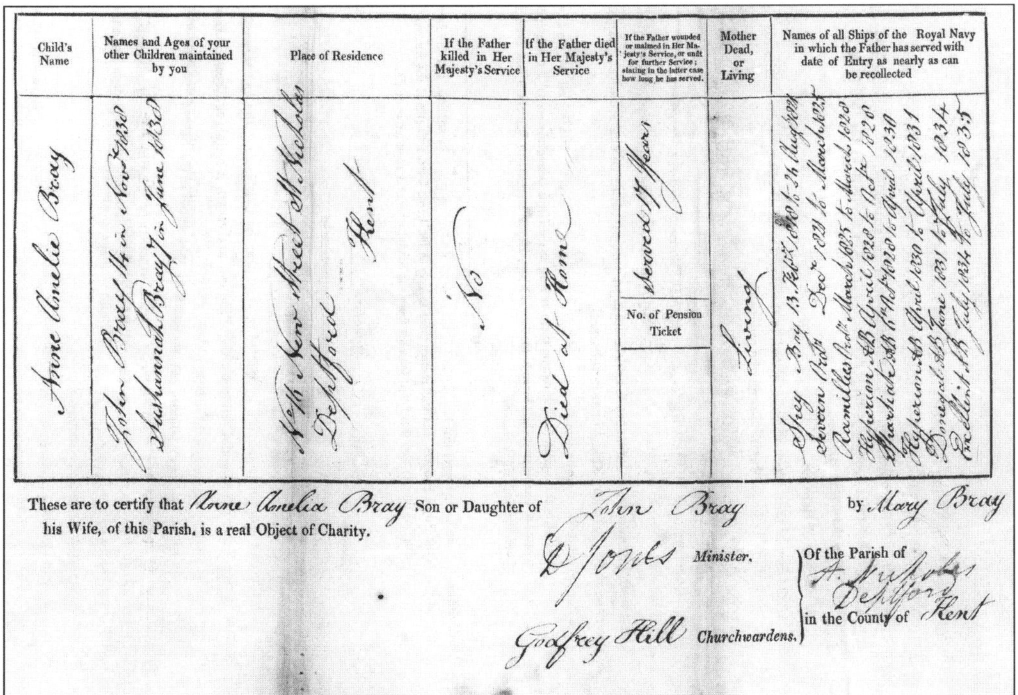

Figure 29 Part of the application papers of Anne Amelia Bray for entry to the Greenwich Hospital School, 1839. (ADM 73/176); (see p96)

5 General genealogical sources

The aim of this chapter is to highlight some of the general genealogical sources held by the Public Record Office and the Family Records Centre, plus one or two other sources, with regard to navy personnel. It should be noted that information such as dates of birth and death are also recorded in service registers and many of the other records mentioned in this guide.

5.1 Baptism, birth, marriage, burial and cemetery records

Below is a list of the key baptism, marriage and burial records held by the PRO that relate to naval personnel (for baptisms, see also under Naval Chaplaincy Service in Appendix 2). Other records, from 1913 onwards, of baptisms on board HM ships and at naval training establishments and Royal Naval Air Service stations can be found in **ADM 338**.

Place	Document references	Nature of records/date range
Alexandria, British Cemetery	**ADM 121/102**	Burials 1822–1916.
Bermuda, Boaz garrison	**ADM 6/439**	Baptisms 1918.
Bermuda, Ireland Island	**ADM 6/434** **ADM 6/435** **ADM 6/436** **ADM 338/11**	Baptisms 1824–48, Burials 1824–48. Baptisms 1847–1946. Burials 1848–1946. Baptisms 1946–54.
Chatham, dockyard chapel	**ADM 338/17–18**	Baptisms 1867–1974.
Chatham, naval barracks	**ADM 338/19–20**	Baptisms 1907–83.
Chatham, Royal Naval Hospital	**ADM 338/22**	Baptisms 1907–61.
Greece	**ADM 121/102**	Burials, Astakos (Dragamesti), 1894–1911. Burials, Corfu, 1907 and 1918. Burials, East Mudros, 1925.
Greenwich, Royal Naval	**RG 4/1669** **RG 4/1670**	Baptisms 1720–73, Marriages 1724–54, Burials 1705–58. Baptisms 1773–1812, Burials 1773–1812.

	RG 4/1671–1675	Burials 1790–1856.
	RG 4/1677	Baptisms 1813–56.
	ADM 73/460	Burials 1844–60.
	RG 8/16	Baptisms 1848–52, Burials 1848–52. Also covers Greenwich Hospital School.
	RG 8/17	Baptisms 1853–8, Burials 1853–8.
	RG 4/1676	Burials 1856–7.
	ADM 73/462	Burials, hospital chapel, 1857–1936.
	ADM 73/463	Register of graves in hospital cemetery, 1857–1966. Includes plan.
	ADM 73/465	Burials, hospital cemetery, 1857–1981. Contains surname index.
	RG 8/18	Baptisms 1859–64, Burials 1859–64. Also covers Hospital School.
	ADM 73/461	Burials 1860–70.
	ADM 73/464	Burials 1888–1966.
Greenwich, Royal Naval Asylum	RG 4/1678	Baptisms 1822–56.
Greenwich, Royal Naval Hospital School	RG 4/1679	Burials 1807–56.
Italy	ADM 121/102	Burials, Brindisi, 1915–19. Burials, Taranto, 1915–18. Burials, Venice, 1918.
Londonderry (Northern Ireland)	ADM 338/50	Burials 1941–6.
Malta, dockyard	ADM 338/51	Baptisms 1845–1959.
Malta (Bighi), Royal Naval Hospital and church	ADM 338/52	Baptisms 1924–77.
Mauritius, garrison	ADM 338/55	Baptism 1915–76.
Portland (Dorset), Royal Naval Hospital	ADM 338/59	Baptisms 1913–77.
Portsmouth, Haslar Hospital	ADM 305/103–115	Burials 1826–1954.
	ADM 305/86	Baptisms 1829–62.
Sheerness, town and garrison	ADM 6/432–433	Baptisms 1813–81.
Sheerness, dockyard church	ADM 6/430	Baptisms 1688–1798, Marriages 1744, Burials 1730–1806.
	ADM 6/431	Baptisms 1798–1812, Burials 1807–26.
	ADM 6/438	Baptisms 1885–1960.
Shotley (Suffolk), Naval Training Establishment	ADM 338/37–41	Baptisms 1905–65.

The *National Burial Index* (*NBI*), compiled by the Federation of Family History Societies (FFHS) and associates, is a database consisting of more than 5.4 million records from 4,440 English and Welsh burial registers. Currently, entries range from 1538 to the end of the twentieth century; some counties are more comprehensively represented than others; and the most extensive coverage is for 1813–37. Eventually, every English and Welsh churchyard and cemetery should be included. Each entry in the *NBI* provides the full name of the deceased, date of burial, age (where given), and the parish or cemetery where the event was recorded.

An index of births, marriages and deaths recorded in the *Naval Chronicle* between 1799 and 1818, compiled by N. Hurst, is available in the PRO Library. Issues of the *Naval Chronicle*, which was a newspaper for officers, can be viewed at the British Library Newspaper Library (for address, see Appendix 2). For the location of officers' marriage certificates held by the PRO, see 2.12.6.

The PRO holds numerous records of births, marriages and deaths of British nationals overseas. Given that the Royal Navy had many foreign bases and its ships sailed to every part of the world, these records can be a useful source for family historians. A detailed overview of these records is provided in *Tracing Your Ancestors in the Public Record Office* by Amanda Bevan (PRO, 6th edn 2002).

If you wish to obtain copies of an ancestor's birth, marriage or death certificate from 1837, you can order these **by post** from the General Register Office for England and Wales in Southport or **in person** at the Family Record Centre in London (for addresses, contact details and websites, see Appendix 2). For full details about how to order copies of certificates (including information about fees), either visit their websites or consult *The Family Records Centre – A User's Guide* by Stella Colwell (PRO, 2nd edn 2002) or *Using Birth, Marriage and Death Records* by David Annal (PRO, revised edn 2002), which also explain how to obtain copies of birth, marriage or death certificates of Scottish and Irish ancestors.

5.2 Census returns

The first comprehensive survey of the population of Britain was conducted in 1801, and since then a census has been held every 10 years, with the exception of 1941. The earliest censuses were merely head counts, but from 1841 more detailed information was collected about every person living in England, Wales, the Channel Islands and the Isle of Man.

The 1841 returns record the full name, age, sex and occupation of each individual resident in every inhabited dwelling or institution (such as prisons, orphanages and hospitals) on the night when the census was held. For those under 15, ages were given exactly. For those over 15 but under 70, ages were rounded down to the nearest five years – so someone aged 53 when the census was taken would be recorded as 50. The ages of those over 70 were rounded down to the nearest 10 years. Some indication of birthplace was included, though it consisted of simply recording whether a person was born in his or her current county of residence, or in Scotland or Ireland, or in foreign parts.

From 1851 to 1901 the census returns provide the following details about each person: full name, age, marital status, relationship to head of household, sex, occupation, and parish and county of birth. They also mention some medical disabilities. Naval officers and ratings ashore on census night figure in the ordinary domestic census returns and in the returns of naval institutions such as Greenwich Hospital.

In 1861 commanding officers of vessels at sea and in port, both at home and abroad, compiled naval ship returns giving the name, age, sex, occupation, marital status and place of birth of every officer, rating and passenger on board the ship. Similar information was collected in 1871, 1881, 1891 and 1901 (see table below). No census returns for naval ships appear to have survived from 1841 or 1851.

Microfilm copies of the returns for 1841 to 1891 can be viewed at the Family Records Centre (for address, see Appendix 2). Transcriptions of the 1881 census returns can be viewed and searched on the internet, free of charge, at www.familysearch.org. The returns for 1901 can be inspected on microfiche, by appointment, at the PRO, Kew. For up-to-date information about accessing the 1901 census returns online at the PRO and FRC or via the internet, visit www.census.pro.gov.uk. Census returns remain closed for 100 years, so those after 1901 are not yet available to the public.

For the 1861 and 1881 censuses, it is possible to search the returns using a person's name as the keyword (for details of indexes for these years, see table below).

Date census taken	Remarks
Sunday, 6 June 1841	No naval ship returns appear to have survived.
Sunday, 30 March 1851	No naval ship returns appear to have survived.
Sunday, 7 April 1861	Document references for naval ship returns: **RG 9/4433–4540**. Microfiche surname index, produced by the Family History Library, Salt Lake City, Utah, contains 120,000 entries and gives an extract of the census information for each member of a ship's crew, together with document reference and folio number. A copy of this index is available at the FRC.
Sunday, 2 April 1871	Document references for naval ship returns: **RG 10/5779–5785**. No surname index available.
Sunday, 3 April 1881	Document references for naval ship returns: **RG 11/5633–5642**. A name index is available on computers at the FRC, and on CD-ROM in the PRO Library. This index provides an extract of the census information for each member of the crew, with full document reference. Transcriptions of the whole 1881 census can be viewed and searched at www.familysearch.org.
Sunday, 5 April 1891	Naval ship returns not collected together in discrete series, but usually found at the end of the returns for the registration district in which the ship was stationed. No surname index.
Sunday, 31 March 1901	Document references for naval ship returns: **RG 13/5325–5335**. These records – which are arranged by ship's name – can be searched on microfiche at the PRO, Kew, by appointment. For current information on how to access these returns via the internet or online at the FRC and PRO, visit www.census.pro.gov.uk.

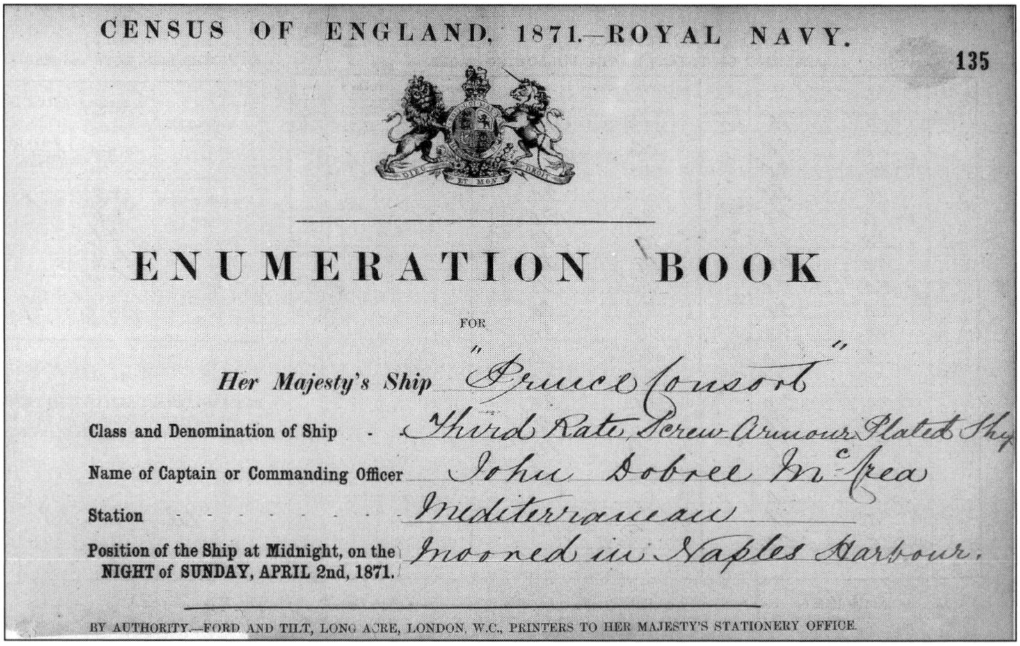

CENSUS OF ENGLAND, 1871.—ROYAL NAVY.

135

ENUMERATION BOOK

FOR

Her Majesty's Ship "Prince Consort"

Class and Denomination of Ship - Third Rate, Screw Armour Plated Ship

Name of Captain or Commanding Officer John Dobree McCrea

Station - - - - - - - - Mediterranean

Position of the Ship at Midnight, on the NIGHT of SUNDAY, APRIL 2nd, 1871. Moored in Naples Harbour.

BY AUTHORITY.—FORD AND TILT, LONG ACRE, LONDON, W.C., PRINTERS TO HER MAJESTY'S STATIONERY OFFICE.

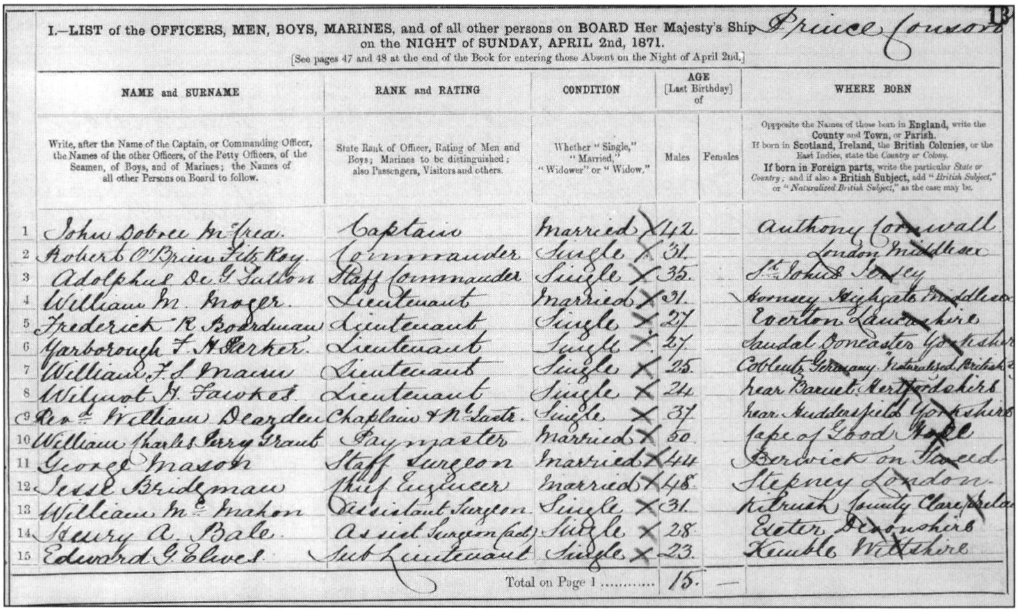

I.—LIST of the OFFICERS, MEN, BOYS, MARINES, and of all other persons on BOARD Her Majesty's Ship Prince Consort on the NIGHT of SUNDAY, APRIL 2nd, 1871.

[See pages 47 and 48 at the end of the Book for entering those Absent on the Night of April 2nd.]

13

	NAME and SURNAME	RANK and RATING	CONDITION	AGE [Last Birthday] of		WHERE BORN
	Write, after the Name of the Captain, or Commanding Officer, the Names of the other Officers, of the Petty Officers, of the Seamen, of Boys, and of Marines; the Names of all other Persons on Board to follow.	State Rank of Officer, Rating of Men and Boys; Marines to be distinguished; also Passengers, Visitors and others.	Whether "Single," "Married," "Widower" or "Widow."	Males	Females	Opposite the Names of those born in England, write the County and Town, or Parish. If born in Scotland, Ireland, the British Colonies, or the East Indies, state the Country or Colony. If born in Foreign parts, write the particular State or Country; and if also a British Subject, add "British Subject," or "Naturalized British Subject," as the case may be.
1	John Dobree McCrea.	Captain	Married	42	—	Anthony Cornwall
2	Robert O'Brien FitzRoy.	Commander	Single	31.		London Middlesex
3	Adolphus De G. Sutton	Staff Commander	Single	35.		St. Johns Jersey
4	William M. Moger.	Lieutenant	Married	31.		Hornsey Highgate Middlesex
5	Frederick R. Boardman	Lieutenant	Single	27		Everton Lancashire
6	Yarborough F. H. Parker.	Lieutenant	Single	27		Sandal Doncaster Yorkshire
7	William F. S. Mann	Lieutenant	Single	25.		Coblentz Germany Naturalized British Subject
8	Wilmot H. Fawkes.	Lieutenant	Single	24.		near Barnet Hertfordshire
9	Revd. William Dearden	Chaplain & Nl. Instr.	Single	37		near Huddersfield Yorkshire
10	William Charles Perry Grant	Paymaster	Married	50.		Cape of Good Hope
11	George Mason	Staff Surgeon	Married	44		Berwick on Tweed
12	Jesse Bridgman	Chief Engineer	Married	48.		Stepney London
13	William McMahon	Assistant Surgeon	Single	31.		Kilrush County Clare Ireland
14	Henry A. Bale	Assist Surgeon (act)	Single	28.		Exeter Devonshire
15	Edward G. Elves	Sub Lieutenant	Single	23.		Kemble Wiltshire
			Total on Page 1	15.	—	

Figure 30 An example of an 1871 ship's census return, in this case for HMS *Prince Consort* which was stationed in Naples Harbour, Italy. (RG 10/5783)

Otherwise, in order to search the naval ship returns you need to know the name of the vessel on which an officer or rating was serving when the census was held. Both the PRO and the FRC hold lists giving document references for HM ships that feature in the 1861, 1871, 1881 and 1891 returns.

The 1881, 1891 and 1901 census returns for Scotland can be searched online via the internet, for a fee, at www.origins.net.

5.3 Wills, administrations, effects papers and associated records

The nature of seamen's work was often very dangerous. The uncertainty of what could happen during long voyages and the risk of death through accident, disease or war were a constant risk. Consequently, many seamen made wills to provide for their families in the event of death.

As far back as 1698 the Admiralty was concerned with the problem of individuals impersonating deceased seamen or their executors, creditors or next of kin in order to fraudulently obtain unpaid wages by forging wills and letters of attorney (a formal instrument by which a person empowers another to act on his behalf). But it was not until 1786 – after proposals in 1716 and 1720 to set up an office for registering seamen's wills had been turned down by the Admiralty, and various Acts of Parliament had been passed to try to stop these criminal practices – that the office of Inspector of Wills was established.

The main responsibility of the Inspector of Wills was to ensure that naval wills were registered properly and that records relating to them were kept. As a result, the PRO holds many naval wills and a variety of records relating to them. These are described in the sections that follow.

5.3.1 Officers', ratings' and civilians' effects papers

5.3.1.1 Officers' and civilians' effects papers 1830–60 (ADM 45)

This series consists of applications by next of kin for unpaid wages or pensions due to deceased commissioned and warrant officers or their widows. These applications usually give the date of death of the officer, his rank, the name and address of the claimant, the date when the claim was admitted and examined, and the total value of the effects claimed. Some applications are supported by birth and marriage certificates or wills. There is a surname card index to **ADM 45/1–39** in the Microfilm Reading Room.

5.3.1.2 Seamen's effects papers in **ADM 80** and **ADM 304**

ADM 80/4–5 contain registers of dead seamen's wages for 1787–1809. Arranged alphabetically by initial letter of surname, they give name, rating and ship's name. The registers of dead men's wages for 1798–1834 in **ADM 80/6–12**, which relate mostly to merchant seamen, provide date, name, amount, how disposed of, and executor's name. Entry books of deceased patients' effects at Bighi (the Royal Naval Hospital Malta) are in **ADM 304/28** for January 1845 to July 1855, and in **ADM 304/32** for December 1851 to June 1860; these give ship's name, date of death, name of deceased, and value and details of effects. Records from Haslar Hospital for 1941–57 giving details of cash and valuables of deceased casualties can be found in **ADM 305/116**.

Lists of sales of effects of seamen who deserted from the home navy during 1814–22 are in **ADM 68/340**. Similar lists for men who deserted from ships and hospitals during 1823–7 are in **ADM 68/341–342** (there is an index of ships in **ADM 68/341**). The lists record date of ending of pay, seaman's name, ship, rating, date of desertion, and amount realized from the sale.

Accounts of funds remaining to Plymouth Hospital from the sale of effects of patients who deserted between May 1793 and September 1806 are in **ADM 68/340**. These list name of patient and ship, date when admitted to hospital, date of desertion, and the sum remaining. **ADM 80/14** records details of money belonging to deserted or deceased pensioners given to Greenwich Hospital during 1863–5.

5.3.1.3 Seamen's effects papers 1800–60 (ADM 44)

This series consists of applications from the next of kin of deceased ratings for their unpaid wages, often accompanied by supporting documents, such as wills and birth and marriage certificates, that include the claimant's name and address. These applications are arranged by the initial letter of the deceased seaman's surname and are numbered individually. Surname indexes to **ADM 44** can be found in **ADM 141**.

5.3.1.4 Registers of seamen's effects papers 1802–61 (ADM 141)

These registers serve as nominal indexes to the seamen's effects papers in **ADM 44** (see 5.3.1.3). They are arranged in an unusual alphabetical order – the initial letter is followed by the next vowel, which is followed by the first consonant after the initial letter, regardless of whether it comes before or after the vowel (see example in 5.3.1.5).

The registers for 1802–24, **ADM 141/1–3**, provide date, surname, number and date of death. Surnames A–F are covered by **ADM 141/1**, G–N by **ADM 141/2**, and O–Z by **ADM 141/3**.

The registers for 1825–48 are **ADM 141/4–6** (surnames A–F being covered by **ADM 141/4**, G–N by **ADM 141/5**, and O–Z by **ADM 141/6**), while those for 1849–61 are **ADM 141/7–9** (A–F being covered by **ADM 141/7**, G–N by **ADM 141/8**, and O–Z by **ADM 141/9**). Details listed in **ADM 141/4–9** include date, name, number, ship or address, and date of death.

5.3.1.5 Example of how to use the ADM 141 registers to find effects papers in ADM 44

A typical entry in an **ADM 141** index is as follows:

Date of notification	Name of deceased seaman	Registered number	Ship or address	Date of death	Number
1807 February 17	Adams William	446	*Leviathan*	6 Aug 1801	P1000
1807 March 12	Adamson John	455	*Renommee*	3 Apr 1806	1012
1807 April 10	Adams William	466	*Swiftsure St George*	6 June 1805	

The details that will enable you to find the application in **ADM 44** concerning the effects of the William Adams who died on the 6 August 1801 are his surname and his registered number (446), which is given in column 3 of the **ADM 141** index. To locate the relevant effects papers, his registered number has to be cross-referenced to the **ADM 44** series list. If you turn to the section in the series list containing the entries for surnames beginning with A, you will find the following listing:

ADM 44/A1	Numbers 1–250
ADM 44/A2	Numbers 251–500
ADM 44/A3	Numbers 501–750
ADM 44/A4	Numbers 751–1000

This indicates that effects papers with the registration number 446 are located in **ADM 44/A2**. When you look at **ADM 44/A2**, you will see that the papers within the box are in numerical sequence, and the application relating to the effects of William Adams bears the number 446.

5.3.2 *Warrant officers' and seamen's wills*

5.3.2.1 Warrant officers' and seamen's wills 1786–1882 (ADM 48)

The documents in **ADM 48** are the original wills, most of them written on printed forms. These were accepted as valid by the Admiralty and deposited in the Navy Office, with orders to issue cheques to the executors. They normally give the testator's name, rank and ship, together with details of his effects and the name (and sometimes the address) of the person who was to receive them in the event of his death (in most cases, his next of kin). As well as being signed and dated by the testator, wills were usually signed by the master and captain of the ship that the seaman or warrant officer was serving on when the will was made. **ADM 48** is arranged by initial letter of surname and is surname-indexed by the registers of seamen's wills in **ADM 142** (which continue for some years after the last dated will in **ADM 48**).

5.3.2.2 How to use the ADM 142 registers to find a will in ADM 48

A nominal card index relating to **ADM 48/1–33** is available in the Research Enquiries Room. Otherwise, in order to find the document reference for a will in **ADM 48** you need to know the date when the will was executed (given in column 7 in **ADM 142/1–14**) or the date of registry (given in column 1 in **ADM 142/15–18**, or column 2 in **ADM 142/19**).

5.3.3 *Registers of deceased ratings 1859–78 (ADM 154)*

The registers in **ADM 154** list the names of ratings who died in service between 1859 and 1878. They note the name of the ship the rating was serving on at the time of his death and whether a will was made, and give the name and relationship of his next of kin. Each of the registers includes a surname index. The following abbreviations appear alongside the names of next of kin (who were usually nominated as the deceased's legal representatives): F = Father, M = Mother, B = Brother, S = Sister, W = Wife. In the amount column in **ADM 154/2–9**, you will find P = Paid and U = Unpaid.

5.3.4 *Miscellaneous probate and power of attorney registers*

Miscellaneous registers of probates and administrations for 1836–1915 can be found in **PMG 50**, arranged alphabetically by initial letter of officer's, rating's or widow's surname. The earliest of these registers, **PMG 50/1**, which covers 1836–49, provides the testator's name, to whom granted (usually next of kin, with relationship given), amount sworn under, date when entered in the Audit and Paymaster General's Office, and when sent. They continue in **PMG 50/2–4** for 1849–70, and **PMG 50/5–9** for 1870–1915. These are similar in content to **PMG 50/1**, but also include the testator's address and date of death.

PMG 51 contains registers of miscellaneous powers of attorney granted by commissioned and warrant officers and their dependants from around 1800 to 1899. They are arranged in alphabetical order by initial letter of officer's surname. Surnames A–K are covered by **PMG 51/1**, while **PMG 51/2** covers L–Z. These two documents, which range from around 1800 to 1839, list the name and rank of the officer, the date when the power of attorney was executed, and in whose favour (name of agent or next of kin, with address). Further registers of this kind can be found in **PMG 51/3** (April 1825 to December 1848), **PMG 51/4** (c. 1830–8) and **PMG 51/5–17** (December 1836 to 1899). These are similar in content to **PMG 51/1–2**, except that **PMG 51/3** sometimes gives date of death and **PMG 51/5–17** do not provide addresses of agents or next of kin.

5.3.5 Miscellaneous records relating to wills

ADM 80/108 records the probate of wills of Greenwich Hospital pensioners and staff during 1732–67. It gives the names of the testator and executors, plus the date of probate, and includes a surname index.

Certificates sent to the Navy Bill Office by next of kin during 1795–1807, in order to obtain letters of administration for deceased officers and ratings, have been preserved in **HCA 30/455–458**. These certificates give the applicant's name and relationship to the deceased, where residing, the deceased's name, rank and ship, and date of death.

A register of wills made at the Royal Naval Hospital Gibraltar between 1809 and 1815 is in **ADM 105/40**. It gives the testator's name and ship, the date of the will, in whose favour, when sent to the Inspector of Wills, witnesses' names, by whom filled in, and the name of the physician or surgeon certifying the sanity of the patient.

Inspector's Branch papers relating to official precedents and solicitors' opinions concerning wills are in **ADM 198/78**, which covers 1833–61 and includes a subject index.

An entry book of wills made by patients in Greenwich Hospital between 1861 and 1869 is in **ADM 80/109**.

5.3.6 Prerogative Court of Canterbury (PCC) wills and administrations 1383–1858

The Prerogative Court of Canterbury (PCC) was the most senior of the ecclesiastical courts that proved wills prior to 1858. It had the responsibility for proving the wills of naval officers and ratings who died abroad; and until 1815 the wills of naval officers and ratings who died with more than £20 of wages due to them.

PCC wills from 1383 to 1858 are in **PROB 11**, and letters of administration from 1559 to 1858 in **PROB 6**. These series, plus the indexes to them in **PROB 12**, are available on microfilm at the FRC and in the Microfilm Reading Room of the PRO, Kew. The **PROB 12** indexes are arranged by year and then (within each year) alphabetically by initial letter of surname. Note that the wills and administrations recorded in **PROB 12** are entered by date of probate, which may be some time – in some instances, years – after the date of death. In the **PROB 12** indexes, entries pertaining to naval officers and ratings often indicate the name of the ship the person was serving on when the will was made, or include the abbreviation 'Pts' (signifying 'foreign parts').

Wills in **PROB 11** usually give information concerning the deceased's next of kin, and details about personal effects and property. Letters of administration in **PROB 6** provide the name(s) of the administrator(s), with relationship to the deceased. From 1796, they also give the estimated value of the deceased's estate and effects.

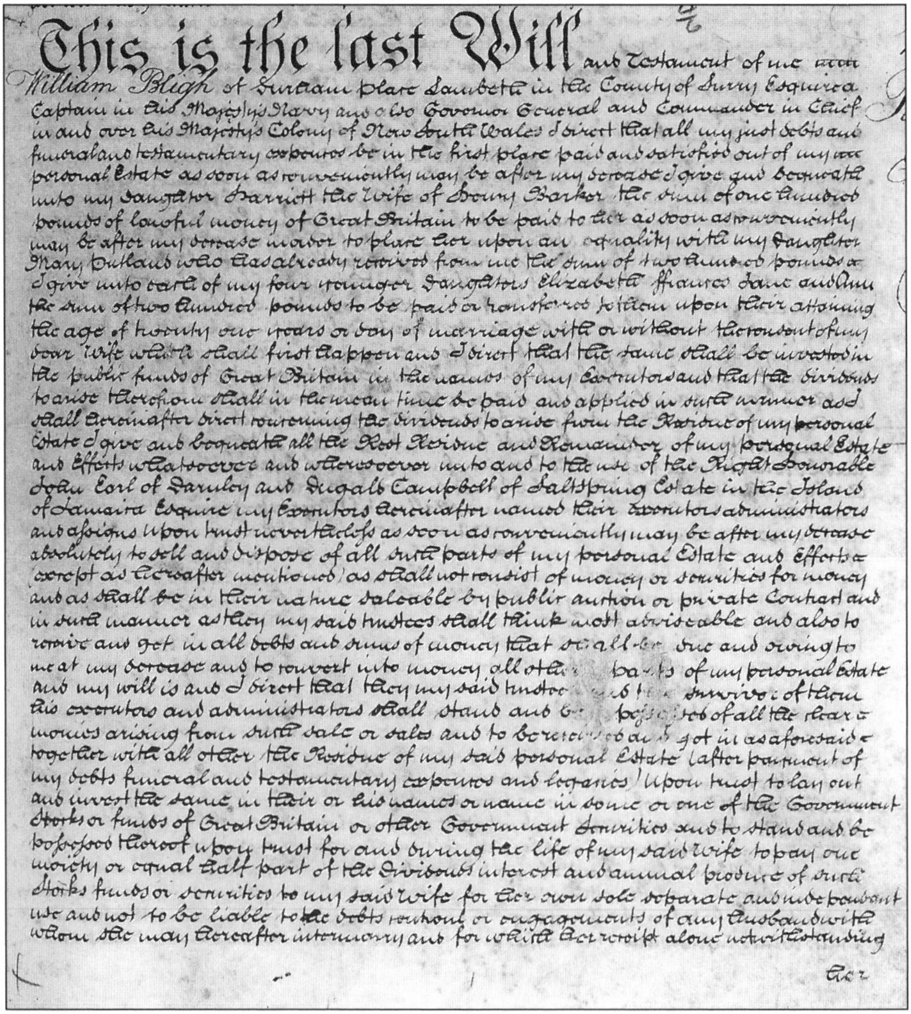

This is the last Will and Testament of me
William Bligh of Durham Place Lambeth in the County of Surry Esquire a
Captain in His Majesty's Navy and also Governor General and Commander in Chief
in and over His Majesty's Colony of New South Wales I direct that all my just debts and
funeral and testamentary expenses be in the first place paid and satisfied out of my
personal Estate as soon as conveniently may be after my decease I give and bequeath
unto my daughter Harriett the wife of Henry Barker the sum of one hundred
pounds of lawful money of Great Britain to be paid to her as soon as conveniently
may be after my decease in order to place her upon an equality with my daughter
Mary Putland who has already received from me the sum of two hundred pounds
I give unto each of my four younger daughters Elizabeth Frances Jane and Ann
the sum of two hundred pounds to be paid or transferred to them upon their attaining
the age of twenty one years or day of marriage with or without the consent of my
dear Wife which shall first happen and I direct that the same shall be invested in
the public funds of Great Britain in the names of my Executors and that the dividends
to arise therefrom shall in the mean time be paid and applied in such manner as I
shall hereinafter direct concerning the dividends to arise from the Residue of my personal
Estate I give and bequeath all the Rest Residue and Remainder of my personal Estate
and Effects whatsoever and wheresoever unto and to the use of the Right Honourable
John Earl of Darnley and Dugald Campbell of Saltspring Estate in the Island
of Jamaica Esquire my Executors hereinafter named their executors administrators
and assigns Upon trust nevertheless as soon as conveniently may be after my decease
absolutely to sell and dispose of all such parts of my personal Estate and Effects
(except as hereafter mentioned) as shall not consist of money or securities for money
and as shall be in their nature saleable by public auction or private Contract and
in such manner as they my said trustees shall think most adviseable and also to
receive and get in all debts and sums of money that shall be due and owing to
me at my decease and to convert into money all other parts of my personal Estate
and my will is and I direct that they my said trustees and the survivor of them
his executors and administrators shall stand and be possessed of all the clear
monies arising from such sale or sales and to be received and got in as aforesaid
together with all other the Residue of my said personal Estate (after payment of
my debts funeral and testamentary expenses and legacies) Upon trust to lay out
and invest the same in their or his names or name in some or one of the Government
Stocks or funds of Great Britain or other Government securities and to stand and be
possessed thereof upon trust for and during the life of my said wife to pay one
moiety or equal half part of the dividends interest and annual produce of such
Stocks funds or securities to my said Wife for her own sole separate and independent
use and not to be liable to the debts control or engagements of any husband with
whom she may hereafter intermarry and for which her receipt alone notwithstanding
her

Figure 31 Copy of the front page of the Prerogative Court of Canterbury's registered court copy of the will of William Bligh – of mutiny on the *Bounty* fame – proved in 1818. (PROB 11/1603, pp68–70)

The following printed name indexes to PCC wills and administrations are available at both the FRC and the PRO:

- for 1383–1700, wills only
- for 1701–49, both wills and administrations (compiled by the Friends of the Public Record Office)
- for 1750–1800, wills only (compiled by the Society of Genealogists).

From 1801, it is necessary to search the **PROB 12** indexes themselves to find references to PCC wills and administrations. For 1853–8, the **PROB 12** indexes are in strict alphabetical order.

An online index to PCC wills for 1820–9 and 1840–58 is accessible on www. pro-online.pro.gov.uk. You can search this index via the internet and at the PRO or FRC, without charge; to view and download images of the wills costs £3 each. It is hoped that by the winter of 2002 this index will have been extended to cover 1830–9, and that eventually all the PCC wills will be accessible online.

A selection of wills of famous people is available on microfilm, in **PROB 1**, in the Microfilm Reading Room. These range from 1552 to 1854 and include Nelson's will (**PROB 1/22**), accompanied by his diary from September to October 1805.

For more detailed information about PCC wills, see *Prerogative Court of Canterbury: Wills and Other Probate Records* by Miriam Scott (PRO, 1997).

5.3.7 Wills and administrations after 1858

Wills and administrations proved on or since 12 January 1858 may be read, for a small fee, at:

Probate Searchroom
Principal Registry of the Family Division
First Avenue House
42–49 High Holborn
London WC1V 6NP

Tel: 020 7947 7022

Website: www.courtservice.gov.uk

You can purchase copies of wills and administrations, either at the Probate Searchroom or by post, so long as you know the date of death. Postal applications for copies should be sent to:

Postal Searches and Copies Department
Probate Sub-Registry
Castle Chambers
Clifford Street
York YO1 9RG

Tel: 01904 666777
Fax: 01904 666776

Microfiche copies of the annual indexes to wills for 1858–1943 (known as the *National Probate Indexes*) can be searched, without charge, at the FRC and in the Microfilm Reading Room at the PRO. They are arranged by year and then alphabetically by the deceased's name. These indexes provide valuable information, such as the deceased's address, date and place of death, names(s) of executor(s) (with relationship to the deceased, if next of kin), and the value of effects.

For further details, see *Using Wills* by Karen Grannum (PRO, revised edn 2001) and *The Family Records Centre – A User's Guide* by Stella Colwell (PRO, 2nd edn 2002), which also provide detailed information about Death Duty records.

5.3.8 Death Duty records

There are many other probate records – such as inventories (lists and value of the deceased's effects) and Death Duty records – that can be used to supplement information found in wills.

Death Duty was introduced, in the form of Legacy Duty, in 1796 and was, with certain exemptions, payable on estates, legacies and personal effects passed on by wills or letters of administration. The Death Duty records (which encompass Legacy Duty, Succession Duty and Estate Duty) from 1796 to 1903 are to be found in **IR 26** and are surname-indexed by registers in **IR 27**. The **IR 26** Death Duty records for 1796–1857 and **IR 27** registers for 1796–1903 can be viewed on microfilm both at the PRO, Kew, and at the FRC. To inspect the **IR 26** Death Duty records for 1858–1903 – which can be viewed only at Kew – you need to give three working days' notice, as they are stored off site. The records in **IR 26** generally include details such as the name and address of the deceased, the date of probate, names and addresses of executors, administrators and next of kin (with relationship to the deceased), details of effects passed on, and the value of the estate.

6 Reserve and auxiliary forces service records

This chapter gives details of the service records held by the PRO relating to the reserve and auxiliary forces formed to assist and complement the Royal Navy over the years.

6.1 Sea Fencibles

ADM 28 contains pay lists, arranged by district and in date order, relating to the Sea Fencibles – a part-time organization consisting of fishermen and boatmen, commanded by naval officers, which was formed in 1798 for anti-invasion defence duties. Records of appointments of naval officers to the Sea Fencibles can be found in **ADM 28/145** for 1798–1810 and in **ADM 11/14–16** for 1804–13.

6.2 Royal Naval Reserve

One of the major recommendations of the 1858 Royal Commission on manning the navy was the establishment of a reserve force of merchant seamen who could be called upon by the Royal Navy in times of emergency. The Royal Naval Reserve (Volunteer) Act was passed, in 1859, on the basis of the Commission's findings. The Act allowed for the recruitment of up to 30,000 men to form the Royal Naval Reserve (RNR), thus making a valuable body of men with sea experience available to the Royal Navy, should a crisis occur.

The number of men enrolled in 1860 was 2,800, which rose to 8,000 in 1861 and 14,000 in 1862. By 1890, 20,000 men had enrolled. RNR commissioned ranks were created in 1861, when the Admiralty was authorized to enrol merchant-navy masters and mates who had the necessary certificates to serve as officers in the RNR. In 1864 engineers and in 1872 midshipmen under the age of 18, from those educated in the *Conway* or *Worcester*, were added to the list of merchant-navy personnel who could be enrolled as officers. The rank of commander RNR was introduced in 1904.

With the expansion of the Royal Navy during the 1890s, it became apparent that whilst ships could be built in two to three years, it took double that time to train a lieutenant. Therefore in 1895 permanent Royal Navy commissions were granted to 100 merchant-navy officers, 90 of whom came from the RNR. In 1898, a further 50 RNR officers were transferred.

6.2.1 RNR officers' service records (ADM 240)

ADM 240 contains service records for RNR officers ranging from midshipman to commander, assistant engineer to chief engineer and assistant paymaster to paymaster, covering 1862–1909; and honorary officers (various ranks) for 1862–1960. Arranged by rank and date of seniority, these records provide comprehensive details of officers' past service both with the Royal Navy and with the merchant navy. Details of merchant-navy service, such as the number of the officer's certificate of competency or the official numbers of the ships on which he served, can be used to search merchant-navy records held by the PRO, which are described in *Records of Merchant Shipping and Seamen* by K. Smith, C.T. Watts and M.J. Watts (PRO, 1998).

In addition to career information, the service records in **ADM 240/1–36** provide details such as:

- date of birth (**ADM 240/1, 2, 7, 12–18, 25–28** and **32–35**)
- where born, year of birth, address, marital status, maiden name of wife, number of children (**ADM 240/3, 8** and **29**)
- date and place of birth with address (**ADM 240/4–6, 9–12, 20–24, 30–31** and **36**)
- year and place of birth, name and address of parents or guardians (**ADM 240/19**).

There is no overall name index to **ADM 240**, but **ADM 240/1–2, 7, 13–18, 25–28** and **32–35** contain surname indexes.

6.2.2 RNR officers' service records: First World War

Service records of RNR officers (executive officers, engineers and telegraphers) who served in the First World War can be found in **ADM 240/37–50**, which are ordered as original documents.

ADM 240/37–41 include surname indexes. Otherwise, surname indexes to **ADM 240/37–50** are available on microfilm in the Microfilm Reading Room, in **ADM 240/84** (Abbot–Cartwright), **ADM 240/85** (Case–Hanxwell), **ADM 240/86** (Harborn–Medway), **ADM 240/87** (Mee–Smiley) and **ADM 240/88** (Smith–Ziman). If you find a reference to an officer in these indexes, you need to note down the numbers alongside his name – for example, '**Harper Tom 6-238**'. You will then need to turn to the piece descriptions for **ADM 240/37–50** in the **ADM 240** series list and look for the volume number given in the index (in this case, '6') among the numbers that appear on the right-hand side of the series list. In this instance the volume number '6' corresponds with **ADM 240/42**, and '238' is the number of the page where Tom Harper's service details are recorded.

The service records in **ADM 240/37–50** usually only record service-related information, such as ships served on, promotions, and medals awarded; they do not provide personal information about the officer such as date and place of birth, although addresses are given. Names and addresses of next of kin can be found in **ADM 240/45–49**.

Another series of RNR officers' First World War service records, **ADM 240/51–83**, is scheduled for release in November 2002; in addition, a series of record cards relating to RNR officers born before 1900 whose RNR service was after the First World War is scheduled for release before March 2003. However, the majority of records of RNR officers who served after this date are still closed. Enquiries about them should be sent to the Navy Records Centre of the Ministry of Defence, in Hayes, Middlesex (for address, see Appendix 2), which can release information to the officer or, for a fee, to next of kin.

Also, it is worth noting that summary details of the careers of RNR officers who served before, in, and after the First World War are given in the *Navy List* (see 2.1).

6.2.3 RNR ratings' service records 1860–1913 (BT 164)

The Admiralty was responsible for the RNR and for its training. But recruitment of merchant seamen and fishermen to the reserve was undertaken by merchant-navy shipping offices at ports in the UK, and their service records were kept by the Registrar General of Shipping and Seamen. Although the reserve was expanded by the introduction of officers in 1861 (see 6.2), initially it consisted solely of ratings.

Only a selection of service records relating to ratings who enrolled in the RNR between 1860 and 1913 has been preserved, and these are in **BT 164**. The ones in **BT 164/1–19** are collated in bound volumes, whereas **BT 164/20** consists of record cards. Each service record or card covers a five-year engagement, so it is possible to find several records or cards for ratings who served more than one five-year engagement.

The records of service in **BT 164** are arranged by type of rating, date when engagement began, and enrolment number. They include a physical description of the rating; details of previous service in the Royal Navy, merchant navy or coastguard; and genealogical information such as year and place of birth, address, and parents' names. There is no overall surname index to these records, but the indexes described in 6.2.4 may prove useful.

Details of service in the merchant navy or coastguard can be used to search the records relating to these services held by the PRO – which are described in *Records of Merchant Shipping and Seamen* by K. Smith, C.T. Watts and M.J. Watts (PRO, 1998) and, for coastguard records, in PRO information leaflet MO 44.

6.2.4 RNR ratings' service records 1914–58

Service records of Royal Naval Reserve ratings who served between 1914 and 1958 – including those who served in the First or Second World War – are available on microfiche in the Microfilm Reading Room, in **BT 377/7**. Some of these records also record pre First World War Service. They are arranged in an alphanumerical sequence of service numbers, and in terms of the kind of information they provide are similar to the records described in 6.2.3. The originals of these documents are held by the Fleet Air Arm Museum (for address, see Appendix 2).

The service numbers of RNR reservists are given in the name indexes in **BT 377/1–6** and **BT 377/8–28** available on microfilm in the Microfilm Reading Room (which include year and place of birth), and in the Royal Naval Reserve's First World War campaign medal rolls in **ADM 171/120–124 (**see 4.7.2). RNR service numbers that have a prefix ending with the letter X (for example, AX or CX) tend to relate to men who served during the Second World War.

Service records of ratings in the Royal Naval Reserve Trawler Section RNR(T) – formed in 1911 and abolished in 1921 – can be found in **BT 377/7**, so long as their service numbers are prefixed by the letters DA, ES, SA, SB or TS. The records of ratings whose service numbers begin with SBC do not appear to have survived. Also in **BT 377/7** are records for ratings who served in the Shetland Royal Naval Reserve, which was formed in 1914 and disbanded in 1921. Their service numbers are prefixed by the letter L.

Records from 1958 onwards are held by the Royal Naval Reserve (at the PPPA address given in Appendix 2), who will release information to the rating or, for a fee, to next of kin.

6.2.5 *Royal Fleet Auxiliary*

The crews of ships serving in the Royal Fleet Auxiliary (RFA), officially formed in 1911, could include Royal Navy and merchant-navy personnel and RNR reservists. Service records for officers and men in the Royal Fleet Auxiliary should be found among those of the branch of service to which they belonged before joining the RFA, for example, many of the RFA officers were RNR officers.

6.3 Royal Naval Air Service and Fleet Air Arm

In 1910 an Air Department was established by the Admiralty. By 1912 it had become the naval wing of the Royal Flying Corps, which also had a military wing run by the War Office's Directorate of Military Aeronautics. From 1 July 1914 the naval wing became known as the Royal Naval Air Service (RNAS), which during the First World War bombed targets at sea and in port, carried out air operations in theatres of war, and was responsible for the air defence of the United Kingdom.

On 3 January 1918 control of the RNAS passed to the Air Ministry, and on 1 April – following the recommendation of a government committee under the chairmanship of General J.C. Smuts – it was merged with the Royal Flying Corps to form the Royal Air Force (RAF). RNAS officers and ratings at the end of the First World War either joined the RAF or reverted to the Royal Navy. After the First World War, the RAF's naval element was run down to a few squadrons and several flights. These remaining naval squadrons were in turn disbanded on 1 April 1923, to form some 400 series flights, each consisting of six aircraft. From 1 April 1924, this small force became known as the Fleet Air Arm (FAA). Although the Admiralty kept control of aircraft carriers and operations at sea, RN officers and ratings were now seconded to the RAF for training and service in the FAA. This division of responsibilities between the Air Ministry and the Admiralty made for an uneasy relationship, and the Admiralty claimed that its efficiency was impaired as it did not have complete control of the FAA.

In July 1937 agreement was reached for the transfer (not completed until 1939) of the FAA to the Admiralty. Initially this applied only to carrier-borne aircraft, and it was not until April 1941 that operational control of the land-based Coastal Command passed to the Admiralty.

6.3.1 RNAS officers' registers of service: First World War

When the Royal Naval Air Service was formed, many officers transferred to it from the Royal Navy. Their previous service in the Royal Navy can be traced in **ADM 196** (see 2.3.1).

Service records of RNAS officers who served during the First World War can be found in **ADM 273**. These records are arranged in service number order, but each register includes a surname index. In addition, a name card index relating to **ADM 273** is available in the Research Enquiries Room. The records of service in **ADM 273** provide details such as:

- date of birth, whether married, name and address of next of kin
- date of entry into the RNAS, previous service in HM forces, previous occupation if entered from civil life
- RAC (Royal Aero Club) certificate number, date and where obtained, by whom recommended (the certificates themselves are held at the Royal Air Force Museum – for address, see Appendix 2)
- appointments (nature of appointment and date when appointed)
- air service (date, seniority, rank)
- naval service (seniority, rank)
- notations at Air Department (e.g. accidents, meritorious work, special flights)
- confidential reports (occasion, date, by whom, conduct, ability, special ability, languages, remarks concerning character, assessments for promotion).

Career details of RNAS officers can also be found in the *Navy List* (see 2.1).

6.3.2 RNAS ratings' service records: First World War

Records of service for ratings who served in the RNAS during the First World War can be found in **ADM 188/560–646**, arranged in service number order. RNAS ratings' service numbers – which are prefixed by the letter F – can be obtained from the name indexes in **ADM 188**, as described in 3.3.2, or by searching the First World War campaign medal rolls in **ADM 171/94–119** (see 4.7.2). The service records of ratings who served in RNAS Armoured Car Squadrons in Russia are located in **ADM 116/1625** and **ADM 116/1717**.

Engagement papers of men who joined the RNAS between 1914 and 1918 are held by the Fleet Air Arm Museum (for address, see Appendix 2).

6.3.3 Fleet Air Arm ratings' service records: 1924 onwards

Service records of ratings who joined the Fleet Air Arm between 1924 and 1938 are held by the Navy Records Centre of the Ministry of Defence, in Hayes, Middlesex (for address, see Appendix 2). Records from 1939 onwards are held at the PPPA address given in Appendix 2.

Further information about the Royal Naval Air Service will be found in *Air Force Records for Family Historians* by William Spencer (PRO, 2000).

6.4 Royal Naval Volunteer Reserve

The Royal Naval Volunteer Reserve (RNVR) was formed in June 1903, by the Naval Forces Act 1903. Volunteers joining the RNVR agreed to serve 'either ashore or afloat', and consequently performed a wide range of duties. On the outbreak of war in August 1914, volunteers reported to their divisional headquarters. Some were drafted into ships of the fleet, but many were ordered – together with reservists from the Royal Naval Reserve and the Royal Fleet Reserve – to join the Royal Naval Division (see 6.5). The RNVR also saw service during the Second World War. Eventually, in 1958, it was amalgamated with the Royal Naval Reserve (see 6.2).

Some RNVR divisional records covering the period 1904–39 are located in **ADM 900/75–86**.

6.4.1 RNVR officers' service records 1914–22

Service records of RNVR officers who served during the First World War are in **ADM 337/117–128**, and a name card index to these records is available in the Microfilm Reading Room. A typical entry from this index is '**Samuel H. C. Luck 3.267**'. To locate the relevant service record, you need to convert the number 3.267 to a PRO document reference. In this example, the 3 is the volume number and 267 is the page number. The conversion table below indicates that Samuel Luck's service record will be found on page 267 of **ADM 337/119**.

Volume 1 = **ADM 337/117**	Volume 5 = **ADM 337/121**	Volume 9 = **ADM 337/125**
Volume 2 = **ADM 337/118**	Volume 6 = **ADM 337/122**	Volume 10 = **ADM 337/126**
Volume 3 = **ADM 337/119**	Volume 7 = **ADM 337/123**	Volume 11 = **ADM 337/127**
Volume 4 = **ADM 337/120**	Volume 8 = **ADM 337/124**	Volume 12 = **ADM 337/128**

The service records themselves include rank, details of appointments, honours and awards, dates of promotion, the officer's address, and that of next of kin.

Service records of RNVR officers from the end of the First World War until 1958 are held by the Navy Records Centre of the Ministry of Defence, in Hayes, Middlesex (for address, see Appendix 2). Records from 1958 onwards are held by the Royal Naval Volunteer Reserve at the PPPA address given in Appendix 2. Both the Navy Records Centre and the RNVR will release information to the officer or (for a fee) to next of kin.

Career details of officers serving in the RNVR can also be found in the *Navy List* (see 2.1).

6.4.2 RNVR ratings' service records 1903–19

On joining the RNVR, men were assigned to divisions and allocated service numbers prefixed by a 'distinguishing letter' indicating the division they had entered. Records of service for ratings who joined the RNVR between 1903 and 1919 can be found in **ADM 337/1–108**. Their records are arranged by division and then by divisional service numbers, so you need to know a rating's service number in order to search them. There is no overall alphabetical surname index to these records, but service numbers are given in RNVR ratings' First World War campaign medal rolls in **ADM 171/125–129** (see 4.7.2); also, some of the divisional service records in **ADM 337** have separate name indexes (**ADM 337/92** and **ADM 337/100**) that provide service numbers. However, even though it is possible to locate a rating's service number through these sources, there is no guarantee that you will find the service record you are looking for, as there are gaps in the records. For some divisions, the Fleet Air Arm Museum (for address, see Appendix 2) holds the engagement papers that men signed on entering the service. These can be useful if you need details about ratings whose records have not survived in **ADM 337**, or to supplement information given in service records. If you are unable to find the service record of someone who joined the RNVR, the reason may be that he saw service with the Royal Naval Division (see 6.5).

The service records of RNVR ratings in **ADM 337** contain details such as name, division and service number, date of birth, place of birth (rarely given), former occupation, whether formerly in the Royal Navy or Royal Marines, a physical description, date and period of engagements, ships or units served in, period of service, and remarks about character and ability.

Service records of men who joined the RNVR between 1920 and 1958 are held by the Navy Records Centre of the Ministry of Defence, in Hayes, Middlesex (for address, see Appendix 2). Records from 1958 onwards are held by the Royal Naval Reserve at the PPPA address given in Appendix 2. Both the Navy Records Centre and the RNR will release information to the rating or (for a fee) to the next of kin.

6.5 Royal Naval Division

At the outbreak of the First World War the Royal Navy found that it had sufficient active personnel for its ships and for replacements in case of shortages, so did not immediately need the services of the 30,000 men in the Royal Fleet Reserve (RFR), Royal Naval Reserve (RNR) and Royal Naval Volunteer Reserve (RNVR). On the other hand, the Army – although it had plenty of untrained men wanting to join it – urgently needed trained men. Winston Churchill, then First Lord of the Admiralty, therefore decided to form a naval fighting force on land to support the Army. Named the Royal Naval Division (RND), it was to consist of thousands of trained men from the RFR, RNR and RNVR, formed into two naval brigades (each with four battalions named after famous British seamen) and another brigade drawn from Royal Marines, Army and Royal Navy personnel, which included both reservists and men on active service.

The Crystal Palace – built for the 1851 Great Exhibition and relocated from Hyde Park to Sydenham in southeast London in 1854 – was renamed *Victory II* and used as a receiving and training depot for men who joined the Royal Naval Division. In June 1916 the RND was transferred to Army control and became known as the 63rd (Royal Naval Division). It was formed into three brigades, numbered from 188 to 190, consisting of four battalions each (190 brigade was formed from Army battalions). In April 1919 the RND was disbanded, having seen distinguished service in the Dardanelles in 1915 and, from 1916, on the Western Front.

6.5.1 RND officers' service records

The service records of officers who served in the Royal Naval Division can be found in **ADM 339/3**, which is available on microfiche in the Microfilm Reading Room. Arranged in surname order, these records include rank, branch of service, private address, name and address of next of kin, service and medical details, and date of death if the officer died in service.

If an officer served with either the Royal Navy, RNR or RNVR before joining the Royal Naval Division, then you may find information about him among officers' service records for the relevant branch of the navy described elsewhere in this guide. Career details of officers who served in the RND are also given in the *Navy List* (see 2.1).

6.5.2 RND ratings' service records

The following table gives the service numbers allocated to men joining the RND:

P.Z.1 to P.Z.3000 and Z.P.1 onwards	Men entered at the Crystal Palace from civil life.
K.P.1 onwards	Men entered at the Crystal Palace from Kitchener's army.
Z.W.1 onwards	Men entered in 1st Brigade, RND, from civil life.
K.W.1 onwards	Men entered in 1st Brigade, RND, from Kitchener's army.
Z.X.1 onwards	Men entered in 2nd Brigade, RND, from civil life.
K.X.1 onwards	Men entered in 2nd Brigade, RND, from Kitchener's army.
R.1 onwards	Men entered from the Army for service in the RND from May 1916.

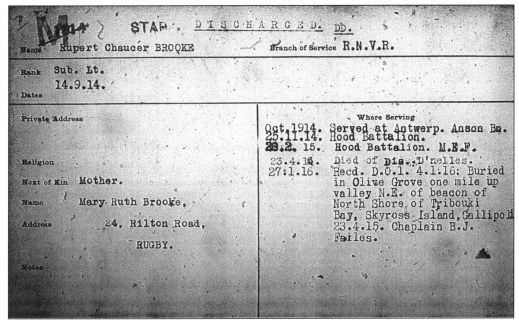

STAR. DISCHARGED. DD.

Name Rupert Chaucer BROOKE   Branch of Service R.N.V.R.

Rank Sub. Lt.
14.9.14.
Dates

Private Address

Religion

Next of Kin Mother.

Name Mary Ruth Brooke,

Address 24, Rilton Road,
RUGBY.

Notes

Where Serving
Oct.1914. Served at Antwerp. Anson Bn.
25.11.14. Hood Battalion.
28.2. 15. Hood Battalion. M.E.F.
23.4.15. Died of Dis..D'nelles.
27.1.16. Recd. D.O.I. 4.1.16: Buried
in Olive Grove one mile up
valley N.E. of beacon of
North Shore of Tribouki
Bay, Skyros Island, Gallipoli
23.4.15. Chaplain B.J.
Failes.

Figure 32 Service record extract and photograph of the noted First World War poet Rupert Brooke. (ADM 339/3; ZPER 34/146, *Illustrated London News*, 8 May 1915)

The records of ratings killed while serving with the RND can be found in **ADM 339/2**; service records for other RND ratings are in **ADM 339/1**. Both **ADM 339/1** and **ADM 339/2** are arranged in surname order and are available on microfiche in the Microfilm Reading Room. They usually give rating, service number, branch of service, date of entry, date and place of birth, address, details of previous service, religion, occupation, name and address of next of kin, a physical description and, if killed in service, date of death and place of burial. If a man served in another branch of the navy before joining the RND, you may also find information about him among records for the relevant service described elsewhere in this guide.

As well as holding the originals of the service records in **ADM 339/1–3**, the Fleet Air Arm Museum (for address, see Appendix 2) has the engagement papers of many of the men who went on to serve in the RND after initially signing papers to join the RNVR or the Army. The engagement papers – which usually provide details such as date, place of birth, and name and address of next of kin – can be used to fill in gaps in or supplement information found in service records. There are no surname indexes for these records, so it is difficult to search them unless you have a rating's service number.

RND unit war diaries and operational orders are to be found in **WO 95/4290–4291** and **ADM 137/3063–3088d**.

6.6 Queen Alexandra's Royal Naval Nursing Service

Before 1883 nursing in naval hospitals was mainly carried out by ex-ratings or marines, who held no nursing qualifications. Earlier trials to introduce female nurses had not proved successful, but some female nurses were employed. Naval hospitals employed both established and hired nurses, whilst on board ships nursing was undertaken by sick berth staff, whose service records will be found in **ADM 188** (see 3.3.2 and 3.3.3).

The Committee on the Organization and Training of the Sick Berth Staff of the Navy and the Nursing Staff of the Royal Naval Hospitals, which was appointed in 1883, recommended in its 1884 report that the existing system of male and civilian nurses be abolished, that trained sick berth staff be employed both ashore and at sea, and that trained female nurses and superintendents of nurses be introduced in certain hospitals. A female nursing service was first adopted at Haslar and Plymouth Hospitals; then extended in 1897 to Chatham and Malta, and by 1901 to all Royal Naval Hospitals. In 1899 the Committee on Training of Medical Sick Berth and Nursing Staff recommended the introduction of the rank of superintending sister in hospitals where three or more sisters were employed. In 1902 the Naval Nursing Service was given royal approval, and its title changed to Queen Alexandra's Royal Naval Nursing Service (QARNNS).

Names of matrons and head sisters first appear in the 1884 *Navy List* (see 2.1). Records of nursing sisters for 1884–1909 can be found in **ADM 104/43**, which includes a surname index and gives name, rank, date of birth, and dates of entry and discharge.

Annual reports about nursing sisters are located in **ADM 104/95** for 1890–1908. Staff are listed by year and in seniority order. Their name, age, hospital where employed and dates of service are given, along with comments about character and work. Further information about nursing sisters and ward masters can be found in the establishment book for c. 1912–27 in **ADM 104/96**. Arranged in rough chronological order, this provides name, rank, and dates of appointment and discharge, with reasons for both.

Genealogical and employment details of nurses serving in the Royal Greenwich Hospital and School between 1704 and 1865 can be found in **ADM 73/83–88**. Applications from ratings' widows for employment as nurses in Greenwich Hospital between 1817 and 1842 are recorded in **ADM 6/329** and **ADM 6/331**.

ADM 104/161 contains a service register for QARNNS for 1894–1929, which includes a surname index. This register gives date of birth, dates of seniority, dates of appointment and discharge, where serving, remarks about conduct and ability, details of training and qualifications, and date of retirement. The name and address of next of kin are also sometimes given. Similar registers for QARNNS reserves for 1914–19, in **ADM 104/162–165**, record name and address, details of appointments, where serving, comments about ability and conduct, leave details, and whether resigned, joined active service or died. Each of these registers contains a surname index, and in some instances there are overlapping references. Career details of QARNNS sisters are given in the *Navy List* (see 2.1).

Records of nurses serving in QARNNS and its reserve who were awarded the Royal Red Cross for special devotion while nursing the sick and wounded can be found in **WO 145/1–3**, which include surname indexes and extend from 1883 to 1994. These documents often contain extracts from the *London Gazette* (see 4.7.6) and provide information such as when and where the award was made and the address to which the decoration was sent (often the nurse's home address). There is a First World War campaign medal roll for Royal Navy nursing sisters in **ADM 171/133** (pp. 569–77).

A service register for massage sisters in naval hospitals, which ranges from 30 April 1917 to 16 July 1925, is available on microfilm, in **ADM 104/171**, in the Microfilm Reading Room. Arranged by date of seniority, it includes a surname index but rarely provides genealogical information such as birth date or name and address of next of kin. Career details of massage sisters are given in the *Navy List* (see 2.1).

ADM 104/159–160 contain registers for pharmacists who served in the navy between 1845 and 1957. A surname index is provided in **ADM 104/159**, but not in **ADM 104/160**. Information concerning the careers of naval pharmacists can also be found in the *Navy List* (see 2.1).

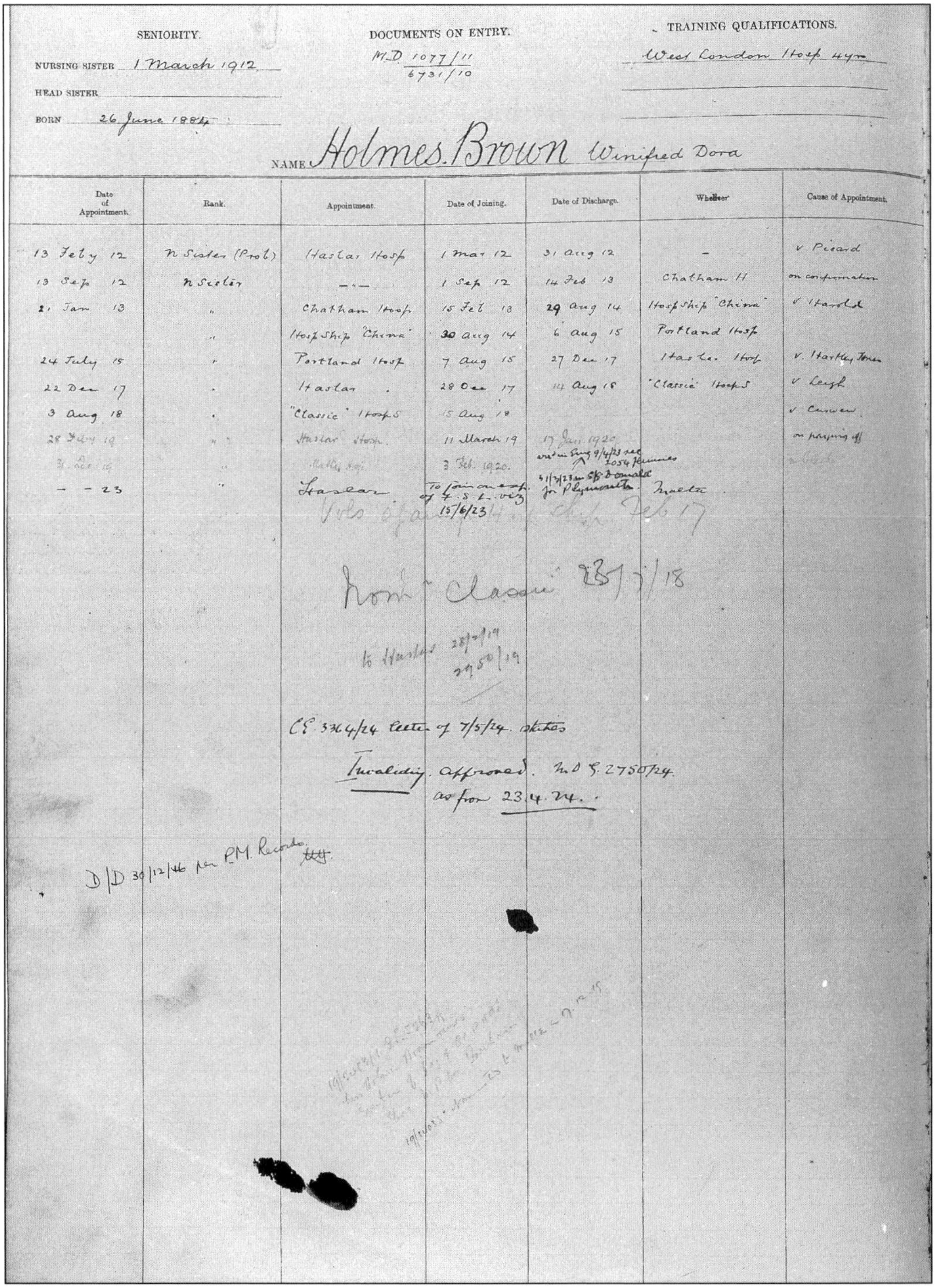

Figure 33 Service record of Winifred Dora Holmes Brown who served in the QARNNS. (ADM 104/161, p115)

6.7 Women's Royal Naval Service

Lady Rocksavage (later the Marchioness of Cholmondeley) first put forward the idea of a Women's Royal Naval Service to Sir Eric Geddes, the First Lord of the Admiralty, on St George's Day 1917. On 26 November Geddes submitted this proposal to King George V, who signified his approval on 28 November. Dame Katherine Fuse was appointed director of this new shore service, whose formation was first mentioned in Admiralty Office memorandum number 245 and in *The Times* of 29 November 1917. When the war ended, there was some pressure to keep the WRNS as a permanent service. However, an Admiralty fleet order of 19 February 1919 announced a process of gradual demobilization, and by the beginning of October 1919 the WRNS had ceased to exist. During the First World War, the total number of women serving in the WRNS reached a peak of 438 officers and 5,054 ratings. The WRNS was re-established, on 12 April 1939.

6.7.1 WRNS officers' personal records and registers of appointments: First World War

Files relating to officers who served with the WRNS between 1917 and 1919, except for those officers who resigned in 1918 for personal reasons, are held in **ADM 318/1–556**. Arranged by name, these files generally consist of dossiers and letters concerning service, appointments and promotions. In some cases they include identification certificates that give the following details: name of holder, address, nationality, trade or profession, religion, date of birth, whether single, married or widowed, a physical description, the officer's signature, and name of next of kin. The **ADM 318** series list also contains a surname index to these records, which can be searched by name using the PRO's online catalogue (accessible at the PRO or FRC and via the internet at www.pro.gov.uk).

Registers of appointments of WRNS short-service officers between December 1917 and July 1919 can be found in **ADM 321/1–2**, which include surname indexes. These registers list date of first appointment, establishment, rank, service from/to, and remarks such as whether transferred to the Women's Auxiliary Air Force (WAAF), whose records can be found in **AIR 80** indexed by **AIR 78**.

6.7.2 WRNS ratings' service records: First World War

The records of WRNS ratings who served in the First World War can be found in **ADM 336/23–29**, arranged in service number order. WRNS service numbers are given in the name indexes in **ADM 336/1–22**. The service records list age, the name and address of next of kin, date of enrolment, names of ships or establishment served in, rating, dates of service, and whether discharged (with cause). Although there are columns for place and date of birth, these are rarely filled in.

A First World War campaign medal roll for the WRNS can be found in **ADM 171/133** (pp581–2).

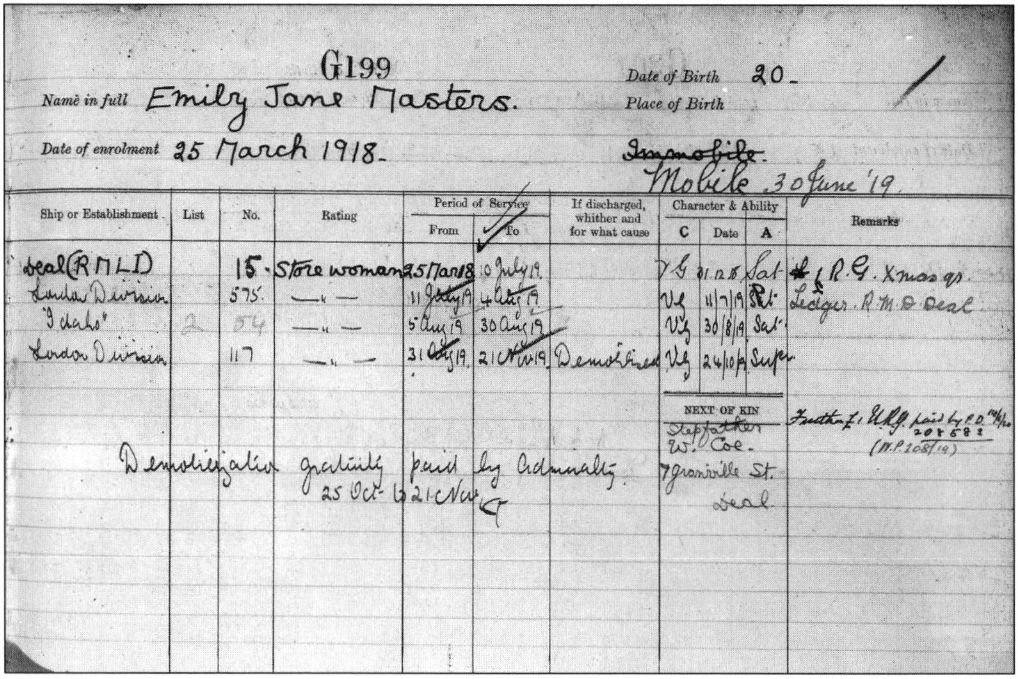
G199

Name in full Emily Jane Masters.

Date of Birth 20.

Place of Birth

Date of enrolment 25 March 1918.

~~Immobile~~ Mobile 30 June '19.

Ship or Establishment	List	No.	Rating	Period of Service From	Period of Service To	If discharged, whither and for what cause	Character & Ability C	Date	A	Remarks
Deal (RMLD)		15	Store woman	25 Mar 18	10 July 19		VG	31.12.18	Sat	R.G. Xmas [illegible]
London Division		575	— " —	11 July 19	4 Aug 19		VG	11/7/19	[illegible]	Ledger R.M. [illegible] Deal
"Idaho"	2	54	— " —	5 Aug 19	30 Aug 19		VG	30/8/19	Sat	
London Division		117	— " —	31 Aug 19	21 Nov 19	Demobilised	VG	24/10/19	Sup	

NEXT OF KIN

~~Stepfather~~ W. Coe. 7 Granville St. Deal.

Demobilization gratuity paid by Admiralty 25 Oct 19 21 Nov [illegible]

Further £1 [illegible] paid by P.O. [illegible] 208583 (W.P. 2081/19)

Figure 34 Service record of Emily Jane Masters who served in the WRNS. (ADM 336/23, G 199)

Engagement papers of WRNS ratings who joined between 1917 and 1919 are held by the Royal Naval Museum, in Portsmouth (for address, see Appendix 2). Enquiries about them should be sent to Lesley Thomas, curator of the WRNS collection at the museum. The papers include date and place of birth, address, details of next of kin, marital status, religion, number of children, starting date, the rating's signature, and in some instances the signatures of parents or guardians.

Service records of WRNS officers and ratings for 1939–55 are held by the Navy Records Centre of the Ministry of Defence, in Hayes, Middlesex (for address, see Appendix 2). Records from 1956 onwards are held by the WRNS at the PPPA address given in Appendix 2. Both the Ministry of Defence and the WRNS will release information to the officer or rating, or (for a fee) to next of kin.

7 ADM 12 digests and indexes 1793–1958

Some of the richest sources of information not only for genealogical research but for all aspects of naval matters and administration are the in-letters (papers or letters received by the Admiralty) in **ADM 1**, the Admiralty and Secretariat out-letters in **ADM 2** and **ADM 13/1–63**, the Admiralty and Secretariat minute books in **ADM 3**, and the Navy Board records in **ADM 106**.

The in-letters in **ADM 1** are a veritable treasure trove for the family historian. These were dealt with by the Secretary of the Admiralty and cover every conceivable aspect of official or semi-official business, ranging from subjects as diverse as the appointment of a housekeeper to the Admiralty to an Admiral's account of a naval action. The arrangement of these records, their survival rate, and the lack of indexes to them for certain periods sometimes make them difficult and frustrating to use, but with patience and persistence they can provide a wealth of detail about individuals who served in the navy.

There are no discrete series of detailed indexes to pre-1792 **ADM 1** in-letters. Various attempts by the Admiralty to provide indexes to some of this material were made – the results of which can be seen in **ADM 12/1–55** – but no single overall index to this material exists. Searches of pre-1792 Admiralty in-letters can be undertaken by using the subject index at the beginning of the **ADM 1** series list, though such searches tend to be speculative and time-consuming.

7.1 The origin of ADM 12 indexes and digests

In the early nineteenth century Admiralty officials were voicing concerns about the lack of a system for controlling the registering, movement and the accessibility of its records. A petition to the Privy Council for the creation of an Admiralty Record Office drew attention to the large number of documents held by the Admiralty in many rooms, without indexes or digests, and the problem of finding information in the documents it possessed. Because of these difficulties it was proposed that all existing letters and papers were to be indexed, and that the task should be given to a Keeper of Records and Papers of the Admiralty. This proposal was approved by an order in council on 16 August 1809. On 21 August 1809 John Finlaison was appointed to the post of Keeper, with a salary of £500 per annum, and in December 1809 he was joined by six clerks to assist him in the work.

7.2 Registration of correspondence

The letters and papers received by the Admiralty in the early nineteenth century were subdivided by the Admiralty Record Office clerks into the following divisions, according to their provenance: Public Offices, Admirals, Captains, Lieutenants, Promiscuous (Miscellaneous), Marines, and Board of Admiralty Minutes. These in-letters were then read by a clerk, who decided under which person's or ship's name they would be registered in the indexes, regardless of who wrote them. If the subject matter was considered important, the clerk would mark on the letter or paper the number of a subject heading, under which it would be registered in the digest indexes. A list of the 104 subject headings – some of them subdivided – that the clerks used for this purpose is available in the Research Enquiries Room (in the series lists these subject headings are referred to as 'codes').

The papers and letters that made up the Admirals, Captains, Lieutenants and Promiscuous divisions were then sorted into alphabetical order and numbered individually, on their front pages, in red ink. Those from Public Offices and Marines were kept in date order and so sorted. The clerk in charge of the indexes then registered the letters in the appropriate indexes. If a letter was not marked to be entered in the digest indexes, the clerk would register it in the alphabetical indexes – recording the name of the person or ship the letter related to, the date of the letter, brief details of its content and the number allocated to it – and would then file it away. If the letter was also to be registered in the digest indexes, the clerk entered in the alphabetical indexes the digest number allocated to it and passed the letter on to the clerk in charge of the digest volumes.

The digest clerk, on being given a letter by his colleague, turned to the relevant subject heading number in the digest indexes and entered a digest (summary) of its content. Once this was done, the work was checked by a senior clerk and the letter was filed away. The resulting indexes and digest volumes are in **ADM 12.**

This method of indexing apparently took Finlaison nine months to perfect. The system of registry described above was applied to Admiralty papers dating from 1793 and continued, with some variation, until 1811. Thereafter it remained virtually unchanged until 1963.

7.3 The format of ADM 12 indexes and digests

ADM 12 indexes and digest volumes – which extend from 1793 to 1958 – are the key means of reference to the Admiralty and Secretariat in-letters in **ADM 1,** the Admiralty and Secretariat out-letters in **ADM 2,** and the Admiralty and Secretariat minute books in **ADM 3.** They are large, heavy hand-written documents, which makes them cumbersome to handle and sometimes difficult to read.

ADM 12/56–1738 and **ADM 12/1742–1851** are arranged in year order. For each year there is a series of alphabetical indexes, plus a parallel series of digest volumes. For example, **ADM 12/771** covers surnames and ships' names beginning with the letters

C–D for 1866, while **ADM 12/778** contains digest numbers 1–142 for the same year. As explained in 7.2, in-letters considered of sufficient importance would be registered in the digest indexes, as well as in the alphabetical indexes.

7.3.1 The index volumes

The alphabetical indexes contain entries by name for commissioned and warrant officers, ratings, persons of distinction, Royal Navy ships (annotated in red ink), foreign naval and merchant vessels (annotated in black ink), and anyone who wrote to the Admiralty. They include references not only to those who sent letters to the Admiralty, but also to persons mentioned in them. In some cases, the letters are accompanied by reports, certificates, maps or other documents.

From 1793 to 1859 letters received by the Admiralty were registered in the indexes in four main untitled columns: from left to right, 'Marines', 'Ships', 'Naval Officers and Ratings' and 'Promiscuous' (miscellaneous). In 1860 the format was changed to three columns: 'Naval and Marine Officers', 'Ships and Persons of Distinction' and 'Promiscuous'. In later years, further columns were added. When searching for a reference to an individual or ship, it is advisable to check all the pages relating to the initial letter, as entries may be found on more than one page.

7.3.2 The digest volumes

The digest volumes are arranged in subject heading number order as listed in the Table of Heads and Sections used by the Admiralty clerks. If an in-letter was considered of sufficient importance to warrant inclusion in the digest volumes, as well as in the indexes described in 7.3.1, it was recorded under one of the 104 subject headings listed in the Table of Heads and Sections. Originally, the subjects or heads of correspondence were arranged alphabetically and then each given a consecutive number or sub-number. However, in 1800, 1843, 1881, 1909, 1935 and 1963 the list of subject heads (copies of which are available in the Research Enquiries Room) was revised and expanded – which resulted in the alphabetical order having to be changed and some subject headings being given new numbers. The digest volumes can be used as subject indexes, or in the manner described in the example in 7.4. The numbers referring to the subject headings are cut into the right-hand edge of each volume, and are therefore sometimes referred to as 'cut numbers'. There is a subject heading at the top of each page.

7.4 How to use ADM 12 indexes and digests 1793–1912

The index and digest volumes can be searched to trace all manner of information both about individuals who served in the navy and about specific subjects. In the example given in this section, they are used to establish why in 1864 George Williams, master of the *Euryalus*, was mentioned in despatches.

7.4.1 Finding the relevant index volume

The first step is to find out which of the 1864 index volumes covers W (the initial letter of his name). As the following extract from the **ADM 12** series list indicates, the document reference for this volume is **ADM 12/745**.

Document reference	Year	Index
ADM 12/739	1864	A – D
ADM 12/740	1864	E – G
ADM 12/741	1864	H – J
ADM 12/742	1864	K – M
ADM 12/743	1864	N – P
ADM 12/744	1864	Q – S
ADM 12/745	1864	T – Z

Document reference	Year	Digest
ADM 12/746	1864	1–14A
ADM 12/747	1864	15–29
ADM 12/748	1864	30–48
ADM 12/749	1864	49–60
ADM 12/750	1864	61–70
ADM 12/751	1864	71
ADM 12/752	1864	72–86
ADM 12/753	1864	87–104

7.4.2 Interpreting columns and entries in ADM 12 indexes 1793–1912

ADM 12/745 (the T–Z index volume for 1864, see 7.4.1) contains the following entries under '**Williams, George, (Master)**':

	Date of paper	How to be found	Subject and marks	Date of execution and letter of branch
Entry 1	Jan 18	B 59	38.2 Lodging Money	19 Jan MM
Entry 2	Feb 5	MIN	Appd "*Euryalus*"	6 Feb W
Entry 3	Feb 16	PRO W 49	Passage 4 March	17 Feb W
Entry 4	May 13	S 231	Expenses	5 Aug MM
Entry 5	Sept 15	S 436	3, 46, 52.26 Praise Simono-Saki	25 Nov M

Date of paper

This column gives the date when the incoming letter was written. In the entries for George Williams shown here, the dates January 18, February 5, February 16, May 13 and September 15 refer to the year 1864. If the date of a letter is given as Oct 23/25 (for example), that means the letter was written on 23 October 1825 but indexed with the correspondence of the next year, 1826.

How to be found

The references and abbreviations used in this column indicate where the correspondence may be found among the Admiralty and Secretariat in-letters in **ADM 1** (for a key to the abbreviations used, see 7.7). Nevertheless, you will sometimes find that, although there is an entry in this column, the original in-letter has not survived in **ADM 1**.

Looking at the entries for George Williams shown above, entry 5 stands out as the one most likely to explain why he was mentioned in despatches – because of the word 'praise' in the 'Subject and marks' column. However, to illustrate how the various references and abbreviations work, it will be useful to examine all five entries, indicating the steps taken.

Entry 1: 'B 59'
The table of abbreviations in 7.7 shows that 'B' means 'Commander-in-Chief, Plymouth', so the **ADM 1** series list needs to be searched to establish which document contains Commander-in-Chief, Plymouth in-letters for 1864. In this instance the document reference is **ADM 1/5865**, but unfortunately no letter marked B 59 has survived in **ADM 1/5865**. However, the content of the letter was deemed important enough to be summarized and entered in the relevant **ADM 12** digest volume (see 'Subject and marks' below). In cases where a letter has been registered in the index but does not have a digest number and searching the relevant **ADM 1** document reveals no trace of the original in-letter, it can be concluded that no other information about the letter will be found.

When converting entries in this column to **ADM 1** references for the years 1793–1839, you will find that the subject index at the beginning of the **ADM 1** series list can be used to locate the relevant document reference more quickly.

Entry 2: 'MIN'
Turning to the table of abbreviations in 7.7, you will see that 'Min' signifies an Admiralty Board Minute. The Admiralty Board Minutes are arranged in chronological order in **ADM 3**; and the documents containing the board minutes for 1864 are **ADM 3/271–272**. No reference to the relevant minute could be found, but the **ADM 12** index entry indicates that it concerned the appointment of George Williams to HMS *Euryalus*.

Entry 3: 'PRO W 49'
The table of abbreviations in 7.7 indicates that 'PRO W' relates to Promiscuous Correspondence (the **ADM 12** term for miscellaneous correspondence), so the next step would be to look at the **ADM 1** series list to determine the document reference for Promiscuous Correspondence relating to names beginning with 'W' (for 'Williams') dated 1864, which is **ADM 1/5912**. A search of this document would need to be carried

out to discover whether it contained a letter marked W 49. This letter was not entered in the relevant digest volume, but 'passage 4 March' in the **ADM 12** index entry suggests that it concerned George Williams's transfer to HMS *Euryalus*.

Entry 4: 'S 231'
The table of abbreviations in 7.7 shows that 'S' refers to the Commander-in-Chief, China; and the **ADM 1** series list indicates that Commander-in-Chief, China in-letters for 1864 are in **ADM 1/5876** (which contains letters S 4–360) and **ADM 1/5877** (letters S 366–502). No trace of a letter marked S 231 could be found in **ADM 1/5876**, and again no digest number is given in the 'Subject and marks' column (see below) of the **ADM 12** index entry. However, it is clear that the letter related to a claim for expenses – perhaps arising from George Williams's journey to join HMS *Euryalus*.

Entry 5: 'S 436'
Researching the previous entry had established the significance of 'S' and the location of in-letters S 366–502 (see above). S 436 was found in **ADM 1/5877** and turned out to be a lengthy report from Vice Admiral Augustus Kuper of the *Euryalus*, dated 15 September 1864, concerning operations in the Straits of Simono-Saki. Kuper's report includes a reference to George Williams, which throws light on how he earned his mention in despatches:

> 'Much credit is due to the masters of the squadron for the skilful manner in which the various ships were manoeuvred amongst numerous difficulties and particularly to Mr G. Williams Master of my ship.'

Subject and marks

The 'Subject and marks' column usually gives a concise description of the content of each letter (such as 'Passage 4 March' or 'Praise Simono-Saki'), which may help decide whether it is likely to be of interest. It may be more rewarding to find the original letter in **ADM 1** (see 'How to be found', above), but if the original letter has not survived, the only option is to see whether details about its content were entered in the digest volumes. This can be determined by the presence of a number or numbers in the 'Subject and marks' column of the **ADM 12** index entry referring to the Table of Heads and Sections available in the Research Enquiries Room. In the example relating to George Williams, only entries 1 and 5 appear to have been judged of sufficient importance for inclusion in the digest volumes.

Entry 1: '38.2 Lodging Money'
Although no trace of the letter marked B 59 could be found in the **ADM 1** in-letters, we can tell that a summary of its content was recorded under the digest heading 38.2, because that number appears in the 'Subject and marks' column of the **ADM 12** index entry. Before ordering the relevant **ADM 12** digest volume, you might want to check what the digest heading 38.2 relates to, so you can decide whether it is worth pursuing this particular avenue of research. You can do this by going to the Research Enquiries

Room and looking at the **ADM 12** Table of Heads and Sections closest in date to the digest entry you are investigating. The Table of Heads and Sections indicates that the digests under heading 38.2 deal with 'Despatches on the Public Services' – travelling expenses allowed to officers for the conveyance of despatches and lodging money. If you decide that it is worth looking at the digest itself, in order to identify the document reference for the relevant **ADM 12** digest you will require the date when the letter was sent, the reference given to it (in this example, B 59) and the digest number (38.2).

Turning to the extract from the **ADM 12** series list for 1864 shown in 7.4.1, you will see that digest number 38.2 is to be found in **ADM 12/748**. So the next step is to order **ADM 12/748** and search for digest number 38.2 (as already mentioned, the numbers are cut into the right-hand margin of the digest volumes). Under 38.2 there is a summary of a letter dated 18 January with the reference B 59, concerning:

> '*Constance* and *Princess Royal*, application from officers for lodging money, cabins not being appropriated, not allowed in the case of *Constance* but allowed in *Princess Royal* while the ship was in dock.'

The entry does not mention which of the two ships George Williams served on. However, to clarify this you could look at the entries in the alphabetical indexes and digests under these ships' names.

Entry 5: '3, 46, 52.26 Praise Simono-Saki'
Because Vice Admiral Kuper's report (in-letter S 436) was found, it may not be necessary to check the relevant digest volumes. However, the digest numbers 3, 46 and 52.26 in the 'Subject and marks' column of the **ADM 12** index entry usefully illustrate that some letters were summarized under more than one subject heading. In the index volumes it is sometimes quite difficult to decipher which digest numbers have been entered, so you need to look at them carefully and make an accurate note of them. Indeed, because of these problems, depending on the nature of your research, it may be quicker and more effective to search for references to Admiralty in-letters by subject, using the digest volumes, rather than the alphabetical indexes.

Date of execution and letter of branch

In early **ADM 12** indexes and digests, there are sometimes references to the action taken by the Admiralty with regard to incoming letters. These references may be used to establish whether there are any pertinent out-letters in **ADM 2** or **ADM 13/1–69**.

In the 1840s the Admiralty developed the practice of collating files of correspondence, which included copies or drafts of out-letters together with relevant in-letters. From 1860, the 'Date of execution and letter of branch' column was added to the **ADM 12** indexes and digests. In this column you will find the date when action on the incoming letter was taken, together with a code – the 'letter of branch' (in the example relating to George Williams, either MM, W or M) – indicating which section of the Admiralty Office dealt with it. This information can be used to find an out-letter in **ADM 1** or **ADM 13** (from 1869 onwards, original out-letters are most likely to be found among the Admiralty and Secretariat papers in **ADM 1**).

7.4.3 The development of cases

From about 1847 the practice developed of collating all papers (in-letters, out-letters, minutes) on a particular subject and keeping them together in a single file. These files began to be known as cases. In **ADM 12** indexes and digests, alongside a subject heading or the name of a person or ship you may find a reference to a 'case' followed by a number (for example, 'case 269'). If it seems likely to be of interest, you will need to convert the case number to a document reference, using the key to cases provided at the beginning of the **ADM 7** and **ADM 116** series lists. Using this key, 'case 269' converts to **ADM 116/124**.

When 'cases' were first introduced, sometimes papers removed from amongst the in-letters in order to form a case were not recorded in the indexes and digests. In addition, a case could extend over many years and yet there may be only one entry recorded in the index and digest volumes – so if you are researching a particular subject, you may find it useful to check the **ADM 7** and **ADM 116** series lists as well. Finally, it should be mentioned that in many instances there are no digest entries for papers removed to form cases.

7.5 How to use ADM 12 digests and indexes 1913–19

With the onset of war, the amount of paperwork dealt with by the Admiralty increased substantially. As a result, two sets of index and digest volumes were compiled for 1915–19 and you will find these listed in the **ADM 12** series list. For a comprehensive search relating to the name of a person or ship or to a particular subject, it is therefore essential to check both sets of indexes or digests for these years.

The Admiralty and Secretariat papers and cases for 1915–19 are chiefly to be found in **ADM 137**, so for the First World War the **ADM 12** indexes and digests serve mainly as an index to **ADM 137**. However, references to Admiralty papers designated ADMTY in the 'Subjects and marks' columns in **ADM 12** indexes and digests should be traced to **ADM 1**; and any references to RNAS (Royal Naval Air Service) papers in **ADM 12** indexes and digests should in the first instance be traced to **AIR 1** (not to **ADM 137**). Generally, the survival rate for documents dated 1919 that are referred to in the **ADM 12** digest and index volumes is very poor.

7.5.1 How to convert a reference for 1915–19 from ADM 12 to ADM 137

Sections 7.5.1.1 to 7.5.1.3 show how the **ADM 12** indexes were used to find information about the capture of Raymond L. Prest, midshipman, Royal Naval Reserve, taken prisoner in 1917. The following steps were taken.

7.5.1.1 Identifying the relevant ADM 12 document

The first step was to find out which volumes of the **ADM 12** index cover surnames beginning with 'P' for the year 1917. The **ADM 12** series list indicated that it would be necessary to search both **ADM 12/1577A** and **ADM 12/1577B**. Nothing relevant was found in **ADM 12/1577A**, but searching **ADM 12/1577B** produced the following entry pertaining to a midshipman named Raymond L. Prest, which seemed well worth investigating.

RAYMOND L. PREST, MIDSHIPMAN, RNR – ADM 12/1577B (1917)			
Number	**Subject and marks**		**Date of outgoing letter**
Jan 30	ADMTY TAKEN P/W		21 C/W
	PRO H ENQUIRY		26/2 NL
	L113 P/W ON GERMAN SUBMARINE		M
	APP 2773 PROMOTED ACTING SUB LIEUT		27/4 CW
	PRO P 85 ENQUIRY		28/5 CW
Jan 30	W0 79 TREATMENT AS P/W		28/4 NL

7.5.1.2 Establishing the HS volume number

Once you have found an entry in **ADM 12** that seems likely to be of interest – in this example, 'L 113 P/W on German submarine' (P/W being short for prisoner of war) – you need to convert the reference in the 'Subject and marks' column to a Historical Section (HS) volume number. This is done by checking the key included in the **ADM 137** series list. This key is arranged in chronological and alphabetical entry order (in this example, L 113 for the year 1917 would be found in HS volume 1303). However, not all the entries in the **ADM 12** indexes for this period can be converted to HS volume numbers, because much of the material has not survived. If an entry in the **ADM 12** indexes cannot be found in the **ADM 137** key, it may be possible to find the information you are searching for in **ADM 1** (which for this period is arranged chronologically) or in the case papers in **ADM 116**. If the letter has been cross-referenced to a digest number, then follow the steps described under 'Subject and marks' (Entry 1: '38.2 Lodging Money') on p196 – bearing in mind that for the First World War there will be two digest volumes for each subject heading (see 7.5).

7.5.1.3 Converting the HS volume number to an ADM 137 document reference

Having found the relevant HS volume (in this case, HS volume 1303), you will need to convert it to an **ADM 137** document reference. So the next step is to turn to the front of the **ADM 137** series list, where there is a key to HS volume numbers. In this example, HS volume 1303 converts to document reference **ADM 137/1303**, which can now be ordered. Most **ADM 137** documents include an index to the letters and reports they contain; in this case, L 113 (the entry pertaining to Raymond L. Prest, prisoner of war on a German submarine) was found on pages 110–16 of **ADM 137/1303**.

Besides confirming that in 1917 Raymond Prest was a prisoner of war, aged 22 or 23, L 113 yielded the following information. Prest had belonged to the crew of HMS *Otway*. When the *Otway* was torpedoed, he was picked up by the *Gaasterland*. Subsequently, on 22 January 1917, the *Gaasterland* was stopped by a German submarine and Prest was taken prisoner.

7.6 ADM 12 indexes and digests 1920–58

The **ADM 12** indexes and digests continue until 1958. For the period 1920–58 their usefulness in terms of finding document references in **ADM 1** and **ADM 116** is greatly reduced, but the digest entries can still be traced – as described under 'Subject and marks' (Entry 1: '38.2 Lodging Money') on p196 – which may be of considerable value if they are the only surviving items of information concerning documents that have not been selected for permanent preservation.

For the period 1939–51, references found in **ADM 12** indexes can sometimes be converted to **ADM 1** document references by using the **ADM 1** packing list, which is among the **ADM** series lists in the Research Enquiries Room. For example, **ADM 12/1768** (the index volume that includes surnames and ships' names with initial letters F–L for 1943–4) contains a reference to '**N. Hyde Stoker 1st Class D/KX 148063 recommendation for award H&A 1049/43**'. Entry H&A 1049/43 (H&A stands for 'Honours and Awards') needs to be located in the **ADM 1** packing list, which is arranged mainly in year order and alphabetically by the original Admiralty reference. The packing list indicates that H&A 1049/43 cross-refers to **ADM 1/14544**. This document contains recommendations for awards to officers and ratings who took part in minesweeping operation 'Antidote' in May 1943, the aim of which was to clear a channel from Galita to Sousse. Searching **ADM 1/14544** revealed that Norman Hyde D/KX 148063 was recommended for a mention in despatches:

> 'For courage and devotion to duty on the occasion of the mining of HMS *Fantome* in operation 'Antidote' in that he was slightly outstanding, but typical of the many engineroom ratings who continued to work between decks in a calm and unconcerned manner when the ship was sinking perceptly [perceptibly] by the stern, reaching an angle when all the quarter-deck was under water.'

These details about Norman Hyde open up other avenues of research. The **ADM 12** indexes for HMS *Fantome* can be searched to see if any operational records have survived; the ship's logs for HMS *Fantome* can be explored; and, equipped with Norman Hyde's service number (given in **ADM 12/1768** and **ADM 1/14544**), his next of kin can apply for his service record.

From 1938 the records in both **ADM 1** and **ADM 116** are arranged by subject headings based on the Table of Heads and Sections used in compiling the **ADM 12** indexes and digest volumes (see 7.3.2); and from 1952 the records in **ADM 1** are arranged in yearly batches relating to their Admiralty branch designations.

Abbreviation	Meaning
A	C-in-C, Portsmouth
Academy	RN Academy, Portsmouth (to 1840)
Acct, Acct Genl	Accountant General
Admty	Admiralty
A G	Accountant General
App	Appointments
Arch	Architect (to 1882)
Army Off	Army Officers
A	Admirals Unemployed
B	C-in-C, Plymouth
Bd of Revis	Board of Revision (1803–09)
Ber Yd	Bermuda Dockyard
B of T	Board of Trade
Brit Cons	British Consuls
Brit Mus	British Museum
C	C-in-C, Nore or Sheerness
Ca	C-in-C, Chatham (1812–14)
Cap ABC	Captains' letters
Cases	Cases (from 1847) [see **ADM 116**]
Cha Commr	Commissioner of Chatham Dockyard
Cha Commt	Commandant of Marines, Chatham
Cha Div	Chatham Division, RM
Cha Yd	Chatham Dockyard
CN	Comptroller of the Navy (1904–12)
C of V	Comptroller of Victualling (1832–70)
Co Gd	Coast Guard Office
Coll of Surg	Royal College of Surgeons
Col Off	Colonial Office
Commr	Commissioners of Home Dockyards
Commr Ab	Commissioners of Dockyards Overseas
Compr St	Comptroller of Steam Machinery (1837–49)
Comp Vit	Comptroller of Victualling (1832–70)
Cont	Controller of the Navy (1860–70)
COP	Commissioners of Out Ports
Coun Off	Privy Council Office
CP	Contract & Purchase Branch (1877–1921)
CSC	Civil Service Commission (from 1855)
Ct Gd	Coast Guard Office
Ct Mar	Courts Martial
Custom Ho	Board of Customs
D	C-in-C, North Sea (to 1815)
	Flag Officer, Particular Service Squadron
	(1878)
	Naval manoeuvres (1887–90)
	Flag Officer, Reserve Squadron (1892–4, 1896–1902)
	Flag Officer, Flying Squadron (1895)
	C-in-C, Home Fleet (1903–04)
	C-in-C, Channel Fleet (1905–09)
D	Dockyard Branch (1870–1903, 1914–15)
Deal Yd	Deal Dockyard
Dept Commr	Commissioner of Deptford Dockyard (to 1869)
Dept Yd	Deptford Dockyard (to 1869)
Devon Yd	Devonport Dockyard
DGM	Medical Director General (from 1843)
DGNO	Director General of Naval Ordnance (1866–8)
DNO	Director of Naval Ordnance (from 1868)
Doc Com	Doctors' Commons
D of W	Director of Works (from 1883)
Dover	Dover Packet Station (1837–60)
Drs Comm	Doctors' Commons
DS	Director of Stores (from 1877)
DT	Director of Transports (from 1832)
DV	Director of Victualling (from 1870)
DW	Director of Works (from 1883)
D Yd Comm	Commissioners of Home Dockyards
DYDS	Director of Dockyards (from 1886)
E	Flag Officer, Downs (to 1815)
EI Ho	East India Company (to 1858)
Elec Tel	Telegrams
F	Second-in-Command, North Sea (to 1815)
Falmo	Falmouth Packet Station (1837–60)
Field Off	Marine Field Officers
FO	Foreign Office
For Cons	Foreign Consuls
For Off	Foreign Office
For Yds	Overseas dockyards
G	Flag Officer, Yarmouth (to 1814)
G	Gunnery Branch (1881–1916)
G Coll	RN College, Greenwich (from 1873)
Gib Yd	Gibraltar Dockyard
Gov of Pl	Governors of Plantations
Gr Hosp	Greenwich Hospital

Abbr	Meaning
H	Flag Officer, Leith (to 1824)
Ha	C-in-C, Baltic (to 1814); C-in-C, Particular Service Squadron (Baltic) (1854–6)
Haul Yd	Haulbowline Dockyard
Hobbs Pt	Hobbs Point Packet Station (1837–60)
H of Comm	House of Commons
Holyhd	Holyhead Packet Station (1837–60)
Home Off	Home Office
Horse Gds	C-in-C, Army
Hosp	Naval hospitals
HPS	Home Packet Service (1837–60)
HSA	Historical Section A (1914–20) [see ADM 137]
HSB	Historical Section B (1914–20) [see ADM 137]
Hydrog	Hydrographer
I	C-in-C, Channel (to 1815)
India Bd	Board of Control (to 1858)
India Ho	East India Company (to 1858)
Insp Genl	Inspector General of Naval Works
Insp Sht	Inspection sheets
K	Flag Officer, Guernsey (to 1815)
Keyham Yd	Keyham Steam Factory, Plymouth
L	Flag Officer, Cork (to 1902); C-in-C, Particular Service Squadron (1844–7); C-in-C, Ireland (1902–22)
L ABC	Lieutenants' letters
Law Off	Law Officers' opinions
Lloyds	Lloyd's
LOO	Law Officers' opinions
L'pool	Liverpool Packet Station (1837–60)
M	Flag Officer, Dublin (to 1815)
Ma	Flag Officer, Lisbon (to 1839); C-in-C, Particular Service Squadron (1848–9); C-in-C, Western Squadron (1854); C-in-C, Fast Service Squadron (1896)
Malta Yd	Malta Dockyard
Mar Cap	Marine Captains' letters
Mar Ct Mar	Marine Courts Martial
Mar Fd Off	Marine Field Officers
Mar Lt	Marine Lieutenants' letters
Mar Off	Marine Office (from 1859)
Mar Paymt	Paymaster of Marines
Mar P Off	Marine Pay Office
Mar Pro	Marine Promiscuous
Mar Town Comm	Commandant of Marines in Town (1804–31)
M Arty	Marine Artillery
MDG	Medical Director General (from 1843)
Min	Board Minute [see ADM 3]
Misc Off	Miscellaneous (Government) Offices
N	C-in-C, Mediterranean
Nav Hosp	Naval hospitals
N Bd	Navy Board (to 1832)
N Off	Navy Board *or* Naval Officers [i.e. Navy Board Officials]
NP Off	Navy Pay Office (to 1836)
NS	Naval Stores Branch (from 1870)
O	C-in-C, North America (to 1815); C-in-C, Halifax (1816–30)
Ord in Cl	Orders in Council
Ord Off	Ordnance Board (to 1855)
P	C-in-C, Jamaica (to 1872, 1874–86, 1891–1902); C-in-C, North America & West Indies (1873, 1887–90, 1903–12)
Palace	Palace
Passage Ret	Passage Returns
Paymastr	Paymaster of the Navy
Paym Genl	Paymaster General
Pem Yd	Pembroke Dockyard
Petitions	Petitions
Phy	Physician
Pkt St	Packet Service (1837–60)
Ply Commd	Commandant of Marines, Plymouth
Ply Commr	Commissioner of Devonport
Ports Commr	Commissioner of Portsmouth Dockyard
Ply Div	Plymouth Division, RM
Ply Yd	Devonport Dockyard
PN	Purchase Naval Branch (1870–7)
Police Off	Admiralty Police Office
Portpk	Portpatrick Police Station (1837–60)
Ports Cmmd	Commandant of Marines, Portsmouth
Ports Commr	Commissioner of Portsmouth Dockyard

Ports Div	Portsmouth Division, RM
Ports Yd	Portsmouth Dockyard
Post Off	General Post Office
Precepts	Precepts
Pro ABC	Promiscuous Correspondents
PS	Packet Service (1837–60)
Pt Serv	Packet Service (1837–60)
PV	Purchase Victualling Branch (1870–7)
Q	C-in-C, Leeward Islands (to 1821)
Qa	C-in-C, Brazil (& Pacific to 1844) (to 1902)
	C-in-C, South Atlantic (1903–4)
	Flag Officer, 2nd Cruiser Squadron (1905–8)
	C-in-C, North America & West Indies (from 1915)
R	C-in-C, Cape of Good Hope
Reg Off	Regulating Office *or* Rendezvous Office
Register Off	Register Office of Shipping and Seamen (1837–51)
Rt Cl Vic Yd	Royal Clarence Victualling Yard, Gosport
RMO	Marine Office (from 1859)
RN Coll	RN College, Portsmouth (to 1873)
	RN College, Greenwich (from 1873)
R of C	Register of Contracts (1864–9)
R Off T	Regulating Office *or* Rendezvous Office
Roy Vic Yd	Royal Victoria Victualling Yard, Deptford
Russ Sq	Flag Officer, Russian Squadron (1795–1800)
R Wm Yd	Royal William Victualling Yard, Plymouth
RWV Yd	Royal William Victualling Yard, Plymouth
S	C-in-C, East Indies (to 1860)
	C-in-C, China (from 1860)
S	Ships Branch (1870–1903, 1912–15)
SA	Air Finance Branch (1914–15)
Sec St	Secretary of State
Sc H Bd	Sick and Hurt Board (to 1806)
Sheer Yd	Sheerness Dockyard
Solor, Solr	Solicitor
Southampton	Southampton Packet Station (1837–60)
SS	Secretary of State
Stat Off	HM Stationery Office
Storek Genl	Storekeeper General (1832–69)
Surg Hall	Royal College of Surgeons
Surv	Surveyor (1832–60)
Sc Wd Bd	Sick and Hurt Board (to 1806)
T	C-in-C, Newfoundland (to 1824)
T	Transport Department (from 1862)
T Bd	Transport Board (1794–1817)
Tel	Telegrams
Town Com	Commandant of Marines in Town (1804–31)
Trans Off	Transport Board (1794–1817)
Treasy	Treasury
Trinity Ho	Trinity House
Trs Bd	Transport Board (1794–1817)
V	Flag Officer, Detached Squadron (to 1856, 1868–70, 1872–3, 1876)
	Flag Officer, Particular Service Squadron (1857)
	C-in-C, Channel Squadron (1858–63, 1865–67, 1871, 1874–5, 1877–1900)
	C-in-C, Atlantic Fleet (1864)
	C-in-C, Channel Fleet (1905–9)
	Victualling Branch (from 1870)
	Flag Officer, Flying Squadron (1869–73, 1876–7)
Va	Flag Officer, Detached Squadron (1874–5, 1880–2, 1886–1900)
	Flag Officer, Cruiser Squadron (1904)
	Flag Officer, 1st Cruiser Squadron (1905–11)
V Bd	Victualling Board (to 1830)
VD	Victualling Branch (from 1870)
Vg Bd	Victualling Board (to 1830)
W	C-in-C, Woolwich *or* Thames
War Off	War Office
Waymo, Weymt	Weymouth Packet Station (1837–60)
Wool Commd	Commandant of Marines, Woolwich
Wool Commr	Commissioner of Woolwich Dockyard (to 1869)
Wool Div	Woolwich Division, RM
Wool Yd	Woolwich Dockyard (to 1869)
X	C-in-C, West Africa (from 1830)
	C-in-C, Home Fleet (1907–13)
	C-in-C, Grand Fleet (1914–19)
	C-in-C, Pacific (1845–1905)
	C-in-C, Australia (1859–1913)

Appendix 1: Finding aids

The PRO has an array of finding aids relating to the naval records it holds. These finding aids, which are listed in the table below along with their location, can be used to quickly locate document references or information that may be of relevance to your research. The location/reference given in the right-hand column is as it appears in the Research Enquiries Room or Microfilm Reading Room.

Document references	Subject matter, date range and type of finding aid	Location/reference (RER = Research Enquiries Room, additional finding aids) (MRR = Microfilm Reading Room)
ADM 1	Index to captains' letters, 1793–1815.	RER: ref to **ADM 1** <vols 3–6>
ADM 1	Naval courts martial, 1680–1701. Nominal card index.	RER/51
ADM 1	Officers' widows' pensions, 1846–47. Nominal microfiche index.	RER Military Memorandum **MN 409**
ADM 1/1–5, 167–180	List of admirals and commodores, 1711–1832.	RER: ref to **ADM 33** <vol. 1>
ADM 1/3506–3521	In-letters relating to Royal Naval College, Portsmouth, 1808–36. Lists of names of candidates and parents.	RER: ref to **ADM 1** <vol. 2>
ADM 6/1–22	Chaplains (mainly refers to warrants). Nominal card index, 1698–1782.	RER/63–64
ADM 6/3–23	Officers' commission and warrant books, 1695–1742. Nominal index.	RER: ref to **ADM 6** <vols 1–6>
ADM 6/15–23	Commission and warrant books, 1735–89. Nominal card index.	RER/59–62
ADM 6/61–72, 182	Index to commission and warrant books, 1742–1846 not comprehensive).	RER: ref to **ADM 33** <vol. 1>

ADM 6/86–118	Lieutenants' passing certificates, 1744–1819. See B. Pappalardo, *Royal Navy Lieutenants' Passing Certificates, 1691–1902* (List and Index Society, vols 289–290).*	
ADM 6/117–118	Lieutenants' passing certificates, 1788–1818. Name index. See B. Pappalardo, *Royal Navy Lieutenants' Passing Certificates, 1691–1902* (List and Index Society, vols 289–290).*	RER: ref to **ADM 107** <vol. 1>
ADM 6/193–196	Pursers' service survey, 1834. Nominal index.	RER: ref to **ADM 6** <vol. 5> Also in **ADM 6** series list.
ADM 6/223–247	Registers of out-pension candidates for admission to Greenwich Hospital, 1737–1840. Nominal card index.	RER/65–72
ADM 6/336–356	Index to commissioned and warrant officers' widows' pensions, 1759–1819 (date of officer's death is given).	RER/73
ADM 7/823	Index to pension books in **ADM 7/809–821**.	RER: ref to **ADM 7** <vol. 1>
ADM 9/1–17	Nominal index to returns of officers' services, 1817–22.	RER: ref to **ADM 9** <vol. 2>
ADM 9/18–61	Nominal index to returns of officers' services, 1846.	RER: ref to **ADM 9** <vol. 1>
ADM 10/6	Alphabetical list of commissioned officers, dated 1844, annotated to form index to **ADM 9/18–61** and **ADM 11/7–8**.	Document to order.
ADM 10/8	Nominal index to writers of captains' letters in **ADM 1/1435–2733**, 1698–1792.	Document to order.
ADM 10/9	Obsolete index to authors of admiral's journals in **ADM 50**, 1755–1848.	Document to order.
ADM 10/13	List of officers registering their commissions at the Navy Board, 1730–1810 (incomplete after 1780).	Document to order.
ADM 12/1–4	Nominal indexes to despatches of commanders-in-chief, 1711–93 (including names of ships mentioned in **ADM 1/1–520**).	Document to order.
ADM 12/5	List and summary of Admiralty out-letters to Commander-in-Chief, West Africa, 1822–45.	Document to order.

ADM 12/6	List and summary of Admiralty out-letters to Commander-in-Chief, North America, 1813–47.	Document to order.
ADM 12/7	List and summary of Admiralty out-letters to Commander-in-Chief, South America , 1813–47.	Document to order.
ADM 12/8	List and summary of Admiralty out-letters to Commander-in-Chief, Cape of Good Hope, 1813–47.	Document to order.
ADM 12/9	List and summary of Admiralty out-letters to Commander-in-Chief, East Indies, 1813–47.	Document to order.
ADM 12/10–11	List and summary of Admiralty out-letters to Commander-in-Chief, Jamaica, 1813–47.	Document to order.
ADM 12/12	List and summary of Admiralty out-letters to Commander-in-Chief, Lisbon and Gibraltar, 1813–47.	Document to order.
ADM 12/13–14	List and summary of Admiralty out-letters to Commander-in-Chief, Mediterranean, 1813–47.	Document to order.
ADM 12/17–20	Subject and name index to Secretary of State's in-letters to the Admiralty (**ADM 1/4084–4156**), 1697–1792.	Document to order.
ADM 12/21–26	Analysis and digest of court martial convictions, 1755–1806 (arranged by offence).	Document to order.
ADM 12/27A	Alphabetical digest of convictions of officers at courts martial, 1810–16 (arranged by name).	Document to order.
ADM 12/27B–27E	'Black Books', digests of conviction of officers at courts martial, 1741–1819.	Document to order.
ADM 12/27F	Index and digest of court martial verdicts, 1812–55.	Document to order.
ADM 12/28A	Indexes to officers tried at courts martial and to ships whose loss led to a court martial, 1750–1803.	Document to order.
ADM 12/29–34	Index and digest of letters to the Admiralty from Public Offices, 1802–7.	Documents to order.
ADM 12/35	Index of persons tried at courts martial, 1806.	Document to order.

ADM 12/48–51	Alphabetical subject and nominal index to Admiralty in-letters, 1807–9.	Documents to order.
ADM 13/70–71	Commissioned and warrant officers' marriage certificates, 1806–66. Nominal card index.	RER/75
ADM 13/88–101, 207–236	Lieutenants' passing certificates, 1854–1902. See B. Pappalardo, *Royal Navy Lieutenants' Passing Certificates, 1691–1902* (List and Index Society, vols 289–290).*	RER
ADM 13/200–205	Engineers' passing certificates, 1863–1902. Nominal card index.	RER: ref to **ADM 13** <vol. 1> Also in **ADM 13** series list.
ADM 20/1–57	Treasurers' ledgers, 1660–1699. Nominal card index.	RER/76–77
ADM 27/22–45	Ships index to naval allotments, 1830–40.	RER: ref to **ADM 27** <vol. 1>
ADM 30/31	Index to midshipmen failing to pass for rank of lieutenant, 1801–10.	RER: ref to **ADM 33** <vol. 1>
ADM 33/41–90B	Index to ships' pay books.	RER: ref to **ADM 33** <vol. 1>
ADM 35/2515	HMS *Victory* pay book for 1805–6, with alphabetical list of crew.	RER: ref to **ADM 35** <vol. 1>
ADM 45/1–39	Officers' and civilians' effects papers, 1830–60. Nominal card index.	MRR/1–8
ADM 48/1–45	Naval wills. Nominal card index to names A–H only, 1786–1860.	RER/86–87
ADM 82/126–127	Nominal index to officers approving wound-compensation claims and to certificates of wounded seamen, 1763.	RER: ref to **ADM 82** <vol. 2>
ADM 101	Medical journals. Card index to names of convict ships.	RER/88–89
ADM 101/128–293	Alphabetical ships index to medical officers' journals, 1850–80.	See **ADM 101** series list.
ADM 106/2952–2963	Surgeons' qualifications, 1700–1800. Nominal card index.	RER/90
ADM 106/3021–3034	Nominal index to Navy Board papers, 1798–1817.	RER: ref to **ADM 106** <vol. 2>
ADM 107/1–63	Lieutenants' passing certificates 1691–1832. See B. Pappalardo, *Royal Navy Lieutenants' Passing Certificates, 1691–1902* (List and Index Society, vols 289–290).*	RER

ADM 107/7, 12–63	Nominal index to baptismal certificates accompanying Lieutenants' passing certificates, 1777 and 1789–1832. See B. Pappalardo, *Royal Navy Lieutenants' Passing Certificates, 1691–1902* (List and Index Society, vols 289–290).*	RER: ref to **ADM 107** <vol. 2>
ADM 107/12–50	Nominal index to Lieutenants' passing certificates 1789– 1818. See B. Pappalardo, *Royal Navy Lieutenants' Passing Certificates, 1691–1902* (List and Index Society, vols 289–290).*	RER: ref to **ADM 107** <vol. 1>
ADM 171/78–88	First World War, Royal Navy medal roll honour sheets. Nominal card index.	MRR
ADM 196/7, 26, 27, 28, 33, 57	Commissioned and warrant officers' service records, 1777–1915. Nominal card index.	MRR
ADM 196/117–124	First World War, nominal manuscript index to executive officers' service records.	MRR
ADM 199	Second World War, war history cases and papers. Subject card index.	RER/58
ADM 242/1–6	First World War, nominal card index to officer casualties and ship losses (the documents to which this index relates have not survived).	RER/129–134
ADM 273	First World War, nominal index to Royal Naval Air Service (RNAS) officers' service records.	RER/135–139
ADM 318	First World War, nominal index to Women's Royal Naval Service (WRNS) personal files.	See **ADM 318** series list.
ADM 337	First World War, card index to Royal Naval Volunteer Reserve (RNVR) officers' service records.	MRR
MT 32	Medical journals. Index to convict ship sailings.	RER/88–89
WO 208/3298–3327	Second World War, POW escape reports. Nominal card index.	RER/327–328
	Ships employed on scientific missions between 1669–1800 (date, ship, commander's name).	See **ADM 55** series list.

WO 208/3298 −3327 (*cont.*)	Ships employed on missions of discovery between 1800–60 (date, ship, commander's name).	See **ADM 55** series list.
	First World War, RN personnel mentioned in despatches, 1914–18. Card index.	MRR
	First World War, Russian honours and orders awarded to RN personnel. Nominal card index.	MRR
	First World War, Royal Navy service book index, applications and recommendations. Nominal card index.	MRR
	First World War, miscellaneous RN recommendations for medals, 1914–19.	MRR
	Second World War, ships and submarines, Alphabetical card index. Provides document references.	RER/52–57
	Second World War, convoys. Card index arranged by convoy number. Provides document references.	RER/123–126
	Second World War, operations. Card index arranged alphabetically by code name. Provides document references.	RER/127–128

* Copies of List and Index Society volumes are available in the PRO Library and can be purchased from the List and Index Society c/o the PRO.

Appendix 2: Useful addresses and websites

British Library, 96 Euston Road, London NW1 2DB (tel: 020 7412 7677, website: www.bl.uk).

British Library Newspaper Library, Colindale Avenue, London NW9 5HE (tel: 020 7412 7356, website: www.bl.uk/collections/newspapers.html).

Commonwealth War Graves Commission, 2 Marlow Road, Maidenhead, Berkshire SL6 7DX (tel: 01628 634221, website: www.cwgc.org).

Family Records Centre, 1 Myddelton Street, London EC1R 1UW (website: www.familyrecords.gov.uk).
For certificate enquiries: tel: 0870 243 7788, fax: 01704 550013, email: certificate. services@ons.gov.uk.
For other enquiries: tel: 020 8392 5300, fax 020 8392 5307, email: enquiry@pro.gov.uk.

Fleet Air Arm Museum, RNAS Yeovilton, Ilchester, Somerset BA22 8HT (tel: 01935 840565, website: www.faam.org.uk).

General Register Office for England and Wales, PO Box 2, Southport, Merseyside PR8 2JD (tel: 0870 243 7788, email: certificate.services@ons.gov.uk, website: www.statistics.gov.uk).

Imperial War Museum, Department of Documents, Lambeth Road, London SE1 6HZ (tel: 020 7416 5221, website: www.iwm.org.uk).

International Council of the Red Cross, Archives Division, 19 Avenue de la Paix, Ch-1202 Geneva, Switzerland. Holds lists of all known POWs for both world wars.

Ministry of Defence, Naval Historical Branch, 3–5 Great Scotland Yard, Whitehall, London SW1H 2HW (tel: 020 7218 5446/5451).

Ministry of Defence, Naval Medal Office, PPPA (Medals), Room 1068, Centurion Building, Grange Road, Gosport, Hampshire PO13 9XA (tel: 023 9270 2174).

Ministry of Defence, Navy Records Centre, DR 2a (Navy Search), Room 31, Bourne Avenue, Hayes, Middlesex UB3 1RF (tel: 020 8573 3831).

National Maritime Museum, Romney Road, Greenwich, London SE10 9NF (tel: 020 8858 4422, website: www.nmm.ac.uk).

Naval Chaplaincy Service, Room 203, Victory Building, HM Naval Base, Portsmouth PO1 3LS (tel: 023 9272 7111). Holds records relating to baptisms in naval establishments and naval ships that have taken place over the last 30 years.

Naval Secretary (OMOBS), Room 169, Victory Building, HM Naval Base, Portsmouth PO1 3LS. Holds service records of RN officers aged under 60.

Naval Secretary's Department, Admin Support, Room 115, Victory Building, HM Naval Base, Portsmouth PO1 3LS (tel: 023 9272 7486). Holds records of naval gallantry awards from the start of the Second World War to the present day.

PPPA, Centurion Building, Grange Road, Gosport, Hampshire PO13 9XA (tel: 023 9270 2174). PPPA (Pay, Pensions, Personnel, Administration) holds service records of RN ratings from 1938 onwards, RNR from 1958, and WRNS and QARNNS records from 1956.

Public Record Office, see 'Using the PRO' (p. xvi).

Royal Air Force Museum, Department of Aviation Records (Archives), Hendon Aerodrome, London NW9 5LL (tel: 020 8205 2266, website: www.rafmusuem.org.uk).

Royal College of Surgeons (England), 35–43 Lincoln's Inn Fields, London WC2A 3PN (tel: 020 7405 3473, website: wwwrcs.eng.ac.uk).

Royal Naval Association, HMS *Nelson*, Portsmouth, Hampshire PO1 3HH (tel: 023 9229 4228, website: www.royal-naval-association.co.uk).

Royal Naval Museum, HM Naval Base, Portsmouth, Hampshire PO1 3LR (tel: 023 9272 7562, website: www.flagship.org.uk).

Royal Naval Submarine Museum, HMS *Dolphin*, Haslar Jetty Road, Gosport, Hampshire PO12 2AS (tel: 023 9252 9217, website: www.rnsubmus.co.uk).

Other useful websites

www.cronab.demon.co.uk
Histories of the sailing ships of the Royal Navy by M. Phillips.

www.familysearch.org
Vast internet resource for the family historian.

www.gazettes-online.co.uk
Online copies of the *London Gazette* for 1914–1920 and 1939–1948 which can be searched by name and date.

www.hmc.gov.uk
National Register of Archives (NRA) website through which searches can be undertaken to establish whether private papers of an individual exist and where they are held.

www.navynews.co.uk
Online news about the Royal Navy.

www.nelson-society.org.uk
Website for those interested in the life of Nelson and the Battle of Trafalgar.

www.royal-navy.mod.uk
Official Ministry of Defence website.

www.ringsurf.com
Friends of the Royal Navy link to a selection of privately developed websites that look at various aspects of the past, present and the future of the Royal Navy.

The Genealogist's Internet by Peter Christian (PRO, 2001) is a useful guide to websites of interest to family historians.

Bibliography

Note: Details of biographical reference works (both naval and general) will be found in 2.1 and 2.2. Details of publications relating to specific topics are given, where relevant, in the text.

Abbott, P.E and Tamplin, J.M.A. *British Gallantry Awards* (Nimrod Dix & Co., 1981)

Bevan, A. *Tracing Your Ancestors in the Public Record Office* (PRO, 2nd edn 2002)

Clowes, W.L. *The Royal Navy: A History* (London, 1898)

Colledge, J.J. *Ships of the Royal Navy* (David & Charles, 1969)

Colwell, S. *The Family Records Centre – A User's Guide* (PRO, 2nd edn 2002)

Davies, J.D. *Gentlemen and Tarpaulins: The Officers and Men of the Restoration Navy* (Clarendon Press, 1991)

Douglas-Morris, K. *The Naval General Service Medal Roll, 1793–1840* (London, 1982)

Douglas-Morris, K. *Naval Long Service Medals, 1830–1990* (London, 1991)

Douglas-Morris, K. *Naval Medals, 1793–1856* (London, 1987)

Douglas-Morris, K. *Naval Medals, 1857–1880* (London, 1994)

Gosset, W.P. *The Lost Ships of the Royal Navy 1793–1900* (New York, 1986)

Hill, J.R. *The Oxford Illustrated History of the Royal Navy* (Oxford University Press, 1995)

Honours and Awards Army, Navy and Air Force 1914–1920 (Hayward, 1979)

James, W. *The Naval History of Great Britain, 1793–1820* (London, 1896)

Kemp, P. *The British Sailor, A Social History of the Lower Deck* (Dent, 1970)

Kemp, P. *The Oxford Companion to Ships and the Sea* (Oxford University Press, 1988)

Keevil, J.J. et al. *Medicine and the Navy, 1200–1900* (Livingstone, 1957)

Lavery, B. *Nelson's Navy: the ships, men and organisation, 1793–1815* (Conway Maritime Press, 1989)

Lennox Kerr, J. and Granville, W. *The R.N.V.R* (Harrap, 1957)

Lewis, M. *England's Sea Officers, The Story of the Naval Profession* (Allen & Unwin, 1948)

Lewis, M. *A Social History of the Navy, 1793–1815* (Allen & Unwin, 1960)

Lewis, M. *The Navy in Transition, A Social History 1814–1864* (Hodder & Stoughton, 1965)

Lloyd, C. *The British Seaman, 1200–1860: a social survey* (Collins, 1968)

Lyon, D. *The Sailing Navy List – All the ships of the Royal Navy built, purchased and captured, 1688–1860* (Conway Maritime Press, 1993)

Marcus, G.J. *A Naval History of England, The Formative Centuries* (Longman, 1961)

Merriman, R.D. *Queen Anne's Navy* (Naval Records Society, 1961)

Newell, P. *Greenwich Hospital, A Royal Foundation, 1692–1983* (Trustees of Greenwich Hospital, 1984)

Pappalardo, B. *Royal Navy Lieutenants' Passing Certificates, 1691–1902*, List and Index Society vols 289–290 (List and Index Society, 2002)

Pappalardo, B. *Using Navy Records*, Public Record Office Pocket Guide (PRO, revised edn 2001)

Rodger, N.A.M. *Articles of War* (K. Mason, 1982)

Rodger, N.A.M. *Naval Records for Genealogists* (PRO, 1998)

Rodger, N.A.M. *The Wooden World* (Fontana Press, 1988)

Smith, K., Watts, C.T. and Watts, M.J. *Records of Merchant Shipping and Seamen* (PRO, 1998)

Syrett, D. and DiNardo, R.L. *The Commissioned Sea Officers of the Royal Navy, 1660–1815* (Navy Records Society, 1994)

Taylor, G. *The Sea Chaplains, A History of the Chaplains of the Royal Navy* (Oxford Illustrated Press, 1978)

Thomas, D.A. *A Companion to the Royal Navy* (Harrap, 1998)

Walker, C.F. *Young Gentlemen, The Story of Midshipmen* (Longman, 1938)

Watts, A.J. *The Royal Navy: An Illustrated History* (Brockhampton Press, 1999)

Wells, J. *The Royal Navy: An Illustrated Social History* (Sutton, 1994)

Winton, J. *Hurrah for the Life of a Sailor! Life on the lower deck of the Victorian navy* (Michael Joseph, 1977)

Index